MW01225102

Poverty and the Production of World Politics

Poverty and the Production of World Politics

Unprotected Workers in the Global Political Economy

Edited by

Matt Davies
Lecturer, University of Newcastle upon Tyne, UK

and

Magnus Ryner
Senior Lecturer, University of Birmingham, UK

First published 2006 by
PALGRAVE MACMILLAN
Houndmills, Basingstoke, Hampshire RG21 6XS and
175 Fifth Avenue, New York, N.Y. 10010
Companies and representatives throughout the world.

PALGRAVE MACMILLAN is the global academic imprint of the Palgrave Macmillan division of St. Martin's Press, LLC and of Palgrave Macmillan Ltd. Macmillan® is a registered trademark in the United States, United Kingdom and other countries. Palgrave is a registered trademark in the European Union and other countries.

ISBN-13: 978–1–4039–9697–8
ISBN-10: 1–4039–9697–0

This book is printed on paper suitable for recycling and made from fully managed and sustained forest sources.

A catalogue record for this book is available from the British Library.
Library of Congress Cataloging-in-Publication Data
Poverty and the production of world politics : unprotected workers in the global political economy / edited by Matt Davies and Magnus Ryner.
    p. cm.
Includes bibliographical references and index.
ISBN 1–4039–9697–0 (cloth)
    1. Labor—Social aspects. 2. Poverty—Economic aspects.
3. International economic relations. 4. Economic policy. I. Davies, Matt, 1960– II. Ryner, Magnus, 1965–
HD4901.P68 2006
331.1—dc22   2006043212

10 9 8 7 6 5 4 3 2 1
15 14 13 12 11 10 09 08 07 06

Transferred to Digital Printing 2007

Contents

Acknowledgements

First and foremost the editors would like to extend their warmest thanks to Jeff Harrod for his friendship, generosity and mentorship, without which this book would not have been possible. There is no doubt that Jeff is much more than a contributor to this book. He sowed the seeds of inspiration for one of the editors through a series of seminars at the Research Centre of International Political Economy (RECIPE), University of Amsterdam, in 1998 and 1999. This was taken further in a long series of discussions and correspondence between the editors and Jeff, beginning at the annual meeting of the International Studies Association in Los Angeles in 2000 and culminating in a few of days of intense discussions at Jeff's home in The Hague in September 2004. We have struggled to think of an appropriate way to acknowledge the breadth and depth of Jeff's contributions to our efforts. His modesty and the importance he put on engaging critically with the approach to global politics examined in this book rendered it impossible to make the book a *Festschrift*. Nor was it appropriate to present him as coeditor, since it would have been unfair to make him editorially responsible for discussions with which he might not entirely agree. Thus we would like to record here our profound thanks to Jeff for his commitment to the project and for teaching us so much.

We would also like to acknowledge the institutional support we received during the preparation of this book. We especially benefited from the facilities of the International Studies Association, and in particular the special workshop grant for the Annual Meeting of 2002 in New Orleans, which made it possible to bring all the contributors together for the crucial meeting at which the first drafts were presented and discussed. Matt Davies also received a supplementary grant from the Office of International Programs at Pennsylvania State University to support that workshop. Different parts of the book were presented and discussed at a number of other meetings and forums, most notably at the Chair's Roundtable at the Department of Political Science, York University, Toronto, in March 2004. We would like to thank Isabella Bakker, who was then the Chairperson at York, for facilitating this roundtable at one of the leading centres for the development of the type of critical IR/IPE advocated in these pages. The roundtable allowed us to discuss some of our ideas with leading figures in the field, including

Isa herself, Stephen Gill, Leo Panitch, Sam Gindin, many of York's very talented graduate students and, of course, Robert W. Cox.

Many other people contributed to the panels and workshops that led up to this book, and we would like to thank them for their incisive comments. They include Vèronique Bertrand-Bourget, Seiko Hanochi, Mustapha Kamal Pasha, Nori Onuki, Christoph Scherrer, Leila Simona Talani, Ritu Vij and Brigitte Young. They also include Paddy Summerfield, Jeff's life partner, who contributed extensively to the discussions in The Hague and designed the cover of the book. Finally, we would like to thank our editor at Palgrave Macmillan, Jennifer Nelson, for her support and patience, and our copy-editor, Keith Povey (with Anne Vickerson and Nick Fox), for Herculean efforts.

MATT DAVIES
MAGNUS RYNER

Notes on the Contributors

Louise Amoore is a Lecturer in Political Geography at the University of Durham, UK. Her current research interest is the governing of worker and migrant bodies through the risk profiling of the war on terror. She is presently working on a book (*Cultures of Consulting*) that traces the rise of management consulting as a technique of governing the global political economy. She is the author of *Globalization Contested: An International Political Economy of Work* and editor of *The Global Resistance Reader*.

Terry Boswell was Professor of Sociology at Emory University, Atlanta, US. His research interests are stratification, the sociology of work and industry, world-system studies, comparative historical sociology and race and ethnicity. His publications include *The Spiral of Capitalism and Socialism* (coauthored with Christopher Chase-Dunn) and *Globalization and Labor: Democratizing Global Governance?* (with Dimitris Stevis). Terry passed away in June 2006, after a long illness during which he kept researching, writing and publishing on the issues that have been central to his life – from world revolutions to labour markets.

Marlea Clarke is a Postdoctoral Fellow in the WSIB-funded project 'Employment Strain: The Hidden Costs of Precarious Employment', which is part of the Labour Studies Programme at McMaster University, Hamilton, Ontario, Canada. She is also a research associate in the Labour and Enterprise Project, Institute of Development and Labour Law, University of Cape Town, South Africa. Dr Clarke completed her MA and PhD in Political Science at York University, Toronto, Ontario. Her PhD dissertation focused on postapartheid labour market regulation, employment shifts and precariousness in South Africa. Her research interests include globalization, precarious employment and labour organizing in Canada and Southern Africa.

Matt Davies joined the School of Geography, Politics and Sociology at the University of Newcastle upon Tyne, UK, in January 2006. Previously he was an Assistant Professor at Penn State Erie, US, and a Visiting Professor at the Political Science Department, York University, Toronto, Canada. His research focuses on questions of culture, everyday life and labour in the international political economy. He is the author of *International Political Economy and Mass Communication in Chile: National*

Intellectuals and Transnational Hegemony, plus articles in *Global Society, New Political Science*, and *The Review of Radical Political Economics*.

Silvia Federici has taught Political Philosophy and International Studies at Hofstra University, New York. A long-time feminist activist and theorist, she has written numerous essays on the international feminist movement, women and globalization, gender and history. She is the author of *Caliban and the Witch: Women, the Body and Primitive Accumulation* and the editor of *Enduring Western Civilization: The Construction of the Concept of Western Civilization and its 'Others'.*

Jeffrey Harrod graduated in Law from University College, University of London, and obtained his PhD in Political Science from the University of Geneva, Switzerland. He was research coordinator at the International Labour Organisation research institute and Professor of International and Comparative Labour Studies at the Institute of Social Studies in The Hague, Netherlands, where he was also Deputy Rector. He has written extensively on labour issues, including *Power, Production and the Unprotected Worker*, and more recently edited *Global Unions? Theories and Strategies of Organised Labour in the Global Political Economy* with R. O'Brien. As a permanent consultant for an international trade union, he has analyzed corporate investment politics and regional and global strategies for key industrial sectors. Currently he is Visiting Professor at the International School for Humanities and Social Sciences, University of Amsterdam, where he lectures and supervises research degrees in International Political Economy.

Teresa Healy is a Senior Researcher at the Canadian Union of Public Employees (CUPE) and the Canadian Labour Congress (CLC). She is also musician and songwriter and her productions include *All Souls' Day*.

Michael Niemann works in the International Studies Program at Trinity College in Hartford, Connecticut, US. He is interested in the spatial aspects of political economy, with a particular focus on southern Africa. He is the author of *A Spatial Approach to Regionalisms in the Global Economy* and various articles in *Africa Today, Alternatives, Journal of African Policy Studies* and *New Political Science*.

Magnus Ryner is Senior Lecturer at the Department of Political Science and International Studies, University of Birmingham, UK. In his written work he has addressed a broad range of issues related to global social welfare and labour politics in an era of neoliberal hegemony. His publications include *Capitalist Restructuring, Globalisation and the Third Way* and *A Ruined Fortress? Neoliberal Hegemony and Transformation in Europe* (coedited with Alan Cafruny).

Dimitris Stevis is Professor of International Politics at Colorado State University, US. His research focuses on the social regulation of global and regional integration, with an emphasis on the environment and labour. He has served as Chair of the Environmental Studies Section and of the Sprout Award Committee of the International Studies Association. He has published book chapters and articles on international environmental and labour politics and is coeditor (with Valerie Assetto) of *The International Political Economy of the Environment: Critical Perspectives*. He is currently completing a book entitled *Globalization and Labor: Democratizing Global Governance?* (with Terry Boswell) and researching the international framework agreements between global union federations and corporations and the views of trade unions on global environmental issues.

List of Abbreviations

AFL	American Federation of Labor
AFL-CIO	American Federation of Labor and Congress of Industrial Organizations
ANC	African National Congress
BCEA	Basic Conditions of Employment Act
BIP	Border Industrialization Programme
COB	Bolivian Confederation of Labour
COSATU	Congress of South African Trade Unions
EPZ	Export Processing Zone
GUF	Global Union Federations
ICFTU	International Confederation of Free Trade Unions
IFTU	International Federation of Trade Unions
IMF	International Monetary Fund
MNC	Multinational Corporation
OECD	Organisation for Economic Co-operation and Development
PRI	Partido Revolucionario Institucional
SER	Standard Employment Relationship
TUC	Trades Union Congress
WCL	World Confederation of Labour
WFTU	World Federation of Trade Unions

Introduction[1]

Matt Davies and Magnus Ryner

Venezuela's poor make up core of political support for the populist President Hugo Chavez. Chavez has not only used income from oil exports to provide the poor with basic services, he has also pursued a foreign policy that is explicitly independent of US interests in the region. Urban marginals in Morocco, living in shantytowns known to locals as 'Chechnyas', have embraced violent strands of Islam, taking their inspiration from factions of the Muslim Brothers of Egypt and the Groupe Islamique Armée of Algeria. It is likely that they were involved in the train bombings in Madrid in March 2004 and were certainly behind the suicide bombings in Casablanca on 16 May 2003 (Belaala, 2004). According to research by the International Crisis Group (ICG, 2004) the 'Mahdi Army' in Iraq not only has a similar political disposition but also has a similar social base in shantytowns such as Baghdad's Sadr City. UN data indicate that if it has not already come to pass, the world is on the verge of becoming primarily urban. Davis (2004) has shown that while some cities do continue to follow the nineteenth-century pattern of urbanization led by industrialization, most contemporary urbanization is taking place in 'second tier' deindustrializing cities that are unable to provide basic services to newly arrived poor migrants. Poverty has become an unavoidable theme in world politics.

International organizations certainly recognize the salience of poverty for world politics. They have reoriented their discourses and practices from promoting development to poverty alleviation. For 40 years economists and sociologists viewed development in terms of industrialization in developing countries in which economic growth would enhance the position of the poor. This tradition declined in the 1980s as 'aid fatigue' increased, the notion of globalization emerged and neoliberal ideas became hegemonic. From the neoliberal perspective, promoting development was not a concern since this *laissez-faire* theory made no distinction between development and promoting markets. Although questions were raised about the distributive effects of the neoliberal model of development and the Washington Consensus, such questions were now posed in terms of the global poor. Within the formal sphere of world politics, the World Bank was the primary producer of the norms and concepts through which policy-makers understand these problems. In 2001, for example, the World Bank introduced the term 'poverty reduction' to formalize, rationalize and legitimize the practices it had developed during the 1990s. Similarly, liberal intellectuals and academics came to conceptualize these problems in terms of poverty alleviation and concerned themselves with the income levels, coping mechanisms and identity of the global poor.

One expression of this consciousness was the theme of the 2001 annual meeting of the International Studies Association (ISA) in Chicago: 'The New Inequality'. Over 2000 delegates were asked to frame their papers, presentations and discussions in relation to questions about the development of poverty in a global context of increased wealth and output. As in the case of the World Bank, this reflected a shift in orientation from development to global poverty. However, unlike the World Bank, the delegates of this conference often conveyed the view that the neoliberal model of development produced rather than reduced poverty. Worse, in those countries where something like development had occurred, income shifts had widened the gap between rich and poor, and in some cases the number of poor had increased.

Another expression of the growing concern with the global poor or underclass can be found in the public sphere in advanced capitalist societies of the North. This can be viewed as a return of the social question that these societies faced at the end of the nineteenth century, but now as a transnational issue. Constituencies with a stake in the welfare state worry that problems associated with job losses are related to the global poor. Thus trade unions, both domestically and internationally, have taken much greater interest in organizing the working poor than in the past. Moreover, inasmuch as the working poor in the South are raising practical and ethical issues associated with world trade, other issue-based social movements and NGOs – such as the US-based antisweatshop movement and the 'clean clothes' campaign – have also concerned themselves with the conditions of the global poor. Finally, various efforts to promote corporate social responsibility have forced corporations to address social and economic factors in their annual reports, especially in respect of the overall impact of corporate activities on poverty and inequality.

However this concern is not always associated with sympathy but perhaps more often with a return of the 'fear of the masses'. One expression of this fear is hysteria about migration. Even the least reactionary elements tend to view the global poor as a problem to be managed. The situation in the United Kingdom is instructive, with politicians competing to be tough on 'bogus asylum seekers' but with New Labour government, as championed by the chancellor of the exchequer, Gordon Brown, flanking this with a G7 initiative to alleviate the Third World debt burden. Furthermore such initiatives tend to go hand in hand with a 'securitization' of the issue, as grave hints of connections between religious fundamentalism, material desperation and political movements are suggested in the foreign policy statements of the world's lone superpower.

The general premise behind this book is that while technocrats, intellectuals and politicians seem to recognize that global poverty is now a central question for world politics, they all lack an adequate conception of the way in which the global poor have contributed to the formation, reproduction, limits and contradictions of the contemporary world order. We argue that such a conception must be based on the way in which production and power relations, broadly conceived, constitute the world order. This requires an analysis of the multifarious ways in which the global poor take part in these production and power relations as unprotected workers. The World Bank's perspectives and the research industry it has provoked do not systematically connect questions of poverty reduction and alleviation to those of work, politics and world order. Any understanding of the relationship between poverty and work and the processes through which the politics of the poor are articulated is missing. To address such questions properly, analyses must explore the articulations of the politics of the poor through the power relations that structure work and production.

The objective of this book is to help fill the gaps left by World Bank-inspired conceptualizations of global poverty. It will do so by engaging with the conceptual framework developed in two collaborative volumes by Robert W. Cox (1987) and Jeffrey Harrod (1987), the first of which has been recognized as a paradigmatic contribution to the foundation of a critical International Political Economy (IPE). We argue that their central concepts of unprotected workers and patterns of social relations of production have been largely ignored by subsequent studies, and that this has been detrimental to the development of a critical understanding of the way in which poverty contributes to the contemporary production of world politics.

Unprotected work and world politics in international studies

Put differently, the general aim of this book is to contribute to the debate on and the development of research into social forces as sources of transnational political economy and international relations. While ethnicity and religion (see for example Huntington, 1993) and the basic insecurity emanating from the interaction of nation states *sui generis* (Waltz, 1979) have been considered key determinants of the terms of conflict, cooperation, war and peace, the politics emerging from experiences in work and production have received far less attention – despite the increased salience of the question of poverty for global politics.

By engaging with the analytical framework developed by Cox (1987) and Harrod (1987), this book seeks to contribute to the understanding of the roles of work and production in transnational relations by focusing on the global growth and development of unprotected work. Unprotected workers are producers who are not socially organized through workplace organizations and are increasingly unprotected by a weakened or unwilling state apparatus. In short, the book focuses on the consequences for transnational relations of the social forces of unprotected work, arising from what has been despairingly referred to as the development of an abandoned underclass in the richer countries and the expansion of the poorest and most vulnerable people in the poorer countries.

The book addresses four thematic questions:

- What is an adequate ontology of transnational relations, and what role and status should be assigned to unprotected work in such an ontology?
- What is the relationship between unprotected work and the formation of political subjects or subjectivity?
- What is the relationship between subject formation and the terms and content of social organization and mobilization?
- What are the spillovers from the emergence of new forms of social mobilization into political society and transnational power politics?

A critical overview of competing approaches to world politics reveals the importance of incorporating a conception of unprotected work. International relations as a discipline still struggles to understand the nature of power relations, conflicts, cooperation and the terms of transformation and change in contemporary world politics. The field has had rather limited success in addressing these issues in dimensions other than that of interstate relations – the privileged object of analysis of realism. Yet the qualitative structural changes in world politics, as suggested by descriptive notions such as 'globalization', indicates that holding everything but the relation of material capabilities between horizontally organized states *ceteris paribus* (Waltz, 1979) is an unsatisfactory approach. As the Multilateralism and United Nations System project (MUNS) of the United Nations University has suggested, the qualitatively new state of affairs in global politics calls for an approach that makes the social context of world politics the appropriate level of analysis of a 'new realism' (Cox, 1997).

Over the last 20 years the field of international relations has seen the emergence of many approaches that break the abstract state-centred mould. We would argue, however, that these new approaches have not adequately conceptualized the constitutive social cleavages and antagonisms that should be the point of departure for analyses of this new realism. For example the 'either–or' dualism of complex interdependence (Keohane and Nye, 1977) restates the realist antagonisms of interstate conflict where the realist game applies, and where the liberal game applies this approach *a priori* defines away constitutive cleavages and antagonisms, thus sanitizing this particular sphere from a consideration of power relations. In our view, despite their contributions in other respects, liberal constructivism and the entire body of global civil society literature do the same by basing themselves on essentially realist, liberal or dualist ontologies (see for example Ruggie, 1998; Archibugi *et al.*, 1998).

The postcolonial and feminist literatures (for example Said, 1993; Marchand and Runyan, 2000) have partially redressed these limitations through their analyses of the power relations in the cultural sphere and their effect on identity formation. This book seeks to explore possibilities of dialogue and synthesis with these perspectives. We would however argue that this literature has, as a side effect of its effort to avoid economism, not adequately reflected on the material context of culture. Hence it is liable to fall into a distorting *ad hoc* analysis that is inconsistent with its ontological commitments and reproduces the problems of the complex interdependence literature. One particularly vivid example of this is the adoption of the term 'informal sector' – a term borrowed from modernization theory – in the quest to understand the feminization of work and globalization from below. This book will help to overcome these inconsistencies by drawing on Cox and Harrod's alternative framework for forms of social relations of production.

At the same time, neither Marxism nor world systems theory adequately conceptualize, in their present form, the social antagonisms that drive world politics, despite taking their point of departure from an analysis of socially determined cleavages and antagonisms. Working from a reified and reductionist conception of class relations and core–periphery relations, such theories postulate abstract universal laws from selectively particular circumstances. This is less of a problem when the objective is limited to understanding the dynamics of globalization from above through an analysis of the dynamics of capital. (Indeed capital as a social force, by its nature, operates through reification and reduction; see for example the important contributions by Harvey, 1990; Arrighi, 1994; van der Pijl, 1998.) However classical Marxists fall short in their analyses of the more heterogeneous and problematic social force of labour.

This book shares the concern of the neo-Gramscian school of IPE with exploring the complex interrelationship of the material, ideational and institutional aspects of historical structures. It should be pointed out, however, that the neo-Gramscian school has not yet developed an adequate conception of labour in its critical theory of world order, though this is due less to its ontological orientation than to its empirical focus. Neo-Gramscian work has hitherto tended to be elitist in focus, concentrating on the terms of factional conflict and cooperation within the capitalist class and state elite (for example Gill, 1990; Murphy, 1994; van der Pijl, 1998). Even when members of this school have concerned themselves with the subject of pressure from below, they have tended to fall into the same trap as postcolonialist studies by privileging the ideological moment and adopting an *ad hoc* analysis of class position (for example Rupert, 2000; Gill, 2002). In other words, while making important contributions to our understanding of social forces in international relations, neo-Gramscian studies have not yet adequately addressed the issues foregrounded in the seminal works by Cox (1987) and Harrod (1987). Hence neo-Gramscian theory remains undeveloped in relation to the premise that it takes as its point of departure:

> Production creates the material basis for all forms of social existence and the ways in which human efforts are combined in productive processes affect all other aspects of social life including the polity. Production generates the capacity to exercise power, but power determines the manner in which production takes place. [Hence one should] approach ... the understanding of current historical change

from the standpoint of a reciprocal relationship between power and production. (Cox, 1987, p. 1)

The present book seeks to redress these oversights by the neo-Gramscian school in order better to realize its latent potential as a critical theory of IPE and international relations (IR). It will do so by engaging with the wide-ranging but analytically subtle categories of production developed in Part I of Cox's *Production, Power and World Order* (1987), and by developing these further through critical investigations informed by empirical and theoretical developments that have taken place since the publication of that work. In so doing it will explore affinities with the social theories of Foucault, Bourdieu, Lefebvre and others, as well as fruitful avenues of dialogue and synthesis with primarily Marxist, post-colonialist, feminist and constructivist strands of research.

The structure of the book

As indicated above, we think that an IPE perspective is particularly suitable for the development of a critical understanding of poverty and its contribution to the production of world politics through unprotected work. Yet serious problems are caused by the fact that the discipline tends to focus on top-down analysis. These are articulated in Chapter 1 by Louise Amoore, who makes the case for the ways in which the kind of research we advocate can contribute to IPE. She calls for the positioning of work as a subject of inquiry for IPE, and of workers as subjects, at the centre of our understanding of the contemporary global political economy. She criticizes IPE as a discipline, and strands of the globalization literature more broadly, for rendering work and workers invisible through the representations implied in its central concepts and categories. This is despite the increased importance that IPE assigns to the politicizing and historicizing of economic relations. Amoore grounds her analysis empirically with references to the instituted practices of multinational corporations. She argues that multinational corporations are increasingly becoming central sites for the articulation of social relations in the world economy. She argues that as these corporations increasingly outsource their production and services – and thus employ unprotected workers – they become fractured into loosely connected sites, deploying insiders, intermediaries and outsiders in a multitude of patterns of social relations of production. Amoore outlines a perspective of work as sets of social practices through which diverse experiences and understandings of global change are constituted. She argues that it is the everyday lives of workers as active subjects that make particular forms of global production possible and that potentially may limit or contest productive practices.

Chapters 2 and 3 reflect upon, outline and discuss the contemporary relevance of the patterns of social relations of production approach that Harrod and Cox developed in their Power, Production and World Order project. In Chapter 2 Harrod discusses the political and intellectual context of his and Cox's original work, which they began at the International Labour Organisation and the International Institute of Labour Studies in the 1970s and published in 1987. He then reflects on what is, in his view, the continuing legacy of the work for contemporary IPE, and offers a critical assessment of how the approach should be developed further. He outlines how he sees their concepts breaking with both modernization theory and, despite their self-professed historical materialism, neo-Marxism. A central problem with these theories is that with descriptive, pretheoretical and 'chaotic' abstractions such as the informal sector and underclass, and indeed the lumpenproletariat, they fail to develop a framework with which to analyze the contribution made to global change by the vast majority of the world's population that exist at the bottom of production-determined hierarchies. The chapter then presents a modified typology of unprotected workers based upon different patterns of power relations of production, in part inspired by Foucault's (1976) conception of power. Different rationalities of power and world views affect subsistence and market-producing peasants, the self-employed, casual, small-enterprise and household producers, and these are distinct from the overriding gender, ethnic or nationally produced perceptions. However the latter interact with the patterns of production in the constitution of subject. Hence the use and manipulation of such perceptions influences or determine the development of social forces. These in turn connect individual experiences as producers, directly or indirectly, to the international political economy and global change.

In Chapter 3 Magnus Ryner makes a case for retaining the Marxist links of Harrod's neomaterialism in the form of a neo-Gramscian analysis. He begins with a metatheoretical section that, drawing on Bourdieu's (1977) theory of habitus, defends Cox's and Harrod's analytical procedure of relating rationalities to production against poststructuralist and other constructivist objections. He then argues that the analysis of patterns of social relations of production corresponds to the 'economic corporate moment' in Gramsci's political analysis based on relations of force. The economic corporate moment is concerned with class sections or 'fractions', which are the sectorally and functionally diverse primordial fragments upon which class identities are politically and ideologically formed in struggle. Hegemonic strategies similarly seek to fuse unity between classes, which in turn underpins consent in states and world orders. The problem with neo-Gramscian analyses in IPE so far is that they have only advanced this three-dimensional analysis of relations of force with regard to capital, not with regard to sections of labour. Hence they have failed to grasp systematically the dialectical tension between the common sense of hegemony, rationality and the disposition of basic consciousness that emanate from the material experience of different sections of labour. As a result they have yet to grasp the terms of counterhegemonic struggles in the world order, which presumably should be their primary objective. The chapter makes a case for returning to the concept of patterns of social relations of production precisely because it provides us with the basis to develop such a sectional analysis of labour. The chapter ends with a preliminary attempt to reconstruct empirically the configuration of sections of labour on the world scale and their attendant tendencies of basic consciousness. It concludes that neoliberal globalization has resulted *inter alia* in increased prominence of the corporate pattern in the core and self-employment and casual social relations of production in the periphery. This seems to imply an ominous polarization between civic privatism among the affluent and millenarianism among the desperately poor, with a common denominator of populism. This is a far cry from benign accounts of a global civil society, and perhaps a critical socioeconomic perspective on the phenomenon that Huntington (1993) has characterized as a 'clash of civilizations'.

In chapter 4 Matt Davies undertakes the difficult task of relating unprotected work to class and subject formation and the ethicopolitical moment. In this endeavour, he draws on Lefebvre's (1984, 1991b) critique of everyday life as well as the debates in German critical theory on the nature of the public sphere. To deal with the complexity of the task, Davies conducts an in-depth analysis of the situation in particular locales, in contrast to Ryner's 'broad sweep' in Chapter 3. In the case of domestic labour, Davies argues that the processes of domination at the levels of state policy formation and implementation (neoliberalism), the transnationalization of capital (globalization) and international relations (imperialism) have contributed both to the emergence of new forms of social subject and to the resurgence of residual forms of resistance. According to Davies the construction of counterpublic spheres, concretely articulated in the everyday spaces of household workers and contributing to the development of struggles amongst and between different forms of subordinate social relations of production, will determine the limits to domination and the possibilities for transformation under the current regimes of capital accumulation.

Hence in Chapters 1 to 4 the emphasis is on the reintroduction, development and inflections of Harrod and Cox's original framework. While the subsequent chapters remain conceptually sophisticated, the focus is on the empirical analysis of dimensions of unprotected work. These chapters assess the merits of the Cox–Harrod approach and reach somewhat different conclusions.

In Chapter 5 Silvia Federici analyses the unprotected work of prostitution. Drawing on a considerable body of empirical material she argues the neoliberalism has had the effect of obliterating, economically and politically, the political gains of sex workers that were advanced in the postconventional politics of the 1970s. Increased social precariousness and disintegration has led to a dramatic increase in the supply of prostitutes and a reduction of their cost, often connected to the control of population movement by a sex industry with overlapping relations between illicit, formal and even state activities. The changes that have occurred in the organization of and workers in the sex industry have resulted in different kinds of sex worker operating in totally different social relations of production, ranging from self-employment to slavery. This is making it extremely difficult for prostitutes to organize themselves to improve their social position. This state of affairs is reflected in feminist divisions between those who advocate prohibitionist legislation against sex trafficking and those who argue for the legalization of prostitution to enable prostitutes to earn a living as self-employed owners of their bodies and means of production. Fedirici argues that neither solution is adequate. The only hope for prostitutes (as for many other workers) lies in the type of struggle that Third World communities are engaging in to reappropriate their means of subsistence and the social entitlements of which they have been deprived by the austerity programmes of the IMF and World Bank. In this endeavour it is also important to link prostitutes' organizations with the international movement for immigrants' rights and against globalization. Federici also offers two critical observations *vis-à-vis* the analysis of Cox and Harrod. The first of these is empirical. Whereas Cox and Harrod tended to associate prostitution with the primitive labour market, the range of social relations in prostitution is much wider and has different implications for prostitutes. The second observation is partly conceptual and partly ethicopolitical.

She cautions against overemphasis on disaggregation at the expense of attention to what it is that unites prostitutes with other oppressed social groups in the struggle to reappropriate their means of subsistence, which she argues tends to perpetuate the ghettoization that is central to the oppression of prostitutes.

In the two subsequent chapters Michael Niemann (Chapter 6) and Marlea Clarke (Chapter 7) engage with Harrod's (1987) framework in two studies of different aspects of the political economy of southern Africa. In contrast to Fedirici, Niemann takes an unambiguously positive view of the approach and its emphasis on multidimensionality, which he sees as appropriate for his object of study. Focusing on the social relations of migrant workers in the mining sector he builds on his previous work on everyday life experiences which incorporated the concepts of social space developed by Lefebvre (1991a). Here he includes patterns of production relations in his analysis. According to Niemann, 'Harrod's sophisticated analysis of the social relations of production offers important insights that can usefully be adapted to understand the everyday work experiences of migrants, not just at the current juncture but also as part of an understanding of the historical trajectory of southern Africa' Niemann demonstrates how Harrod's analysis can be fruitfully reconciled with the sophisticated spatial reformulation of the Marxist dialectic of commodification that Lefebvre offers. Niemann presents a critical geopolitics in which the deepening of 'abstract space' implied in the model of development adopted by the postapartheid Republic of South Africa, excludes from consideration, and clashes with, the historical movement of unprotected migrant workers in the region. This topic is certainly deserving of further consideration and research. Niemann concludes that it is a sad irony that 'postapartheid southern Africa, although now free of racist power politics, is marked by new international relations, driven by market forces rather than the desire to further human development'.

Marlea Clarke (Chapter 7) investigates the dual and contradictory process of labour market restructuring and post-apartheid democratization that is currently underway in the Republic of South Africa. By means of an investigative strategy that incorporates segmentation theory in labour studies with a sympathetic but critical reading of Harrod (she questions some of his typology), Clarke explores the dramatic rise of unprotected work in the country, despite the participation of COSATU unions in labour market reform under the ANC government. In this regard Clarke argues that labour is caught up in a contradictory process, shot through with strategic dilemmas, because of its ongoing alliance with the ANC. COSATU pursues concession bargaining through tripartite forums in order to gain the best deal possible for organized labour within the ANC's compensatory neoliberal model of development while at the same time attempting to persuade the government to relax its neoliberal orientation. Whilst Clarke understands the reasons for this strategy, she considers that it is resulting in organized labour playing a significant role in shaping, producing and reproducing the increasingly casualized social relations and institutions in postapartheid South Africa. The consequence of this is a dramatic increase in unprotected work, which Clarke investigates with particular reference to the textile sector. In the long term the strategy is likely to undermine trade union strength, in part because the percentage of unionized workers in the labour force will decrease and in part because unions will be alienated from unprotected workers who do not feel that the unions are representing them. The question then is, can the tradition of social unionism be revived in a new strategic orientation that seeks to build alliances with unprotected workers? Such an orientation would imply a change of emphasis from tripartite interest intermediation to union organization.

The problem of relating the experience of work to political society is the central theme of the next two chapters of the book. In Chapter 8, Teresa Healy draws on Cox and Harrod's work to advance a neo-Gramscian analysis. Unlike Ryner (Chapter 3) Healy does not restrict her analysis to the economic corporate moment, rather she investigates the relationship of this moment to class and gender formation and ethicopolitical struggle, conditioned by what she calls the 'condition of hegemony' in Mexican society, as shaped by 'passive revolution' and 'organic crisis'. She demonstrates how the approach can be fruitfully synthesized with a feminist political economy, and argues that gender relations have always been of importance to Mexican social formation. In Mexico the feminization of work is fundamentally transforming state corporatist relations, in which male trade unionism has been a constituent part (associated with the Partido Revolutionario Institucional (PRI) power bloc) of neoliberalization. On the basis of research on the automotive sector, Healy concludes that the current situation is one of impasse. On the one hand the current amalgam of hollowed-out state corporatism (which ensures coercive transformation) and the enterprise model (which ensures flexibility and commodification) has not become hegemonic in Mexican society and it continues to be contested, not the least by workers themselves. On the other hand gender relations continue to divide male and female worker identities (the 'worker-father' and the '*maquila* girl'), and this division is pre-empting an effective counterhegemonic strategy based on a redefinition of the 'universal worker'. It is also fuelling coercive neoliberalization, flexibilization and feminization – what Healy calls the 'maquilization' of the dominant social relations of production in Mexican social formation. In other words Healy, returns to the questions of diversity and unity raised by Federici in Chapter 5, though for her Harrod's disaggregated analysis of the economic corporate level provides a useful way to think about the struggle for unity.

In Chapter 9 Dimitris Stevis and Terry Boswell turn to the larger question of international organizations and labour, which is of considerable importance for the politics of ghettoization and unity at the international level. Their concern is with the extent to which unprotected workers are included in or excluded from the politics of representation in international labour organizations (especially The International Confederation of Free Trade Unions (ICFTU) and the Global Union Federations (GUF)). In order to relate unprotected worker categories to a political analysis they introduce a typology aimed at capturing (in descending order) the quality of labour representation: 'agents', 'subjects', 'objects' and 'phantoms'. Their empirical research suggests that although in the immediate postwar period unprotected workers were excluded from representative labour politics (or at most were used as objects in the Cold War struggle), the defensive posture of unions in response to neoliberal globalization has resulted in a more inclusive politics of representation. Whilst this has happened mostly at the discursive level, it may signal a long-term shift of international labour politics. The authors also show that not only structural constraints but also deliberate strategies pursued by international union organizations can have a significant effect on outcomes.

The final chapter examines the implications of the analyses in the preceding chapters. There is nothing about the current state of world affairs to suggest that poverty will soon cease to be a concern in global politics. Consequently we conclude with a proposed research agenda for global politics that is grounded in the politics of power relations in production and the importance of unprotected work for the maintenance and transformation of the world order.

Note

1. The first part of this introduction owes much to joint discussions and drafting with Jeffrey Harrod.

1
Invisible Subject(s): Work and Workers in the Global Political Economy[1]

Louise Amoore

As argued in the Introduction to this book, despite increased recognition of the importance of poverty for world politics, the policy and academic literature lacks a sense of the way in which the global poor contribute as subjects to world politics via production and work relations. Focusing on the related globalization and global/international political economy literatures, this chapter argues that this is in large part because the contemporary problematic of these literatures has encouraged a particular mode of knowledge to dominate explanations of social change. Academic and popular discussions of all matters global have predominantly asked 'what is happening' type questions. It has become common to seek to explain the nature of the beast itself, with reference to technological and market structures as the driving forces of change. In this formulation the everyday lives of people are positioned passively outside the process, receiving the imperatives of global restructuring. For workers this implies that transformation of their everyday lives will follow essentially, necessarily and automatically from new production technologies, the competitive impulses of global markets and the demands of shareholder capitalism. Where agency-centred questions have been raised in the globalization debate, these have tended to focus on the decisions and actions of powerful transnational, state or corporate elites. Here the actions, experiences and articulations of workers are simply contained within corporations, transnational trade unions and state formations as sites of global restructuring.

This chapter argues that the dominant representations of global restructuring have rendered the voices, experiences and practices of workers, and particularly unprotected or unrepresented workers, unheard and invisible.[2] Not only does this invisibility produce a serious deficit in our understanding of the dynamics of global change, but it also causes us to avert our eyes from the very sites where work is taking place in the global political economy. As multinational corporations increasingly outsource their production and services they become fractured into loosely connected sites, many of them employing unprotected and precarious workers. In line with an emergent literature that looks at the relationship between globalization and everyday social practices, this chapter outlines a perspective of work as sets of social practices through which the experiences and understanding of global change are constituted (see Sinclair, 1999; Davies and Niemann, 2002; Marchand and Runyan, 2000). In contrast to the view that globalization necessarily and causally transforms work (casualizing, flexibilizing, feminizing and so on), this chapter argues that it is the everyday lives of workers as active subjects that make particular forms of global production possible and that potentially limit or contest productive practices. The chapter calls for *work* as a subject of inquiry and *workers* as global subjects to be positioned centrally in our understanding of the contemporary global political economy.

The first section explores the representation of transformations in work and work organization in the dominant discourses of globalization, and the ways in which workers are rendered invisible by such representations. In the section that follows the treatment of production and work in studies of the global political economy is discussed. When workers are made visible in analyses, which workers feature and which remain excluded? Finally, a social practice approach to work is outlined and tentative insights are drawn (see Amoore, 2002, for a more detailed account). It is argued that in order to restore and capture the concrete experiences of workers it is necessary to address the articulation of conflicts, tensions and compromises in the everyday social practices of work.

Global restructuring and invisibility

The concept of globalization has been variously described as 'vague', 'ambiguous', 'the cliché of our times' and 'wishful' (Jones, 1995, p. 3; Held *et al.*, 1999, p. 1; Scholte, 2000, p. 1). Yet it is precisely the empty and mythical nature of the concept that has endowed globalization with such seductive power, inviting people to fill the void with distinctive meanings and to deploy the concept as a means of governing social life. The dominant representations of globalization celebrate a process of change that is the inevitable outcome of the expansionary ambitions of a global economy and transborder technology:

> Lately, technology has been the main driver of globalisation … It would be naïve to think that governments could let integration proceed mainly under its own steam, trusting to technological progress and economic freedom, desirable as that would be. Politics could never be like that. (*The Economist*, 23 September 2000, p. 19)

In this reading states, societies and political activities get in the way of an economic and technological process of transformation. A kind of no alternative logic prevails, whereby it is assumed that practices will be restructured to conform to a neoliberal deregulatory model. Political and social aspects of change are abstracted from the economic and technological imperatives so that particular governments, trade unions, and welfare institutions, for example, are cast as obstructions to successful transformation. The social costs of global restructuring are commonly perceived as temporary by-products of adjustment to the imperatives of change. People in general and non-elite groups in particular are rendered invisible in such readings of globalization. They are positioned as passive receptors of global imperatives who, if they are sensible, will seize the opportunities of a globalizing world economy.

The dominant essentialist image of globalization outlined is the representation most commonly encountered in the restructuring programmes of work and labour. A vocabulary of globalization and imperative change in the form and nature of work can be found in many forums. Among them, the OECD states that 'the globalisation process requires economies to be more adaptable and workers more willing to change' (OECD, 1996, p. 13). The emphasis here is on the responsibility of workers to accept the inevitable and adapt to prescribed changes. World Bank reports provide a similar image: 'governments and workers are adjusting to a changing world. The legacy of the past can make change difficult or frightening. Yet realization of a new world of work … is fundamentally a question of sound choices – in the international and the domestic realm' (World Bank, 1995, p. 11). In this framing of the problem, it is a changing world of globalizing production and technology that is driving the process of transformation towards a new world of work. The message is that in order to respond effectively to globalization it is necessary for production costs to be reduced through the removal of barriers to the free market in factors of production – predominantly in labour. Globalization is cast as an indomitable process, equated with a shift to new forms of work organization in line with lean production, just-in-time, teamwork and *kaizen*. Workers are assumed to move towards more flexible working practices and atypical forms of employment such as part-time, temporary, zero-hours and fixed contract, outsourcing and homeworking. Labour has become a resource that must be commodified and restructured in line with global logics. Indeed the restructuring of work is presented as a panacea for the pain of globalization, so that failure to adapt to the new realities will incur the 'costs of inaction' (OECD, 1996, p. 21). This image of a globalization that is friendly if it is accepted and harnessed is a major theme in governmental reports (for example IMF, 2000, p. 2; World Bank, 2001, p. 179; United Kingdom HMSO, 2000).

It is not difficult to see how the dominant discourse on the restructuring of work has obscured the possibility of agency being exercised by workers themselves. Any discussion of the potentially contested nature of restructuring is confined to an instrumental role in implementing prescribed reforms. The globalization process is taken as a given and separate reality from social and political restructuring, which can only respond in a passive form. Indeed worker agency is represented as contrary to the flexible and adaptable workforce that is required. Put simply, there is an implicit warning that the organized actions of workers will incur the wrath of the not-so-friendly face of globalization.

Making visible? Perspectives on work and globalization

Critical accounts of globalization have tended to expose and counter the dominant discourse by means of an emphasis on the power of particular individual and collective agents to drive or resist global change. Power is thus understood as a resource that is held or resisted by identifiable agents, predominantly transnational managerial elites or nationally situated labour groups. As a result, transformations in labour and work are assumed to derive from the concrete and visible actions of multinational corporations (MNCs) as key actors in production (Stopford and Strange, 1991; Sklair, 2001), the disciplinary forces of neoliberalism (Gill, 1995) and, more rarely, the actions of fledgling global trade union movements (Cox, 1999; O'Brien, 2000; Radice, 2000). Meanwhile others point to the 'embeddedness' of MNCs in national structures (Sally, 1994) and to competing models of national capitalism – particularly industrial relations institutions and systems of production – that give distinctive character to divergent patterns of change in forms of work (Crouch and Streeck, 1997).

As will also be elaborated in the next two chapters, though these approaches provide us with a valuable antidote to the techno-economic determinism of many accounts of global transformation, they employ a limited view of power and one that serves to depoliticize the everyday actions and practices of workers. When labour is acknowledged in analyses, this tends to be in the form of organized and represented workers in trade unions. As Burnham (1999, p. 3) has compellingly argued, the category of 'labour' is explored only insofar as it equates with 'trade union bargaining power'. It is not difficult to see how even critical accounts of the restructuring of production could feed a depoliticization of labour by reinforcing the image of a spent force. The prevailing common sense begins to see the elite-level actions of national governments and corporate managers as the sole legitimate 'researchable' agents in the restructuring of work.

In subsuming work into understandings of production and capital, international political economy (IPE) analysis does tend to treat labour as a singular force and workers as a naturalized category of class that maps onto a global proletariat. As Thompson (1963, p. 10) noted, 'There is an ever-present temptation to suppose that class is a thing.' The insights of his historical mode of thought are particularly significant given the way in which the problem of class consciousness is framed in the light of contemporary changes:

> One of the most puzzling developments of the closing decades of the twentieth century has been the precipitous decline of working-class consciousness and organisation at a time of great numerical expansion of the world proletariat ... It was not unreasonable to expect the capitalist crisis of the 1970s would enhance rather than dampen the class consciousness of the expanding world proletariat. (Silver and Arrighi, 2001, p. 53)

To take seriously the historical contingency of workers' consciousness and experiences is to problematize the above assumption that class consciousness, as a monolithic entity, rises and falls in response to capitalist shifts. Workers express a multitude of contradictory and contingent subjectivities when deciphering their experiences of restructuring, and are differentially inserted into relationships with one another and with global sections of capital. The contradictions and compromises of workers' experiences thus provide a window on the tensions and inequalities of globalization. Some intraworker dynamics and relationships actually intensify and enable the programmes of flexibilization that are enacted in the name of globalization. Workers have competing experiences and expectations of the restructuring of their practices – some of those who are formally protected may experience uncertainty and work intensification elsewhere, and some of those who are formally unprotected may be well protected via other means.[3] To assume that workers constitute a single and coherent group not only seriously underplays the participation of some workers in enabling flexibilization, it also underestimates the concrete acts of resistance that emerge in the spaces between of formal organized channels. Trade unions themselves increasingly acknowledge both the importance of unprotected sites for global campaigns and the potential contradiction within the sites' relationships with other workers.

In sum, societies, firms and classes are too often assumed to contain workers, and are rarely unpacked to reveal the political and social forces engendered by these workers (Vilrokx, 1999; Amoore, 2000). As a result, while the invisibility and obfuscation of worker subjects in the globalization discourse is challenged, alternative sources and forms of invisibility emerge in IPE inquiry. The need to address new sources of the invisibility of workers is rendered all the more acute by the restructuring process, which serves to fracture the firm into a myriad of loosely connected or contracted fragments. Consequently an exploration of the restructuring of work in particular social spaces cannot meaningfully abstract the workforces of individual firms from their relationships with the practices of agencies, satellite plants, workshops and households. There are a number of dimensions to this fragmentation, each of which contributes a layer of invisibility.

First, the rapid growth in outsourcing,[4] contracting out, and the use of temporary employment agencies has moved production to sites that are not immediately visible if the firm is treated as a bounded entity. As a result contemporary studies of MNCs must confront the fact that new flexible working practices do not sit neatly within the bounded firms that tend to be the focus of IPE inquiry. As an MNC outsources some of its core and most of its non-core activities, understanding the social practices of the workplace extends to the practices of homes, sweatshops, supply-chain workshops with a contract workforce, and other *ad hoc* and unprotected sites of production. The use of unprotected labour in production for the global economy has led scholars to focus on the increased use of child labour[5] and bonded or slave labour in less-developed countries (see Klein, 2000; Bales, 1999). In the OECD countries, the growth of precarious and unprotected forms of employment has pushed workers towards individualized forms of flexibility that carry high degrees of personal risk (Moody, 1997; Coyle, 1997; Beck, 2000b). The next two chapters will introduce Cox and Harrod's conception of 'patterns of social relations of production' as a way to understand dynamics such as these (see Cox, 1987; Harrod, 1987).

The trend towards fractured firms that outsource production and business activities exacerbates a second key layer of invisibility, that of gender. As corporations replace full-time protected workers with part-time, temporary or contracted unprotected workers they also tend to replace men with women (Corporate Watch, 2000). The invisibility of the role of women in international relations (IR), IPE and industrial relations studies has, of course, been widely documented by feminist scholars (for example, Enloe, 1989; Marchand, 1996). However the apparent feminization of work that has accompanied global restructuring makes it particularly important to view women as actors in global restructuring and recognize gender in terms of the power at work within the process of change (Murphy, 1996; Marchand and Runyan, 2000). At one level this implies making women's experiences and activities visible in our analyses: '$16 trillion of global output is invisible, $11 trillion produced by women' (United Nations, 1995, p. 97). Here it is the non-monetized care, family and community, agricultural and domestic work of women that is absent from our understanding of the global political economy. At another level, however, making gender visible is about revealing the gendered nature of the power relations surrounding the global restructuring of work. Focusing solely on firms and trade unions as representing and containing workers perpetuates a gendered invisibility that sanitizes and naturalizes processes of restructuring.

Finally, and relatedly, an invisibility persists with regard to the reconfiguration of public and private within the restructuring of work. Brodie (1996, p. 387) depicts restructuring as a 'recoding' and 'renegotiating' of the boundaries between public and private. To apply Brodie's analysis to working practices, recoding is manifested in the permeable boundaries between home and work. The previously private realm of home and household has increasingly become a site of production for the global economy. The International Labour Organisation (ILO, 2000a, p. 114) has reported a rapid increase in the number of homeworkers who provide 'optimal flexibility' in the industrialized and developing countries. Households in the global North and South have become simultaneous sites of production and consumption. The clothing industry, the electronics and assembly sectors, and ancillary activities such as catering and repairs have found their way into homes. Homeworkers are predominantly low paid and unprotected, with pay based on piecework with no formal employment contract. Households are also the sites in which the global growth in domestic services has taken place. A 'new domestic labour' is said to be 'flourishing' (Ibarra, 2000, p. 454) in a climate of 'deliberate economic interventions' by the governments of the North to individualize and privatize care services (Chang, 2000, p. 3). Given IPE/IR researchers' predilection for data on change in production and work, it is perhaps unsurprising that the work of immigrant domestic workers remains hidden. The ILO standard classification of occupations fails to describe the roles of migrant domestic workers and provides no data on the extent of this work (Anderson, 2000). Indeed a recent report for the ILO on the relationship between human trafficking and the growth of domestic service agencies in the UK was gagged by the British government. As a result of the deliberate obfuscation of the 'global feminization of labour intimacy' (Chang and Ling, 2000), the highly visible expansion of financial and productive globalization continues to be isolated from its invisible other.

As a consequence of these layers of invisibility, there is a serious obfuscation in representations of the power dynamics of the global restructuring of work. The growing gap between the 'two IRs' of international relations and industrial relations has concealed the connections between workplace and world order (Harrod, 1997) making an IPE of labour and work ever more necessary, yet problematic within prevailing ontologies.[6] The legacies of positivist IR/IPE inquiry persist in the tendency to view power as a tangible entity or resource, and to seek out power-wielding people as the subjects of research. Work is thus equated with monetized economic activity and workers are conceptualized as a commodity, so those whose working practices are unprotected or subordinate receive little or no recognition in IR/IPE research. In a sense it is assumed that those who do not possess power as a resource are not significant to our understanding of the global political economy. Unprotected workers are the passive victims of someone else's power. It is this 'someone else' whom orthodox (and some heterodox) IPE researchers feel they should be concerned with, whether international organization, MNC, government or transnational class. So to be a significant, research-worthy global agent, one needs to have the ability and resources to transcend distance – to possess mobility, flexibility, distance-shrinking telecommunications and portable skills. At a time when work is increasingly undertaken in a range of unprotected spaces, addressing the blind spots in existing IPE research is rendered all the more important.

Globalization and the everyday practices of work[7]

There is currently, then, relative invisibility with regard to the meanings and concrete experiences that workers, and particularly unprotected workers, themselves ascribe to the pressures and transformations of globalization at work. A range of studies have suggested the need to explore the relationship between everyday social practices and the processes of global restructuring. For example Rose (1999), drawing on Foucault's (2003) studies of governmentality, views the transformation of working practices from the vantage point of workers' subjectivities. The feelings, wishes and aspirations of workers become bound into a web of techniques that link the state, firms and individuals in the governance of work. According to Rose's understanding, restructuring relies not only upon the material transformation of production, but also upon 'technologies of the self' that govern how workers think about themselves, their working lives, their risks and responsibilities.

From the fields of IPE and IR a diverse scholarship is emerging that seeks to revalue the more mundane experiences of working, commuting, producing and consuming that constitute contemporary global change. For example, a number of scholars have sought to raise the profile of the prosaic, ordinary and everyday practices of world politics (Campbell, 1996; Sinclair, 1999). Such approaches serve to demystify the global political economy by interweaving international or global social relations with the daily practices of workers, families and consumers (Davies and Niemann, 2002; Amoore, 2002). On the one hand this positions subordinate people at the heart our understanding of contemporary global change; on the other hand, and following the work of feminist scholars, it provides some degree of concrete human purchase on the slippery abstract structure of the global political economy (Enloe, 1989).

It is proposed here that incorporating the theory and practice of everyday life into our understanding of global restructuring can serve to heighten the visibility of workers who have previously been obscured from view. Considered through the lens offered to IPE by the study of everyday practices, the restructuring of work becomes characterized by contests, tensions and compromises over the reality and representation of change. One element of such contestation is addressed by those IPE scholars whose research has exposed the direct role of organized labour in shaping world order (Cox, 1987; O'Brien, 2000; Harrod and O'Brien, 2002). Harrod's (1987, 1997) work on the unprotected worker has also laid the foundations for those who wish to uncover subordinate economic activities in the global economy. However there is still work to be done on workers' concrete experiences of and the meanings they attribute to global restructuring. Tensions permeate the process of change as established and known practices confront demands for adaptation. Such tensions are exacerbated as the restructuring of work produces and reproduces patterns of inclusion and exclusion, and constructs and corrodes social alliances (Sinclair, 1999). Everyday social practices may occasion 'silent resistance' (Cheru, 1997, p. 153) as the experiences of unprotected workers inform shared feelings that may serve to challenge restructuring programmes (see Scott, 1990). Capturing the tensions, contradictions and forms of silent resistance in the restructuring of work effectively challenges the representation of workers as passive and adaptive. Underpinned by an ontological commitment not to view labour simply as a factor of global production, work is explored here as sets of everyday structured social practices that may enable, contest or confound the emerging social relations of globalization.

Contradictions at work

Investigating the transformation of work by focusing on social practices reveals a series of contradictions that serve to undermine the dominant representation of a benign process of restructuring. First, at the heart of neoliberal representations there is an assumption that flexible forms of work and employment are compatible with human security. Indeed it is claimed that failure to deregulate labour markets and seize the opportunities offered by new forms of work will result in a loss of security through increased unemployment and diminished competitiveness (OECD, 1997). When it is acknowledged that there may be tension between flexibility and security, the problem is presented in terms of 'striking the right balance' so that employees can enjoy 'greater involvement in their work, more job satisfaction and the possibility of developing skills and long-term employability' (European Commission, 1997, p. 8). This representation of the benefits of flexible working appeals to images of autonomous workers in an information society, while obscuring the concrete experiences of workers for whom flexibility means acute personal insecurity. For example the European Commission's green paper (ibid.) focuses on the balancing of work and home life that is made possible by teleworking, but it makes no reference to home-workers or domestic care workers whose working time is more variable and uncertain.[8]

Examination of the tensions between flexibilization programmes and everyday social practices reveals that general deregulation and new forms of work organization are simply replacing one problem of poverty (unemployment) with another (income inequality and insecurity) (ILO, 1995). Indeed implicit in OECD figures is a correlation between those societies that have implemented a jobs strategy and those with high a drop-out rate from education, widening income inequalities and a growing group of disadvantaged people (OECD, 1997). The experiences that workers have of restructured working practices reveal that, as Rose (1999) has argued, the feelings and emotions of workers have themselves become a domain for management. Interpreted in this way, programmes of labour flexibilization can be said to rest upon acute insecurity and instability on the part of workers. Indeed there is growing evidence that the most flexibilized labour markets are now experiencing the greatest growth in people trafficking as the risks of restructuring are being displaced onto the most marginal and vulnerable groups (Amoore, 2004).

Second, there is a contradiction between deunionization and levels of contestation. The restructuring of working practices along UK/US-style neoliberal lines is widely associated with an assault on traditional industrial relations, or what Harrod calls tripartist practices (see Chapter 2). Recommendations to deregulate collective bargaining to the level of individual firms assume that the contests of centralized industrial relations can be eradicated. However an exploration of the ways in which concrete industrial relations practices are challenged by restructuring reveals a different picture. The loss of formalized channels of collective bargaining in radically restructured workplaces does not result in a diminution of contestation and dissent.[9] Rather the traditional channels are replaced with less organized and more fragmented tacit forms of resistance and challenge based on common experiences and what Cox (1987, p. 22) calls 'collective images'. Nor can the neoliberal assumption that trade unions distort labour markets, thereby inflating wages and creating income inequality and unemployment, be upheld. As Coates (1999, p. 133) has put it, 'inequality is not a product of trade unions. It is a product of unregulated labour markets'. A focus on working practices suggests that the transformation of industrial relations is simply not universal: it is contingent upon workers' position in relation to other networks of employment, family, welfare and so on. As formalized, traditional forms of industrial relations practice are diminishing, it is important that we investigate the new relationships that are emerging within the firm and extending into unprotected workspaces.

Finally, the image of empowerment found in the flexibilization doctrines is undercut by the concrete realities of intensified control and surveillance in the workplace. Images of empowerment abound in global blueprints for new forms of work and work organization. In an elite group are the 'symbolic analysts', whose new 'weightless' portfolio careers offer flexible alternatives to traditional structures (Reich, 1991; Coyle, 1997), through variants of what Harrod calls in Chapter 2 the corporate pattern of social relations of production. Yet even for these apparently free agents, their experience can be 'net slavery' if 'the stock options turn into pink slips when the company goes belly up' (Ross, 2001, pp. 81–2). Then there are the workers for whom teamworking, quality circles and working time flexibility are said to offer empowering alternatives to the Taylorist style of scientific management. Workers' actual experience of hyperflexible working has much in common with the monitoring and surveillance of Taylorism, intensified by the use of self-monitoring and team targets. At the end of the supply chain, in the *maquiladora* factories and export processing zones (EPZs) in less developed countries, are the predominantly women workers for whom the image of empowered participation in the workforce is replaced by the realities of abuse, exploitation and personal injury (see Chapter 8 of this volume; Lui and Chiu, 1999; Soldatenko, 1999).

The disparities between workers' experiences of production in a global era will be explored further below. Here the aim is to emphasise the common patterns of control and power that lie behind the images (or what Harrod in the next chapter calls 'rationalities') of empowerment for many worker groups. In terms of everyday working practices, globalization has come to be associated with a hiving off of peripheral activities into branch plants, microfirms, households or the informal economy. This is the concrete reality behind the much-hyped promise of a flexible and productive global workforce. In a very real sense production has exploded into a galaxy of stratified, loosely connected workspaces that are nonetheless closely controlled through webs of corporate power. In the case of teamworking, which has been presented as a potentially autonomous and innovative experience, workplace studies demonstrate the reality of monotony, repetition, diminished skills and increased surveillance and control (Danford, 1998; Pollert, 1999; Amoore, 2004). At the heart of change in everyday working practices is the experience of increased individualization, intensified risk and heightened tension between individuals and groups. The image of individual empowerment emerging out of globalization and flexible forms of work is a constructed discourse that inhibits workers' efforts to organize.

Divisions at work

Alongside the contradictions outlined above, a practice-centred perspective reveals patterns of inclusion and exclusion that are significant to the restructuring of work. New forms of work organization and the rise of flexible and mobile forms of work imply challenges to past practices and a reconfiguring of working relationships. What Scholte (2000, p. 85) has called an emerging 'global consciousness', though, should not necessarily be read as a unifying characteristic. Instead it is based on an association of globalization with increased risk and short-termism, the intensification and speeding up of work, and feelings of individualization and acute competition. As Beck (2000b, p. 3) puts it, 'flexibility means a redistribution of risks away from the state and the economy towards the individual'. If workers come to know and recognize change in the global economy through the lens of their own experiences and via their relationships with other workers, this changes the picture somewhat. There is now a need to explore the stratified social practices of different groups and individuals, and to avoid the assumption that these necessarily represent a 'class experience' or an expression of the general interests of civil society (see Panitch, 2001).

The diversity of workers' experiences is explored here in terms of 'insider', 'intermediary' and 'outsider' practices, though of course, many groups cut across these ideal-type boundaries and there are significant patterns of inclusion and exclusion within the groups. The divisions at work are overlaid by other social divisions and inequalities so that, for example, some workers' experience of increased insecurity is ameliorated by financial security, and by inclusion in the defining of the terms of flexibility. For others the risks of flexibilization are exacerbated by social exclusion and poverty. Similarly workers' position in terms of societal, firm and legal status will condition their particular relationship to flexibilization programmes. The worker groups outlined here are in no sense bounded or static. Workers may move between insider, intermediary and outsider roles, and some may experience them simultaneously. Rather than viewing these as categories of work or workers, the constantly shifting boundaries of inclusion and exclusion can be seen as central to the means by which the contemporary restructuring of work is governed. It is precisely the ambiguity of the relationship between insiders and outsiders that operates as a disciplinary force, so that the insiders are governed by the threat of being cast outside, and the outsiders are promised the opportunity of becoming insiders. It should be pointed out that this typology of social practices is not applicable to the entire global workforce, but only those who come within the reach of corporate restructuring in a broad sense (see the discussion in Chapter 3).

Insider working practices

Insider workers predominantly take on one of two central roles in the reorganization of work. The first is direct participation in defining the terms of new forms of work and work organization, and in reinforcing the global image of flexibility and mobility. Labelled 'portfolio people' by management guru Charles Handy (1995), these business analysts, policy advisors, consultants, auditors and marketing and advertising agents are engaged in the constitution and packaging of knowledge about the future of work. The intensified risks borne by these groups, such as their lack of a company pension package and job security, are compensated by the potential rewards – working autonomy, high remuneration and the ability to afford a private pension plan. As Coyle (1997, p. 91) argues, there is a stark contrast between those working in the 'weightless industries' who can use the new flexibility to 'turn themselves into stars', and those for whom flexibility 'boils down to being exploited'. For the insider groups, their increasingly mobile and flexible lifestyle serves to reinforce their own security through a particularly extreme variant of what Harrod (Chapter 2) calls the corporate pattern of social relations of production. Indeed as Beck (2000b) suggests, the security and mobility of these groups rests upon the relative insecurity and immobility of other groups who are excluded from a defining role. Stability is not experienced by insider groups in terms of a single workplace, but in terms of the ability to enter multiple workspaces as consultants, commentators and managers of change. It should not be assumed, however, that such elite groups do not contest the effects of working arrangements on their lives. For instance after the firm Merrill Lynch was put on *Working Mother* magazine's 'best employers' list in 2000, a group of women stockbrokers, who had sued the company for sex discrimination, drew attention to their case by hiring light aircraft with banners and storming a shareholders' meeting (*New York Times*, 30 January, 2001, p. 3).

The second key group of insiders consists of core skilled workers whose working practices enable restructuring, though perhaps not as consciously as the first group. The highly skilled German craftspeople in manufacturing, and the software programmers in the British service sector, for example, have become wrapped up in the discourse on restructuring. Their stock options, bonus-led pay structures and performance-related pay, together with the nature of their work, ties their interests to particular programmes of flexibility, either through a pure form of the corporate pattern or what Ryner in (Chapter 3) calls an increasingly 'hollowed-out' form of tripartism. In the UK, US and to a lesser extent Germany there has been a common tendency for skilled workers to play the labour market in a way that mirrors the 'leanness' of corporate organizations: 'Well-paid technicians, engineers, and designers became independent contractors ... . "Employees without jobs", they moved from company to company, "pollinating" the seeds of innovation, according to the new flexible style of corporate organization' (Ross, 2001, p. 79).

The assumption that has dominated IR and IPE accounts of workers – that they constitute potential forces of resistance to globalization – is highly problematic. Core worker stockholders and mobile skill traders have become emblematic of the possibilities of flexible work, and have featured heavily in governmental and media reports and advertising images. In the words of Rose (1999, p. 117), management programmes are accompanied by 'individual portraits of the successful entrepreneur and high achiever'. Of course the uncertainties of global restructuring and the concomitant demands of everyday working life are more comfortably reconciled for insider groups than for those who work on the margins of the space they so fleetingly occupy.

Intermediary working practices

Intermediary workers can be defined as those whose practices serve a 'buffer' function at the interface between the demand for flexible labour and the need for employment and work. In essence the intermediaries insulate the insiders from responsibility for the risks and reprisals of the reorganization of work. They take radically different forms, ranging from recruitment and employment agents, to informal subcontractors and the individuals and gangs who supply undocumented, unprotected or slave labour (Bales, 1999). At one end of the scale, management and human resource consultants move fluidly between insider and intermediary functions, maintaining the mantle of external expertise that is, necessary to legitimate their role in prescribing work reorganization and to lend an air of objective neutrality to restructuring. Currently, for example, there is a trend to use British management consultants on short-term contracts to oversee the privatization of industries in Continental Europe. Similarly PricewaterhouseCoopers and Cap Gemini Ernst & Young (CGEY) have been contracted to monitor the implementation of labour codes of conduct for garment and electronics multinationals. Their independence as intermediaries has been questioned by international trade union confederations, though it is clear that for their corporate clients they are diffusing the risks and responsibilities of outsourcing. As the chairman of CGEY describes it, the professional service firms 'provide a more complete solution' by engaging in both 'audit' and 'non-audit' activities (*The Economist*, 7 July 2001, p. 87).

While professional service workers are situated at the boundary between insider corporate interests and outsider worker groups, intermediaries can also serve as traders and buyers of the services of unprotected outsider groups. One such group comprises subcontractors who buy in contingent labour for a specific contract with a client corporation. In the automotive component, electrical and garment manufacturing sectors, and in service sectors ranging from logistics and transportation to cleaning and catering, such subcontractors are employed by MNCs to absorb the slack in their lean production systems. Intermediary contractors diffuse the responsibility for stock inventory, terms of employment and labour costs down the line to smaller firms, 'shop houses' and homeworkers. A number of recent tragedies in the UK have illustrated the dangers of this. In October 2000 a student working part-time in rail maintenance was killed on a stretch of track in London. Railtrack, which owned the line at that time, had contracted the maintenance to Balfour Beatty, which had then subcontracted to McGinley Recruitment, which in turn had employed the student via an agency. The RMT union, commenting on the incident, stated that 'if this young lad has been placed in danger by his employer, then action must be taken'. Of course the problem was that the string of intermediaries made it difficult to determine who the employer actually was. Not only unprotected workers such as students, but also migrant workers in the UK have died in similar accidents when subcontracted to fruit picking and other food industry gangmasters (see Amoore, 2004).

In effect the enormous growth of outsourcing and subcontracting in production and services has diffused risk disproportionately along a supply chain, reducing the responsibility (or perception of responsibility) the customer firm has for work done in their name. In terms of working practices, many intermediary traders and buyers outsource to firms or individuals that are known for poor pay and intense workloads, and for their use of temporary, unprotected or illegal labour (EIRO, 2000; Klein, 2000). Research into the roles and practices of these intermediary actors is almost totally absent from the contemporary agenda in IPE. And yet a focus on the diffuse webs of production and supply begins to reveal an array of complex relationships between worker groups. Nonetheless experiences of the 'outsiders' among them remain relatively invisible in studies of the contemporary global political economy.

Outsider working practices

Outsider groups are those who are excluded from defining the terms and nature of the new forms of work and working practices. This is not to say that their working practices do not play a significant part in shaping or contesting transformation. Though we may not consider them to exercise power in a direct sense, their practices and relationships lie at the heart of the webs of power that constitute contemporary restructuring. The much-prized labour mobility and flexibility of the management gurus' 'portfolio people' is reproduced through the practices of outsider 'precarious people' (Cox, 1999, p. 87) – a reserve army of contingent workers in factories, offices and homes. The outsiders cannot be defined in terms of a single class, and indeed the overwhelming trend is towards a fracturing of common working identities, a 'patchwork quilt characterised by diversity, unclarity and insecurity in people's work and life' (Beck, 2000b, p. 1). In this sense the outsiders are themselves divided into an array of disparate individuals and groups in order to destabilize and disrupt the potential for organization and to provide optimal flexibility:

> Every corporation wants a fluid reserve of part-timers, temps and freelancers to help it keep overheads down and ride the twists and turns in the market … One thing is certain: offering employment – the steady kind, with benefits, holiday pay, a measure of security and maybe even union representation – has fallen out of economic fashion. (Klein, 2000, p. 231)

Thus although outsider groups are fluid, segmented and difficult to identify, it is precisely for these reasons that they must be included in our understanding of global restructuring. The 'rise of the permatemp' documented by *Time Magazine* (12 July 1999) is indicative of the ironic permanence of temporary and contingent work. Despite barriers to the formal organization of their interests and direct efforts to position workers in competitive rather than collaborative relationships with one another, as Harrod's study of the patterns of social relations of production for unprotected work seeks to grasp in the following chapter, the experiences of outsider workers fall into common patterns and conflicts that must be understood if meaningful dialogue between protected and unprotected workers is to take place. First, there is a consciousness of individualism and 'hypercompetitiveness' (Vilrokx, 1999; Sinclair, 1999). The use of human resource management techniques such as benchmarking the performance of production plants,[10] coupled with the 'storming' effects of just-in-time (JIT) production,[11] cause workers to feel that the greatest threats exist within the supply chain itself. The volatility and irregularity of production that is commonly associated with efforts to respond to the perceived demands of global markets is understood by workers to be created by the manipulation of orders to fit JIT, to suit shareholder reports or to respond to last-minute short-run contracts. Similarly outsider groups associate the use of quality circles and teams with attempts to encourage them to compete with one another, and this is commonly resisted by tacit and infrapolitical means (Scott, 1990).

Second, and relatedly, outsider groups widely associate globalization with a diminution of collective identity and group representation. This phenomenon has been widely documented by industrial relations scholars in their studies of deunionization. However the changing practices of the unions themselves reveal much about the character of contemporary change in the workplace from what Harrod (Chapter 2) calls 'bipartism' and 'tripartism' to 'corporate' and 'enterprise' patterns. UK and US trade unions have responded to challenges by becoming individual service providers for their 'consumers', thus reinforcing individualization and excluding contingent and non-standard workers (Williams, 1997). Stabilizing and protecting core workers has the effect of further destabilizing the already precarious contract workforce. For a flexibility-seeking corporation the existence of a protected and stable core of workers increase the incentive to create a buffer of temporary or outsourced working practices. This contributes to the polarization of the core group of workers, who may organize to protect themselves from restructuring (or to negotiate role in the form of restructuring), and a larger group of workers in contingent, outsourcing or homeworking roles whose practices may undermine these efforts, making dialogue problematic (Gallin, 2001). The polarization of worker groups is taking place in close spatial proximity, so it cannot be understood purely by reference to geographical development divisions. Research has shown, for example, that restructuring has produced dramatic increases in socioeconomic and spatial inequalities in the cities of the developed world (Sassen, 1994; Enloe, 1996). Feelings of belonging and alienation transcend distance, so precarious workers in the advanced industrialized world may share some of the characteristics of developing country workers in the same supply chain.[12] Indeed their practices may be remarkably similar and they may feel that they are competing directly for their personal security.

Finally, the social practices of paid work are becoming increasingly similar to the social practices of unpaid work in the home. The British media has observed this trend in terms of 'family life mirroring the workplace' as 'services such as cleaning, cooking, childcare, Do-It-Yourself and laundry' are being contracted out (*Guardian*, 6 February 2000). Thus as Young (2001, p. 316) argues, 'the growing participation of professional women in the labour market is accompanied by the largely "invisible" development of paid work in the private household'. To trace the webs of power in the restructuring of a large European or North American MNC is to cross the boundary between public and private, to see the relationship between 'flexible' professionals and the 'flexible' cleaners and childminders who work in their homes. In terms of the categories Harrod will introduce in the next chapter, this can be seen as the rearticulation of the working practices of the MNCs (tripartism, but increasingly corporate and enterprise patterns, and subcontracting and self-employment) in relation to household and casual patterns of social relations of production.

Meanwhile, for the most flexible contract workers the 24-hour demands of care and household work are contemporaneous with the demands of production for the global economy. These 'precarious workers' (Cox, 1999, p. 87) experience what one woman worker has termed 'knife-edge flexibility' in paid working practices and rigid constraints in unpaid family work. Another worker, commenting on her husband's opposition to her new working time arrangements, could see no clear boundary between paid cleaning work for the MNC and the unpaid and informal work outside: 'I don't know why they fuss on so much about the new hours. I have worked like this as far back as I can remember. It is the same here as at home.'[13] In industries such as textiles, garments and electronics, where the production chain extends into unprotected sites, women at this ultimately flexible end of production take on considerable personal risks. Their labour is a complex blend of private household and public enterprise production, and as a result they are often not legally acknowledged to be employees. Work that takes place in *ad hoc* workshops, in family living rooms or on kitchen tables tends to be both unprotected and invisible (Sassen, 1994; Hsuing, 1996). The rise of the 'multi-activity society' (Beck, 2000a, p. 42) interweaves the social practices of work, family, leisure and consumption, giving rise to new political questions and potential sites of political organization.

Politics at work

A focus on the contradictions and divisions that arise from the restructuring of work demonstrates that work and workers need to enter the globalization debate on a level that reveals the political nature of changing practices. Is it possible to sketch the terrain of an emergent politics of transformation in working practices? As large firms disperse their activities and workers experience greater insecurity, can we identify spaces of potential political organization? At one level the most visible political contests could be said to be the strategic activities of nationally or transnationally organized trade unions (O'Brien, 2000; 2001). Here the contradictions of globalization may create the pressures and opportunities for 'global social movement unionism' (Lambert, 1999), and extend IPE inquiry into the political economy of labour (Harrod and O'Brien, 2002). The activities of trade unions in forming alliances with NGOs, participating in highly visible antiglobalization protests (Waterman and Wills, 2001) and adapting to engage with workers in the informal sectors suggest that organized labour could become a political mechanism for a global civil society (Somavia, 1999; IILS, 1999).[14]

However at the level of social practices the study of firms, unions and organizations as primary sites of political activity in the global political economy is problematic. Put simply the fracturing of traditional sites of production leads us to question the representativeness of trade unions and other institutionalized political agencies. In a report for the ILO, Hyman points to the gap between the image of a homogeneous labour internationalism and the concrete experiences of different worker groups:

It is evident that the traditional core constituency of trade union membership has dwindled, while there has been expansion at two extremes: those with professional or technical skills who may feel confident of their individual capacity to survive in the labour market; and those with no such resources but whose very vulnerability makes effective collective organization and action difficult to achieve or perhaps even contemplate. (Hyman, 1999, p. 3)

We are reminded that mechanical and organized forms of solidarity are formulated and constructed in ways that are historically particular (Thompson, 1963; Hyman, 1999). As production is actively shifted into unprotected domains, restructuring programmes have rendered past myths of solidarity more difficult to sustain, making it impossible to assume 'the existence of a "normal worker" ', and emphasizing the need for 'organic' solidarities based on 'direct experiences, immediate milieux and specific patterns of social relations' (Hyman, 1999b, p. 3; 1999a, p. 96). Challenges to existing workplace political institutions have broken past patterns of solidarity and allegiance. There are clear dangers but also opportunities here. The dangers lie in assuming that the workplace, in becoming deunionized, has also become depoliticized, thereby reinforcing the emerging disparities in working practices. The opportunities lie in recognition of the common experiences, feeling and challenges within these diverse practices. In contrast to the idea that labour must operate globally in order to match the scale of MNC activity (see Herod, 2001), workers' everyday thoughts and actions defy a global/local opposition. The apparent global activities of organizations such as the Clean Clothes Campaign, Women Working World Wide, HomeNet and the Self-Employed Women's Association are informed by the everyday experiences of workers in precarious sectors. Likewise the struggles that are labelled local, such as plant-level industrial action and campaigns, or the everyday acts of disruption in a stretched lean production system, are undertaken within frameworks of thought that blend the near and the far in personal histories. Contrary to the assumption that the crisis of industrial relations has removed politics from work, the form and nature of change in work and its organization remains politically open, contingent and contested.

Concluding remarks

The starting point of this chapter was the recognition that the dominant representations of global restructuring have rendered the voices, experiences and practices of workers unheard and invisible. At a time when IPE and IR scholars are calling for the politicization and historicization of their subjects, the concern of this chapter has been the people who remain invisible in analyses, and why these people are considered to be insignificant. Where political struggle and agency have been uncovered in IPE inquiry, this has predominantly been related to individuals, groups and institutions who are perceived to wield the power necessary to engage with the debate on global restructuring. It is national governments, corporate agencies, international economic institutions and (much more rarely) trade unions, civil society associations and new social movements that feature in the contents pages of IR/IPE texts and journals. When workers do feature they are assumed either to be contained within the parameters of the aforementioned collective agencies or to be outside these boundaries as passive victims of change. Thus in a very real sense the capacity of ordinary people to comprehend, contest or give consent to global restructuring is seriously underestimated. This chapter has attempted to reopen some of this political terrain by asking which groups are visible in IPE analyses, and exploring the grounds on which others are considered insignificant and excluded.

A first question to be raised in considerations of the relationship between the global political economy and ordinary working practices, is whether unprotected and precarious workers actually matter to our understanding of the global political economy. Do they have a rightful place on our research agendas? This chapter has argued that shedding light on the experiences and practices of a range of workers' groups is not simply about highlighting grassroots or ground-level political activity. Indeed it has shown that the conceptual categories of 'global' and 'local' are significantly problematized and transcended by the concrete thoughts and practices of people in their everyday lives. Not only does the neglect of unprotected workers further entrench them at the margins of globalized social relations, but their invisibility also obscures central aspects of transformation in the global political economy. Even for those who study the activities of MNCs in mainstream IPE, an understanding of 'life in the supply chain' brings significant insights. The fractured firm moves production into unprotected sites, cutting across public–private boundaries along complex supply chains, so that it becomes difficult to trace lines of responsibility and relations of power and control. The failure to bring workers' experiences into the global restructuring debate allows MNCs to commit this sleight of hand and exclude the matter from our analyses. While business management studies extol the virtues of 'successful outsourcing', for example, IPE is slow to produce critical readings of the social power relations of outsourcing practices.

Raising the profile of unprotected workers not only exposes the new sites in which work is done for the global political economy, it also reveals political contestations over the reality and representation of the restructuring of work. Following the analysis of this chapter, workers do not simply passively respond to a global force that is somehow greater than them and beyond their reach, rather they both constitute and contest the meaning of that force in their everyday lives. In their frameworks of thought and action, workers engage with the restructuring of their own practices: differentially, unevenly and contradictorily, and within the constraints of prevailing webs of power. The assumption that the perceived dictates of globalization and flexibilization are transmitted uncontroversially through the layers of organizations, states, firms and workers is subjected to serious challenge. The insecurity that is evident in concrete working practices directly undermines the benign images of security, empowerment and choice that accompany doctrines of flexibility. It is clear that complex patterns of inclusion and exclusion emerge from transformations in the nature and form of work, with increased security for some resting upon and requiring intensified risk for others. For the insider 'portfolio person' the risks of flexibility can be reconciled comfortably with the opportunities offered by mobility. Meanwhile, for the most 'flexible' precarious worker at the end of the supply chain, risk and insecurity are intensified. An understanding of such relationships is vital to the mapping of political terrain that may formally and informally connect organized workers. Viewed in this way the restructuring of work is inherently political, contested and contingent. If we choose to depict or ignore particular realities of global change, highlighting the sanitized spheres of technology and corporate strategy, we leave the 'messier' realms of work and labour in deep shadow. In doing so we risk obscuring the politics of restructuring that gives the character and form to contemporary change in the workplace and in wider world politics.

Notes

1. I wish to thank the editors of this volume plus Isa Bakker, Jeff Harrod, Paul Langley and Mustapha Kamal Pasha for their comments on previous versions of this chapter. I acknowledge the financial support of the British Academy.
2. This focus on the relationship between epistemological bias and invisibility owes much to the work of Tooze and Murphy (1996), who suggest that poverty and the poor have been made invisible by the predilection of the fields of international relations and international political economy for empiricist epistemology and positivist methodology. For further discussion of the positivist and empiricist underpinnings of international theory see Smith (1996).
3. I owe this point to discussions with Dimitris Stevis.
4. The Outsourcing Institute (2000) estimates that outsourcing is growing in the US at around 15 per cent per annum. While it is clear that the practice is growing in all the OECD countries, its rate is difficult to estimate as the boundary between inside and outside provision is increasingly fluid. For example some German firms part-purchase suppliers, thus technically making production 'in-house' but maintaining the external relationship. Cleaning, maintenance and catering are commonly outsourced by British companies, though is rarely recognized and reported as outsourcing, as it is not considered to be a production function. In the case of research on outsourcing business journal articles on how to outsource are burgeoning (see Elmuti and Kathwala, 2000), though there is little critical analysis of the nature and effects of outsourcing (see Bittman *et al.*, 1999).

5. The ILO estimates that around 250 million children (5–14 years old), are working in economic activities worldwide. For 120 million of them this work is full-time and precludes schooling; the remainder combine work with schooling (ILO, 1998a).
6. Harrod and O'Brien (2002) bring together the insights of labour studies, IPE, industrial relations, international relations and the sociology of work. The collection addresses the common problematics that global restructuring brings to these disciplines.
7. The relationship between globalization and social practice is explored in Amoore and Langley (2000). The ideas presented here owe much to that joint work.
8. The term homeworker denotes people working at home on tasks that are generally low paid, insecure and undertaken on a piecework basis, usually with no contract. In contrast a teleworker may be a manager, a senior professional or an other type of employee who works from home.
9. During 1999 in the UK 12 days per 1000 employees were lost due to industrial action. In the same year in Germany, where trade unions remain central despite declining density, one day was lost per 1000 employees (EIRO, 1999).
10. It is not uncommon for workers to be made directly aware of their individual performance *vis-à-vis* competitor plants and contractors. This can take the form of daily or weekly bulletins of benchmark performances, or screens on the factory floor displaying targets.
11. Just-in-time (JIT) production implies a reduction of slack or buffers in the system, requiring minimal materials and labour inventory, and an electronic data system that links the customer to the firm and the supply chain. For large electronics MNCs this commonly manifests itself in weekly or biweekly estimates of production runs, necessitating instantaneous responses in working practices.
12. Soldatenko's (1999) study of Latina garment workers in Los Angeles reveals the complexity of the shared experiences and feeling of alienation. The intraworker and interethnic conflict in sweatshop situations problematizes the treatment of workers as a collective body of resistors. A central theme in the explosion of the subcontracting chain is what Soldatenko refers to as the difficulty in 'forging an effective culture of resistance' (ibid., p. 319).
13. Confidential interviews with contract workers at an electronic component multinational, 24 February 1998.
14. The Clean Clothes Campaign Network, for example, includes trade unions, women workers' groups and networks, and worker education bodies. The aim is to improve the working conditions of garment workers worldwide.

2
The Global Poor and Global Politics: Neomaterialism and the Sources of Political Action

Jeffrey Harrod

In conventional discussions of international politics it might be considered strange, if not eccentric, to start with an analysis of a small enterprise in an Indian industrial town or the pitch of a hawker in the Philippines. Yet, strangely, and perhaps without knowing it, this starting point is inherent in the position of those who argue that global politics will be determined by the actions of the global poor. For example, in a research report produced for the RAND corporation, Nichiporuk (2000, p. 20) notes:

> Finally, the squalid living conditions in the rings of slums that now surround many third world cities are becoming a fairly permanent condition. Many of the recent migrants live in these areas and their desperate straits can prove to be fertile ground for radical and revolutionary groups that seek new recruits for battle against the existing regime.

Similarly the writers of the 1999 *Human Development Report* are unequivocal about the source of global unrest:

> Social tensions and conflicts are ignited when there are extremes of inequality between the marginal and the powerful. Indonesia shows what can happen when an economic crisis sets off latent social tensions between ethnic groups – or between rich and poor. Recent research on complex humanitarian emergencies concluded that

'horizontal inequalities' whether ethnic, religious or social are the major cause of the current waves of civil conflicts. (UNDP, 1999, p. 36)

More purposefully, Gill (1996, p. 216) argues that 'the subordinated classes – including the marginalized of the political economy – are neither indifferent nor inactive in face of their oppression. Indeed these people have the capacity to undermine and disrupt the privileged circuits of production and consumption.'

The poor may also become active in global politics in a way not envisioned by those who view poor people as a mass of protesters, as noted by the Office of the US Assistant Secretary of Defense (1998, p. ii) concerning the background of recruits to the US armed forces: 'Socioeconomic representation in the volunteer force is a key interest because of concerns that our Nation's defense might fall heavily on the poor and the underclass.' The implication of these quotations is that a formal army composed of the poor will engage with an informal army of the poor reacting to the conditions of poverty.

Thus for some the global poor are a potential source of resistance to current global policies, while for others they are a threat to stability, wealth accumulation, power and privilege. The latter perceived threat invokes the 'fear of the mass' that was so prevalent in earlier epochs (Balibar, 1993) and characterized the socially and politically bipolar class societies in the Third World in the middle of the twentieth century. Since that time there has been a perceptible shift in the demonology of the perceived precipitators of social turbulence or change. In the 1960s the 'demons' were peasants and peasant armies, in the 1980s they were workers in unions (Harrod, 2004) and now they are the urban poor, in all their religious, ethnic or antisocial configurations. This shift is reflected in the development and international social programmes of major financial institutions and national administrations, which in the past decade have increasingly concentrated on poverty alleviation, as in the case of the World Bank, or on poverty issues such as 'livelihood practices' in national development cooperation programmes.

If it is the case that the poor are either a threat or a force for change, then what is needed is an analytical framework or approach that can help show why this is the case. Such an approach might also reveal the nature of the political attitudes, consciousness and forms of action of poor populations and the trajectories that social and political action might take. As indicated in the previous chapter, the international relations, international political economy and globalization literatures, by their very design, are not well equipped to deal with this question.

The purpose of this chapter is to address this need. The first section focuses on the productive activities of people. It examines the power relations that surround work and the attitudes and world views that people derive from their experience of this, which in turn are important to the part played by such people and the potential for social and political change and development. The approach adapted, here called neomaterialism, can be applied to the whole of the world's labour force. In the second section the approach is applied to a contemporary section of the labour force that is variously called the underclass, the labouring poor, urban marginals or precarious workers and can be found among the majority of the conventionally defined global poor. The section argues that a neomaterialist approach in which blanket segments of productive populations are disaggregated using the criteria of work and power relations can make an important contribution to the analysis of contemporary world political events.

Neomaterialism: restoring work and production to contemporary analysis

Essentially the neomaterialist approach takes the most important activity of humankind (productive work), observes that this involves different patterns of power relations, argues that the world views of individuals are developed from or influenced by these patterns, and that such world views are important to mobilization and political action. This means that the preferred method for disaggregating the global labour force is according to the patterns of power relations surrounding production, rather than nationality, occupation, ethnicity or gender.

This approach to politics and society was launched in 1987 in two free-standing but linked volumes that elaborated a theory of social forces in the process of change in global society: *Production, Power, and World Order: Social Forces in the Making of History* (Cox, 1987) and *Power, Production and the Unprotected Worker* (Harrod, 1987). Part 1 of Cox's volume outlined this approach, which had been partially developed in the early 1970s (Cox, 1971) and which he and Harrod had worked on until the publication of the two volumes. The Harrod volume also contained some personal viewpoints on the nature and application of the approach. Cox's *Production, Power, and World Order* was deservedly acclaimed as a seminal work, especially Part 2, whose focus on world orders associated it with the neo-Gramscian approach and made it a core text in international political economy. The broader approach to society, change and its comprehension in Part 1 and the statement, elaboration and application of it in Harrod's book has received less attention.

This section recounts some of the first steps in the process of revising, refining, elaborating, improving and, in some cases, departing from the original presentation of the approach. It starts from the position that while the approach can be integrated into the structure and perceptions associated with Marxist materialism, as it has been through the elaboration of Gramscian historical blocs, it need not be. Further, while it could be considered materialist in that its focus is on work and production, it need not be the version of materialism made familiar by Marx and Marxists.

Patterns of power relations in production

The neomaterialist approach was developed, admittedly with resort to intuition and the use of ideal types, by surveying the global labour force (defined as those engaged in expending energy for socially valued output) to identify distinguishable patterns of power relations in work and production. In this regard the power relations between an entrepreneur and a non-unionized employee are held to be different from those between an indebted peasant and a moneylender, or between those with a secure contract of employment and those who are casually employed. At the heart of all power relations is the degree of domination, subordination and authority in the productive process. Differences in degrees of power and authority, combined with different types of power holder and subjects of power, create different patterns of power relations. These patterns can be observed universally and thus the identification of them is not contingent upon country, region or other sociopolitical variables.

Some of these patterns[1] are dominant in that the groups and actors within them and the dynamics of their particular power relations substantially affect the nature of other patterns, while subordinate patterns are led by events and outputs from the dominant patterns. The combination of dominant and subordinate patterns in any identifiable cluster is viewed as a distinct political economy that may or may not be a nation state. Thus the power relations between important trade unions and corporations clearly affect, in terms of wages, conditions of work and labour law, people in other patterns, such as the self-employed, unorganized small enterprise workers and small-scale farmers.

Each of the patterns is dynamic; that is, power relations are dynamic and patterns can be transformed or eliminated. More importantly, persons employed in one pattern may move from that pattern to another, or may be in several patterns at the same time. For example these are four facets of the power relations experienced by a self-employed person, defined as someone who produces without employing other people. The work of and production by the self-employed person is determined by the suppliers of materials or services, the regulators of the conditions of production (often state agencies), the customers and the competitors. The size of the returns from work is determined by the nature of the engagement of the self-employed person with these powers. If someone is employed by the self-employed person then a new actor enters the power relations. Now the pattern becomes more typical of a small enterprise, and the previously self-employed person becomes an employer with power over the employee. Thus the four-faceted pattern has become a five-faceted one and the roles and attitudes of the persons involved will change.

It is also argued that power relations in production are the source of the rationalities, ideologies, world views and institutionalized practices that enable, disguise or psychologically mitigate acceptance of the authority, domination and inequalities within and resulting from the power relations. The strength of such rationalities and the internalization of them by subordinate producers affect the nature and direction of change in these relations. The development of world views or counter-rationalities and the political action they precipitate or determine are an essential part of social change.

In the period from the mid 1970s to the mid 1980s, 12 patterns were discerned (Cox, 1987, pp. 32–50; Harrod, 1987, pp. 14–19), but since then – confirming the dynamic nature of the approach – some of these have become less important (Ryner, 2002) and some – those associated with command economies – have been eliminated. In addition the original nomenclature of some of the patterns has now become inappropriate. Viewing the current world labour force from such a perspective, eight distinct patterns can be discerned. These patterns could be labelled 1–8 or A–H, but for purpose of image and identification words are used to help capture the core relationships and the most important persons or organizations in the pattern. Thus the current patterns are referred to as tripartite, corporate, state corporatist, peasant, casual, enterprise, self-employed and household (for further clarification and elaboration, see Chapter 3).[2]

To illustrate these patterns we shall place them in a hypothetical political economy. In this political economy a small proportion of the workforce belongs to organized unions and there is tripartite bargaining among the state, companies and unions (the tripartite pattern); a smaller proportion of administrative workers have an enduring attachment to state agencies or a corporation (the corporate pattern); a larger proportion works in enterprises where the employers have power over the employees but less power than that enjoyed by corporations (the enterprise pattern); a large section of the labour force consists of partially or intermittently employed people (the casual pattern); a residue of people engage in household services, for example child rearing and food preparation (the household pattern); and a mass of small tenant farmers are engaged in agriculture (the peasant pattern).

Within these different patterns there is a divide between workers or producers who are protected by workers' organizations, state structures and corporate practices, and those who have less protection from the power and authority surrounding their productive work. The patterns of power involving the latter, the unprotected worker, or more accurately the less protected worker, are examined in detail in Harrod (1987) and are the concern of the second section of this chapter.

This is a stripped-down account of an approach to society and world politics that begins with power at its lowest and most immediate level – the workplace. It is not the intention here to present the details and arguments in support of the approach, but to suggest that there is a need to revise current perceptions and to show what the approach might contribute to political analysis where other approaches have fallen short and left something to be desired.

Launching a different approach: revising traditional perceptions

There are three basic elements to the neomaterialist approach: production and class, power, and rationality and consciousness. Each of these differs from their use in traditional Marxist materialism and their use in approach differs from conventional political sociology.

Production, class and materialism

Marx's theorizations of production had a specific and rather narrow meaning that was associated with capitalism and the theories of alienation and surplus value, and on that definition Marx and his glossators built a huge and sophisticated philosophical, sociological, political and economic theory of capitalism. However the focus on capitalism as a society-wide 'mode of production' became problematic when societies with only limited possession of the characteristics of capitalism became the subject of analysis. Capitalism, like all constructs, was a relative concept but it was relative only to the past (feudalism) and to a non-existent future (communism). It appeared that only the present was capitalist.

Generations of non-European revolutionaries and intellectuals struggled with what would now be called the Eurocentric idea that the industrial present in Europe, and particularly in the Britain of the 1850s, was the end of extant history. Indeed such ethnocentrism was expressed in the communist and Marxist literature of the times. As Cox notes:

> The term *capitalist* is not used in this study to apply to a single mode of *production*. Indeed, the capitalist mode of development has spawned several distinctive modes of social relations of production. To bracket these all together as a single capitalist mode of production confuses things that are significantly distinct. (Cox, 1987, p. 406; see also Harrod, 1987, p. 29)

The unsatisfactory nature of the narrowness of the Marxist view was made apparent by two developments. One was the attempt by European intellectuals in the 1970s to explain the current historico-political juncture in Marxists terms; that is, a century away from Marx's original predictions. The other involved revolutionaries and thinkers outside Europe in places where industrialization was in its infancy. Nicos Poulantzas, writing in 1968, and Mao Tse Tung, writing in 1926, can be taken as representative of these developments and can also been viewed as initiating the move towards a neomaterialist position.

Poulantzas set himself the task of modernizing Marxism, essentially by emphasizing the importance of the so-called capitalist state. His *Political Power and Social Classes* (1973) contains many elements of a neomaterialist approach: a plurality of 'modes of production'; dominant and subordinate modes comprising a 'social formation'; power blocs within the capitalist state and so on. His book can be viewed as the most important and thoughtful expression of the intellectual development it represents. However his refusal to leave the confines of Marxism and his assumption of the overall domination by the 'capitalist mode of production' means that, despite his reference to a plurality of modes in social formations, he never specifies these unless they are historical. Eventually the potential of flexible analysis and the greater scope implied by the plurality of modes in social formations is abandoned and he concentrates on the capitalist social formation. The social formation is conflated with one mode of production (ibid., pp. 15–16). Poulantzas' unpreparedness to depart too far from Marx's theory of capitalism causes even greater problems when it comes to class, and especially the bourgeoisie. 'Fractions' of the bourgeoisie present even greater problems, for while fractions connected with production – industrial and commercial – are acceptable there is no place, for example, for the bureaucracy (ibid., pp. 84–5).

The neomaterialist approach, which takes the multiplicity of power relations in production to its logical conclusion, easily accommodates 'fractions' as dominant producers in dominant patterns. The state becomes the arena for contests between such groups, which seek rents and support from the state with such ferocity that class unity with other groups may be abandoned. In such cases Lasswellian notions of power and standard political science analyses of power, if linked to production, become useful indicators of political outcomes. Such is currently the case with the increased power of corporate elites whose power stems from organizational corporatism (Harrod, 2005).

Mao Tse Tung, in his 1926 pamphlet *Analysis of Classes in Chinese Society*, laid the ground that was subsequently addressed by Poulantzas, but Mao was concerned with the lower classes rather than the bourgeoisie. Mao was faced with a social formation that no European Marxist had had to consider from the standpoint of revolution, and certainly not from strategies involving war and casualties. Informed by the Marxist focus on production Mao listed categories, if not ideal types, of subordinate workers in different classes and situations in contemporary China. Thus he divided the so-called 'petit bourgeois' into three groups: self-employed artisans and land-owning peasants (the 'semiproletariat'; land-renting peasants and small handcraft workers; and the 'lumpenproletariat'. Missing from his account was household production and the role of women in it, which he corrected in a publication in 1927:

> As for women, in addition to being dominated by these three systems of authority, they are also dominated by the men (the authority of the husband). These four authorities – political, clan, religious and masculine – are the embodiment of the whole feudal-patriarchal system and ideology, and are the four thick ropes binding the Chinese people, particularly the peasants. (Mao Tse-Tung, 1964, p. 43)

Mao examined the consciousness of these groups of subordinate workers, produced by the power relations, using the groups' potential attitudes towards the revolutionary movement as a yardstick. (At that time he noted a development that was relevant to the current Chinese situation: that peasants who had lost their land and handicraftsmen who were unable to get work joined mutual aid societies that became secret sects with cult overtones.)

Both Poulantzas and Mao dismembered Marx's capitalist class and working class; devised new modes, forms or patterns of production; divided class fractions into dominant classes or distinguishable subordinate groups; countered the Eurocentric and 'workerist' bias; and thus laid the groundwork for a new, eclectic and more encompassing materialism than that of a general theory of capitalism. But both of them, Poulantzas intellectually and Mao practically, refused to admit or declare their essential deviation from Marx. Poulantzas disguised his deviation by resort to high theory and refinement of definitions, and Mao, at least in 1926, declared that despite his profound and expert assessment of the revolutionary potential of various groups the almost non-existent industrial proletariat was to be 'the leading force in our revolution' (ibid., p. 14).

This implicit criticism of the narrower Marxist view (some argue that it was started by Marx himself in the *Eighteenth Brumaire*) was not able to produce an alternative variation. To some extent the dialectic within Marxism has not produced a synthesis. To consider production as more than a facet of capitalism, that producers may be as divided by their specific experiences in production as they are united by their position of relative subordination, is part of that process and any neomaterialist approach is but a step in that direction.

Power

Power is at the core of the neomaterialist approach in that it is power that allocates work and production, configures the distribution of the product and disciplines the producers, and in the course of this it constructs rationalities, resulting in specific forms of consciouness and world views. There have been three basic approaches to the study of power. The first concerns the power of large organizations at the apex of societies, such as the state, the church and the corporation. The second involves class or group power, in which organizations are seen as vehicles for such power. The third is to do with the more diffuse power found in forms of discipline and authority aimed at ensuring regularity of behaviour.

The first of these approaches is the traditional one in political science. It is now commonplace to assume that humanity is characterized by intraspecies violence and that it is necessary to construct norms, rules, laws, symbols and centres of power to avoid self-destruction (Harrod, 2003; Cooper, 2003). Power in this purview essentially resides in the state. Significantly, intraspecies violence is rarely ascribed to greed for material goods or services, or factors such as territory or, security, despite the fact that these were common motives in antiquity among warring tribes. This view of power either ignores or discounts the more primary uses of power, which may indeed support state power.

The second approach to group or class power, which is related to production and materialism, was adopted by most sociologist and political philosophers in the nineteenth and twentieth centuries. Putting class power and its materialist objectives into the supreme position resulted in a theoretical contradiction between state and class power that has never been fully resolved. The problem was that the focus on a limited number of classes obscured the complexity of dynamics and attitudes.

The third approach begins with the smaller units of power and, perhaps inductively, builds up an understanding of the larger, more abstract exercise of power. This is the initial focus in the neomaterialist approach. The Foucauldian view of power is relevant here, although neomaterialists would not necessarily accept all of Foucault's typology (Bevir, 1999). Foucault (1976) is scathing about the idea of a centralized, mechanistic, materialist, capitalist class power and sees no virtue in studying it. He distinguishes between what he calls the power of sovereignty, which is exercised over the earth and its products, and that which is exercised over human bodies and their operations, including labour, which he calls disciplinary power.

The latter type of power confirms the need, as emphasized in the neomaterialist approach, to study power by beginning at its lowest levels, one of which is the workplace. The possibility of an autonomous state power is not denied. However it may be mediated by those who operate state agencies – civil servants, the police – because they themselves are producers and reflect the power relations of their work, based as they are on the production of intangibles in a logical, bureaucratic, hierarchical and secure framework.

The focus in neomaterialism, then, is on the disciplinary power found at the point of production: the workplace. It is the power that 50 per cent of people worldwide experience directly and daily for at least 60 per cent of their wakeful hours. Conventionally it is the power most intensively studied in the sociology of work, labour relations, industrial relations and human resource management. An understanding of such power and its impact on consciousness and therefore politics is the contribution that the neomaterialist approach can make to political science.

Rationalities, consciousness and world views

Production and power can be studied for functional and manipulative purposes, but when they are specifically connected to political and social change then a more encompassing neomaterialist approach is created. The connection between authority and discipline at the workplace and societal politics is constructed through rationalities and the consciousness and world views that such authority and power produces in people.

It is not possible here to elaborate on the relationship between the exercise of power and its outcomes in detailed political, psychological or sociological terms. But a neomaterialist approach will have only limited value in political analysis if it cannot be shown that there is a fundamental and constitutive connection between the daily experience of power and different groups' attitudes, world views and political actions. It is therefore necessary to give some indication of avenues to be explored in this area.

What should be noted first is that commentators from a variety of positions, some of whom were quoted at the beginning of this chapter, assume that redressing the material inequality produced by asymmetric power relations is a source of political and social change. If ethics and morality are connected with material equity, then material equity has been a constant concern of human thought and society. From this has arisen the assumption that inequality inevitably results in the use of violence to redress it and therefore inequality is undesirable. The fundamental question is, why should this be so? This question was been posed with great force in the last quarter of the twentieth century when serious political and economic philosophers and politicians advocated acceptance of inequality, as well as the institutionalization of asymmetric power relations and their material outcomes as the basis of a socially free and wealthy society (Giddens, 1998). This question is important to the neomaterialist approach because part of the power dynamics is produced by resistance, to some degree and in some form, to the exercise of disciplinary power or authority in the workplace.

When considering this question it is necessary to depart from the confines of social science to find the answer. Technology developed for human biophysics is producing indicators that may eventually help to resolve some of the perplexities of philosophical and social analysis. For example d'Aquili and Newberg (1999), using new brain scanning techniques, claim that the mind functions on the basis of cognitive 'operators' that will always seek causes for 'breaches of natural laws of causality'. For social scientists much will depend on the definition of such breaches. Is it likely that the causal imperative is involved when the brain receives information that indicates arbitrary inequalities? A reason may be demanded when the internal self confronts external arbitrariness encapsulated in questions such as why is he/she/they richer/poorer than me/us? If this is the case then we arrive at a biological determinism for the demand for equity in the context of socially constructed and arbitrary material inequities – socially constructed greed is confronted by neurobiology. It also provides a neurological basis for ethics and morality and suggests that if there is a rational imperative for maximizing individual gain, then there is also a counter logic that demands the provision of a cause of or reason for the unequal result so achieved.

While d'Aquili and Newberg talk of a universal brain function, Brown (1991), by constructing a list of human universals, provides possible answers to questions about the illogicality of material differences. Brown argues that there are core elements of human nature that are not mediated or constructed by culture and society to the extent suggested by earlier anthropologists. He lists amongst his human universals the presence of economic inequalities – the poor and rich are everywhere. But at the same time another human universal, consciousness of economic inequality, means that the poor and rich know they are everywhere (for a recent study see Cohen, 2003). Studies from disparate areas of human knowledge are important to the neomaterialist approach because if there is evidence to support the proposition that inherent in the human brain is a demand for equity, then a world view will always be developed that emphasizes fairness, that is, opposes arbitrariness. In this case the core arena in which these factors are in play will certainly be the power relations involved in work and production (Harrod, 1999). It will also indicate that it is necessary to construct socially elaborate explanations for the resultant inequality. For this reason the neomaterialist approach places emphasis on rationalities, as constructs or explanations, consciousness and world views as perceptions of inequality and its solution.

Within the framework of neomaterialism these latter concepts have special meanings. Consider, first, a rationality that takes the form of a sociopolitical construct, myth or discourse which seeks to explain the unequal material circumstances of human groups – such a construct is always larger than an individual consciousness and can be discovered objectively. Something approximating this rationality has been used by almost all writers and philosophers who have set out to consider the nature of society and governance. Thus a rationality could be seen in Weberian terms as inauthentic legitimization, or as a Foucauldian regime of truth. It might also be conceived of as internalization of the norms of ruling class governance, as in Gramscian hegemony, the Marxist superstructure or Habermasian 'systematically distorted communication'. What all these have in common is that they are constructed views that in some way or other disguise an ill-defined reality. For this reason 'rationality' is used here as a generic term for a constructed concept that satisfies the need for an explanation of the causes (to use the terminology above) of real social and economic illogicalities. It is a construct that at its essence is a power-cloaking device (Harrod, 2001b).

In the neomaterialist approach there are two levels of rationality. At the macro level are rationalities that could be considered as societal and, in the contemporary world, global, and those which are discrete and specific to particular patterns of power relations in production. A macro rationality that is global in scope forms a framework in which discrete forms of power relations are able to develop. The sources of macro rationalities are religion, governance, the economy and biology, and each can be associated with organizations such as the church, the state, the corporation and the household.

The rationality of the church is that the unequal or arbitrary outcomes of power relations resulting, for example, in rich and poor are explained by 'God's will'; the rationality of the state is that it is 'the people's will'; the rationality of the corporation is explained in terms of 'market forces'; and for the household it is 'familial patriarchy' (Harrod, 2005). In each case these are cited as a last resort to explain an 'uncaused cause', when all logical explanations supported by evidence have been exhausted. As will be discussed in the next section, given that macro rationalities are not constructed for a specific pattern of power, they engender contradictions that, under certain circumstances, make it possible for the macro rationalities to be used for mobilization by opposing or revealing power.

The discrete rationalities are part of a power complex that alters the allocation of power and distribution within each pattern of power relations. Examples of discrete rationalities are the divine right of landowners in the peasant pattern of power relations, harmony within diversity in the corporate and state corporatist patterns, paternalism and the 'working boss' ethic in the enterprise pattern, and the 'woman's work' rationalization for inequality in the household. Different uses of macro and discrete rationalities can be observed in different patterns of power relations. The household pattern of power relations relies on patriarchal and religious rationalities to ensure differential allocation of and rewards from work for women members of the household, the justification of land ownership for indebted, rack-rented peasants draws on the agency of a supreme being, and the rationality that governs relations in large enterprises relies heavily on the idea of corporate loyalty and the immutability of bureaucratic organizations.

We turn now to the concept of consciousness, which is understood here as awareness, realization or cognizance at the individual level of power relations and their outcomes. Consciousness need not be oppositional, as is often assumed in materialism, for at the individual level rationalities may provide a satisfactory answer to perceived inequities (Mansbridge and Morris, 2001). However, collective action by those in any of the patterns is predicated on their consciousness of power relations. Without such a consciousness there would be no workers' organizations in the enterprise pattern, the institutionalization of these as unions in tripartism, producer cooperatives in self-employment, mutual aid and local associations in the household pattern, or chiliastic events in the peasant pattern.

World views are the collective perceptions derived from individual consciousness. The development of consciousness and world views in any particular pattern of power relations is a product of the mixture of extant macro rationalities and their use by different groups, and the discrete rationalities of the specific form of power relations.

World views can be seen as a collection of concepts that allow the construction of a coherent image of the world, and in particular which element of the world needs to be altered or eliminated in order to improve the situation for the group concerned. World views often determine the course of political action, and in particular the effectiveness of mobilization appeals. The world view of a self-employed person, buffeted by competitors for his or her means of livelihood, is characterized by insecurity and political action by that person is aimed at restoring security (Harrod, 1987). A civil servant in the corporatist relations of a state bureaucracy is not characterized by the need to achieve security but by the need for institutionalized fairness, and therefore political action involves organization, occupational loyalty and defence of state power. The enterprise pattern produces a world view of continued inequity of outcomes and arbitrary authority, and political action is aimed at redressing the power of authority in the workplace via collective action. Thus for each of the patterns a consciousness and a form of political action can be discerned. The objective conditions produced by the power relations and the consciousness will determine individuals' ability and willingness to participate in dramatic political movements and events.

In presenting, reconsidering and refining the neomaterialist approach outlined above, it should be noted that such an approach contravenes a whole range of norms relating to organizational structures and sub-structures, conventions and specializations in the academic practices of social science. The divergences from mainstream analyses conducted in the last quarter of the twentieth century include the fact that the approach, although materialist, is not classically Marxist; that the idea of subordinate producers engaged in different production patterns challenges the concept of the 'working class'; that although global, the approach is not based on the nation or nation-state; that it proposes that occupation, gender, economic and ethic divisions in the global labour force are by themselves not useful and meaningful categories when considering the processes of social change; and that the normative or cognitive discussion is centred on rationalities rather than ideologies.

These differences from, contradictions of and misfits with conventional scholarship mean that there is no easy place for the neomaterialist approach within current knowledge and academic structures. This is a problem for the sociology of knowledge; to point out the lack of a place for the approach is not to defend specific details of the approach, especially as it was presented in the mid 1980s. At that time many aspects were missing and historical rationalities were not incorporated in the way in which they might now be, some of the nomenclature was clumsy, and the linkage with more commonplace concepts was not sufficiently emphasized.

However the redefinition and refinement of the approach mean that a strong case can now be made for the proposition that approaching social and political analysis through the portal of work and production, and their accompanying patterns of power, deserves greater recognition and bestowal of importance than is currently afforded. The exposition of the approach here is a defence of the position taken earlier that:

Any approach should be welcome which can integrate or accommodate into policy and strategies the different dynamics, power groups, and consciousness emerging from different patterns of power relations. In general, as noted in the opening chapter, in policy planning, in devising strategies for political and social change, and in investigating the nature of human societies any social scientist or general observer of the human condition who ignores, or fails to analyze rigorously, the variety of patterns of power relations in production is likely to produce at best uneven or at worst self-defeating results. (Harrod, 1987, p. 325)

These are some of the arguments behind, and elements of, the ongoing construction of neomaterialism. The test of any theory or approach, however, lies not in its relationship with its antecedents nor in its vitality in a theoretical discourse as such, but rather in its ability to explain contemporary developments and reveal into the matrix of ideas, perceptions and material circumstances that create social and economic dynamics. A brief consideration of the place of the global poor in world politics within a neomaterialist framework is outlined in the next section in order to illustrate its utility for these purposes.

The global poor/unprotected workers/ underclass in world politics

In the current discourses on the global poor there is a common materialist assumption that infects most liberal social theories of change – namely that material deprivation provokes political action to bring about positive social change (in the sense of redressing inequalities). In these accounts a normative element interferes with analytical rigour: sympathy for the poor and rejection of current trends leads to the idea that protest actions by the poor may be empowering rather than murderous, liberating rather than despotic, and caring rather than inhumane. In conservative accounts it is assumed that material deprivation is the sole source of anti-establishment and extremist fervour.

These accounts offer little insight into or understanding of what it is about the material conditions of poverty that causes the poor to erupt into social action. They also offer little comprehension of divisions that exist amongst the poor, not in respect of degree of material deprivation, nor in terms of ethnicity or gender, but in terms of world views developed from the daily experience of coping with work, production and the attendant power relations. The neomaterialist analytical framework described in the first section of this chapter offers a basis for reestablishing some rigour in the analysis of the political actions of the global poor; that is, the potential for constructing coalitions of groups with different forms of power relations, and forming (rather than assuming) social movements to redress injustices. It should be noted, however, that such a neomaterialist analysis would not have an inherently normative bias. The approach may be useful for the armies of both liberation and oppression (as was evident in the quotations concerning military operations in the introduction to this chapter).

In the dominant patterns of power relations in a political economy, employees or workers – be they unionized workers in tripartite relations or employees in corporatist relations – have secured a degree of protection against arbitrary and authoritarian action in the workplace with regard to issues such as dismissal, conditions of employment and work, and remuneration. Thus workers in these patterns have obtained some degree of human rights in the workplace; that is, some security of employment and therefore livelihood, and some protection against the power inherent in employers' ownership of property or status. In the 1980s (Cox, 1987; Harrod, 1987) these were described as 'established workers', but now 'more protected' would be a more accurate term. In addition the least protected workers in the patterns of power relations in production were designated as unprotected workers. A nomenclature problem is evident here in that 'unprotected' implies an absolute state, while transformations between different patterns of power relations suggest that there are degrees of protection and only at the extremes can the difference between established and unprotected workers be concretely identified.

Of the eight patterns of power relations defined in the first section of this chapter, the least protected workers can be found in five of them: the peasant, casual, enterprise, self-employed and household patterns.

In the peasant pattern, at one end of production is the subsistence household, which consumes 75 per cent of its own production. Here there is little external authority and thus the power relations are those of allocation and reward within the household. At the other end is the peasant, whose returns from work are determined by the power relations between him or her and the landowner, middleman or moneylender, which respectively correspond to the peasant's classification as tenant farmer, market-dependent or indebted. In the casual pattern are casual workers whose power relations with the production authority (the surrogate employer) are often infrequent as their employment is time-limited and irregular. Thus in household production, defined by the production of household services, the authority and power structure is constructed between the members of the household; in the enterprise pattern the power relations are between employer and employee.

In each case the power held by dominant or authority-wielding individuals may be derived from macro structures and organizations within the political economy. Thus landowners' demands may be enforced by the state and army; employers' power is based on labour market coercion, which is itself dependent on the absence of state intervention; male-headed household production depends on patriarchy; while casual employment is often enforced by reference to ethnicity and/or large differences in wealth.

As outlined in the first section of this chapter (and as will be elaborated in the following chapter), each of these patterns of power relations produces different conflicts, dynamics and forms of consciousness, and therefore different transformational paths. In other words, in each pattern there are different ways in which the dynamics produce change or can be used to induce change. Thus the individual, fragmented and psychologically dominating relationships surrounding production by servants, scavengers, bag-carriers, shoe-cleaners and the casual pattern of power relations create a consciousness of despair that can foster responsiveness to millenarianist and populist movements. With self-employment, as it has been defined here, consciousness arises from individuals' relative ability to control their own labour, plus the ability to handle the power of competitors, suppliers, customers and regulators. This results in resistance to collective efforts and changes in the *status quo*, except for time-limited functional adjustments between the powers that indirectly control production. The enterprise pattern of power relations has within it a dynamic that promotes the creation of workers' organizations within the workplace, which seek to counter employers' potential manipulation of the work process, the labour market and consciousness to attempt to prevent such workers' organizations arising. These power relations are conducive to a consciousness based upon the workplace, collective action and other factors that have been evident throughout the last century of industrial action. Finally, the power relations of household service production, in which women are usually subordinate, are sustained by and linked to a wider patriarchal ideology that aims to foster acceptance of male authority.

The neomaterialist approach thus indicates that if unprotected workers, as described above, make up the 'global poor', the 'slum dwellers', the 'underclass' or the 'urban marginals', they nevertheless are unlikely to share a uniform consciousness or world view that many authors and commentators would expect to mobilize them into political action. Even an overarching consciousness or identity mediated by ethnicity or gender will be expressed in movements and organizations mediated by the occupational power patterns that determine leadership potential and structure. Thus mobilization would be by a coalition of unprotected workers working in different patterns of power relations and having different world views. The creation and development of their 'social space' (see Chapters 4 and 6 of this volume; see also Bakker and Gill, 2003), the existence of which is necessary for concerted resistance, would also be mediated by differences in power relations, as would their attitude towards forming coalitions with organized labour (see Chapter 9). Likewise transnational processes would be accepted or rejected in accordance with different power relations and world views. Any blanket mobilization attempt would have to take account of these differences or be doomed to failure.

Although the above propositions could be usefully engaged with and refined, contemporary scholarship and discourse continue to pursue concepts that hide rather than reveal the differences in world view among, and therefore political actions taken by, the global poor. It is useful to consider these differences as heuristic device to illustrate the importance of an approach that disaggregates the global poor according to the different power relations in production.

Work-empty concepts and discourses

Understanding the nature of and potential for change offered by unprotected workers means restoring to social science in general awareness of the importance of labour, work, production, the workplace, human rights at the workplace and the power relations and patterns of distribution that issue from all of these. The study of the impact of production power relations on consciousness has been retarded by the contemporary retreat from the study of work and labour as inputs to political action. This is despite the fact that the aphorism 'you are what you do' has yielded, in discussions of occupational identity, some indications of consciousness when an occupation or the nature of an occupation has cocoincided with a pattern of power relations.

The post-Cold War rejection of materialism and adoption of the rationality of the market have rendered the words work and power (other than state power) subversive in an era in which materialism has been eliminated from any meaningful discourse, and in which citizenship and humanity is defined in terms of race, colour, religion, nationality, identity, language and gender but rarely in terms of occupation or power position in production. In contemporary discourse the major activities of humanity – work and production – have no place, and therefore any theory that attempts to incorporate them has no place either.

The patterns of power that make the unprotected worker the most subordinate in any political economy have been obscured by a number of concepts and practices that are contested by the neomaterialist approach. Concepts that impede a more rigorous analysis are the 'informal sector' and, in the richer countries of the world, the 'underclass'. Likewise the current practice of disaggregating populations on the basis of ethnicity, gender and space excludes work and production.

The informal sector

For almost a quarter of a century, use of the blanket term 'informal sector' has hidden the diversity of work and the associated power relations that exist in the materially poorest urban areas of the poorer countries. The term stemmed from the need to categorize activities that did not fit into the generally accepted categories: agriculture, industry and services (the primary, secondary and tertiary sectors). After some years of alloting the activities of the informal sector to the tertiary sector the idea of the informal sector was developed by the International Labour Organization (ILO, 1972) in accordance with that organization's constitutional structure and ideological bias (Harrod, 1972a).

In the 1990s many authors, drawing on literature produced in the 1970s, could see no need to disaggregate the informal sector, and certainly not on the basis of work and production relations (Cameron, 1992). The core definition used in these studies was that by Portes *et al.* (1989): that the informal sector is based on the household and concerns income-producing activities that are not associated with contractual and legally regulated employment. On the basis of this definition, case studies of countries and informality were often disaggregated according to space, gender, ethnicity, labour markets and, occasionally, vague occupational grounds. Hence some scholars who approached the informal sector with politics and mobilization in mind did engage in some disaggregation, but not on the basis of work or production relations. For example Staudt (1998 p. 170), drawing on the Gramscian concept of hegemony for her study of spatially determined borders, saw informality pitted against 'formal, hegemonic forces', and argued that 'the informals and political community holders standing front and center at our borders have crossed territorial, regulatory, gendered and employment lines in a region called North America'.

The underclass

The concern about the global poor and the growth of inequality in the rich countries has brought to the fore two other concepts that, unlike the concept of the informal sector, involve a dimension of political change. However these are still blanket concepts that allow for little political analysis of divisions and segmentations other than ethnicity, gender and region. Such is the case with the concept of the underclass. According to Murray (1999) the levels of criminality, labour force drop-out and illegitimate births by low-income women show that the under-class in the US is greater than ever but it is no longer a political issue as it has been 'dealt with'. The concept of an 'underclass' is becoming a commonplace in Western Europe, even outside countries that, based on income distribution, could be said to have the largest underclass, such as the UK and France (Harrod, 2004).

As with the definition of the informal sector, the definition of the underclass is work-empty, although it does include essential power over-tones. The underclass, as conventionally defined, is being swollen by once secure workers as a result of deregulation and flexibilization. The consciousness of those who move to a lower employment status will presumably be affected by their lack of protection and greater subordi-nation compared with their previous situation (Maurin, 2004). If they have moved from a dominant form of bipartite, tripartite or corporate power relations to the enterprise or casual pattern, how will this affect their behaviour? In Japan, for example, will they be involved in social change as both organizational corporatism and small enterprise paternalism collapse?

There are some in the underclass who have never worked and do not intend to, but this is not due to laziness, as is often claimed, but to the attraction of 'freedom in desperation' acquired from never being sub-jected to power relations in production. The negative view of structured work is the antithesis of industrial work and the disciplinary power inherent in any pattern of power relations in production. The escape route for those who suffer authority badly is to become self-employed, where the power relations are diffuse and less direct, split as they are between regulators, suppliers, competitors and customers. If such a course is not possible then 'floating marginals' become individual adjuncts to people working in other patterns of power relations in produc-tion, increasing the number of people who might depend on the income from a 'nine-to-five' work. Will the growing number of inactive or low-waged individuals become part of the underclass? They share with the traditionally unemployed and partially employed the absence of struc-tured workplace power relations and the discipline associated with it. They share with the casually hired and fired the same public spaces and insecurity of income.

As with the informal sector, the underclass needs to be disaggregated by work and power relations in analyses of the political behaviour of those in the class, including voting behaviour.

The poor divided by ethnicity, gender and space

The current approach to the study of specific political economies is conceptually to separate the poor from the rest of the population according to economic or material consumption criteria, and then to divide them on the basis of, for example, ethnicity, gender and region.

Analyses of mobilization, of new social movements and of politics therefore adopt disaggregation criteria other than those of work and production. Thus new social movements are based on such criteria as human rights (ethnicity), women (gender) and environment (space) (Diani, 2000). Even the best analyses of the transnational aspects of identity politics (Nasr, 2000) exhibit a problem with level – an identity descends as religion from heaven or is constructed from existing psychosocial inputs without reference to what the individuals do or produce. Others divide power by degree and locality, creating local 'uppers' and 'lowers' (Williams *et al.*, 2003). The literature also reflects the continuing malaise of the conventional ways of looking at sections of the poor: Mwangi wa Githiniji and Cullenberg (2003) use forms of payment to disaggregate the peasantry; Prandy (2002) unifies traditional class analysis with a continuum that is similar to the transformation of, or movement through, patterns of power relations in neomaterialism.

Use of the conventional criteria for disaggregating the global poor may be necessary for policy-makers in situations where immediate or palliative actions are required, and even for political purposes, as in the case of movements for the empowerment of women, which naturally require a gender disaggregation. But when the issues are larger and these are possible threats, such as the question of whether the poor will be at the forefront of change or constitute a potential army of disruption, a more inclusive approach is necessary.

Conclusion: connecting to world politics

The key linkage in the case of unprotected workers and world politics (especially with regard to urban unprotected workers, whose individual physical production does not have an impact on the wider society or global politics) is between power relations of production and the consciousness it produces. The neomaterialist position is that it is power relations in the workplace, and not material poverty alone, that produces a consciousness in unprotected workers that causes them to seek out movements, myths and ideologies that deny the reality of powerlessness and seem to restore the power necessary to comprehend the self.

More practically there are two direct links between some producers in the unprotected worker category and political events in global society. The first is their position in the political economies of major global military and economic powers, and the second is the global response to direct local actions by different subgroups of unprotected workers and the active or passive support of others.

Space prevents more than a few examples of these connections. With regard to the first type of link a brief discussion of the concept of the underclass is important. Is it the case that in political economies with a large proportion of people trapped in casual work, own-account activities have a distinct political character? Could it be proposed, for example, that the greater the proportion of unprotected workers in a political economy the greater the need for political manipulation based on a lowest common denominator that appeals to abstract emotional notions, including nationalism? Holman (2004) argues that European politics is increasingly characterized by a new populism in which there is an appeal to an inauthentic nationalism to provide a myth of security based on nation that is denied by corporate/political elites' preference for transnational forms of accumulation (Nitzan and Bichler, 2000). That there will eventually be external diplomatic and military manifestations of this tendency is inevitable. Traditionally, international relations scholars would start at the latter point, but the neomaterialist approach requires the starting point to be pushed back to the workplace.

The second link concerns those who are trapped in the casual pattern and therefore are highly dominated and deprived of structured work and relations, and thus of material subsistence. It has already been observed that such groups respond to millenarianistic movements that promise salvation, dignity and future release from material deprivation and its accompanying spiritual desolation (Harrod, 1987). Militant Islam is one such movement. Ismail (2000, p. 393) writes about the situation in Cairo: 'the mobilization potential of militant Islam seems to lie in its ability to ground its ideological principle in the social antagonisms and the opposition positions that are part of the urban landscape'.

While the conclusion that militant Islam has popular dimensions is not uncommon (see Hoogvelt, 1997), the power relations in production approach suggests that militancy cannot simply be placed in an urban landscape or in ethnic identity, and even less so in poverty. The power relations involved in the casual pattern cause a loss of dignity, health and spirit to a greater degree than those associated with other forms, such as the small enterprise pattern or self-employment. It can therefore be suggested those in the casual pattern will be more likely to support messianic millenarianist movements, as currently seems to be the case in Indonesia, Nigeria and the Philippines. The neomaterialist approach is able to accommodate contemporary trends and developments in that it suggests that the most exploited, most marginal and apparently powerless people may yet precipitate global change. This connection to change and security politics was made even before the current war on terror was declared. For example, 'upon the millenarianism inherent in militant Islam is balanced the emergence of militant Muslim regimes and on that event the concept of "rogue states" and in turn, on that the development of additional military strategies and defensive missile systems' (Harrod, 2001b, p. 13).

To understand global politics requires an approach that includes a global political sociology and is based on important universals of the contemporary world population. There are many global universals, but the universal of work and production and the power involved in its control and distribution is the one most intimately connected with politics and change. The purpose of this chapter has been to argue that the neomaterialist approach offers an effective means of comprehending the politics of the global poor.

Notes

1. Note by the editors: different terminologies have been used to describe these relations of production: Cox (1987) refers to them as modes of social relations of production, while Harrod (1987) sometimes refers to them as forms and sometimes as patterns of social relations of production. In order to distinguish them from Marx's 'mode of production' and the philosophical distinction between form and content, in this book they are called patterns of social relations of production unless points are made of an intellectual-historical nature.
2. Note by the editors: this nomenclature, then, differs from that used in the 1987 books, and except in the case of points of an intellectual-historical nature it will be used throughout this book.

3
Workers of the World … : The 'Economic Corporate Moment' of Contemporary World Politics[1]

Magnus Ryner

In the previous chapter Jeffrey Harrod provided an account of his and Robert Cox's approach to the study of unprotected work through 'patterns of social relations of production' (Harrod, 1987; Cox, 1987). This was in part a retrospective account and in part a consideration of possible future developments of the approach. He also made the case that his neomaterialist approach was better equipped to analyze poverty as a social force of world politics than the approaches that dominate at present. He made this case through a critique of both Marxism and fashionable approaches that are characterized by 'work-empty' discourses.

With the objective of consolidating the case for this approach, this chapter amplifies Harrod's line of reasoning in two ways. First, it provides a systematic theoretical critique of the ontological claims upon which 'work-empty' and reductionist Marxist theories are based. Particular attention is paid to the ontological foundations of post-structuralism and constructivism, which have become increasingly influential theories of world politics and whose claims must be addressed if one is to render convincing the contention that focusing on work is an appropriate route to obtaining a critical understanding of contemporary world politics. In other words a particular interest of this chapter is to pre-empt any objections of Cox and Harrod's approach to consciousness that might be raised by those who draw on linguistic and semiotically based concepts. It argues that Bourdieu's (1977) concept of *habitus* – defined as transposable and durable dispositions that are inherent in particular material practices – justifies Cox and Harrod's argument that a particular pattern of social relations of production generates a disposition towards a particular 'basic consciousness', which in turn is produced dialectically from the antagonisms generated by the rationalities associated with the pattern in question. This general ontological defence is the subject of the first section of this chapter.

Having shown the importance of approaching the subject matter by means a disaggregated and composite analysis of patterns of social relations of production, the second section offers a more systematic sketch of the composition (or 'matrix') of the patterns of social relations of production and the attendant dispositions towards 'basic consciousness' that characterize the contemporary world order. This is admittedly an initial sketch and it should be tested and refined through more systematic empirical research. At the same time, as the lessons of the 'hermeneutic circle' have taught us, detailed empirical research is dependent on an understanding of the whole whose parts it sets out to study (Johansson and Liedman, 1993). It is hoped that this chapter will provide this 'preunderstanding'.

This chapter differs from Harrod's in one other important way. Rather than claiming to usher in an entirely new neomaterialism it seeks to demonstrate that the approach can fruitfully be deployed within a modified Marxist historical materialism, as pioneered by Gramsci (1971). In contrast to Harrod, this chapter takes the view that Marxism would be abandoned at too high a cost, given the contribution of its method of abstraction to identifying the generative mechanisms and emergent causal powers associated with capital as a social relation and commodification, which can be viewed as the central articulating principle of the contemporary global political economy.

From such a perspective, the patterns of social relations of production correspond to, and offer an improved elaboration of, what Gramsci called 'the economic corporate moment' of the 'relations of force' (ibid., p. 181). For Gramsci this 'moment' is that in which the members of a group of producers spontaneously become aware of their similarities but have yet to forge a 'hegemonic moment' when this realization can be extended to a larger social and political grouping. Thus they are susceptible to the hegemony of other social groups. However the economic corporate moment also sets limits on hegemonic projects emanating from other groups and may generate tensions and contradictions. In applying Gramsci's concept to the contemporary world order and using Cox and Harrod's approach, this chapter extends the range of workers considered beyond Gramsci's traditional Marxist definition, which was conditioned by the particular circumstances of industrial capitalism in the nineteenth century.

Patterns of social relations of production: a theoretical defence

The problem of economic reductionism

Relating dispositions of consciousness to class position could be viewed as economic reductionism, the critique of which goes at least back to Max Weber's studies of religion and capitalism *contra* Marxism. In recent times constructivism and post-structuralism have offered such a devastating critique that one might consider the matter settled. For post-structuralism, Lacan's psychoanalysis has demonstrated that consciousness, and indeed the unconscious, is forged semiotically rather than economically. Furthermore, as Derrida shows, the differential relationship between signifier-elements and the signified in semiotic formations (discourses) is ambivalent, fluid and contingent. This undermines any possibility of a literal correspondence between an economic base and a cultural and political superstructure (for an overview, see Hall, 1988).

It is hard, then, to make the case for any mechanical correspondence between class position and conscious subject formation. On the other hand Eagleton's (1991) sarcastic retort that presumably this means that it is a mere coincidence that financial capitalists are not revolutionary socialists suggests there is a problem here. Hence while one can accept that concrete subject formation is the result of a contingent and constructivist practice, it is dubious to suggest that the 'play of difference' is entirely free.

In contrast Bourdieu's concept of *habitus*, which invokes a broader conception of practice, provides relief here. Defined as 'durable and transposable *dispositions*' (Bourdieu, 1977, p. 72) it eschews any implication of mechanical correspondence. There is no automaticity in dispositions, and they are quite consistent with the idea that political consciousness and action may ultimately be subject to contingent semiotic constructions. However by invoking the term disposition, Bourdieu suggests that the socioeconomic context in which such constructions are made is not totally pliable but instead offers an uneven terrain of potential articulations. Lacan might be right in insisting on the semiotic nature of subject formation, even at the level of the unconscious. However Bourdieu is equally convincing in suggesting that the very existence of the social presupposes certain homogeneous 'unconscious principles of the ethos', the 'commonplace' and 'conventional and conditional simulations'. Without these 'homogeneities of the habitus', it is hard to see how one agent's practices and discourse becomes 'sensible', 'reasonable', 'intelligible' and 'taken for granted' by another agent. In other words it is this homogeneity of 'common conditions of material existence ... which enables practices to be objectively harmonised without any conditional calculation or conscious reference to norms' (ibid., pp. 79–80).

Rationalities of production and basic consciousness

The homogenizing conditions of *habitus* should not be understood as exclusively economic. Indeed Bourdieu points to the particular importance of the 'hysteresis effect' of family socialization for *habitus* (ibid., p. 83). Furthermore the articulation of an Islamic millenarianism (as discussed in the conclusion of Chapter 2 of this volume), for instance, is obviously only likely to occur in a cultural space where an Islamic civilizational intersubjectivity is prevalent (Cox, 1995). Subject formation, then, takes place against the backdrop of a broader everyday life, and extra-economic bodies such as nations may form a distinct *habitus* in the long term (see for example Elias, 1989; Harrod discussed this in terms of 'macrorationalities' in the previous chapter). Identification of the aspects of *habitus* that are associated with transposable social relations of production, as well as the differential positions defined by class divisions, is only one task in the method of abstraction. Cox (1987) and Harrod (1987) call these 'rationalities of production'.

Rationalities of production are nevertheless very important in everyday life insofar as work denotes the general 'expenditure of human energy in order to convert or transform material substances into other forms' (ibid., p. 8). On the one hand the everyday life of the family (which is also a site of production) and the broader public sphere are materially produced and distributed by the socioeconomic order and social divisions of labour (Negt and Kluge, 1993; Lefebvre, 1974; Harvey, 1990). On the other hand 'the everyday naturalisation of arbitrary power-relations' in class-divided production serves an essential socioeconomic function and as such helps to constitute production rationalities (Harrod, 1987, pp. 13–14, 32–4). Bourdieu (1977) calls this *doxa*, by which he means that arbitrary power is represented as an objective and natural order of things, or as Harrod put it in the previous chapter, an arbitrary invocation of causality where there is a 'breach of natural laws of causality'. The dispositions of socioeconomic subjects are produced by the contradictions and antagonisms generated by the dialectic between these two processes.

Gramsci's 'economic corporate moment'

According to Bourdieu (1977) one of the fundamental effects of the 'orchestration of *habitus*' is the production of a 'commonsense world'.

Common sense is, of course, also crucial to Gramsci (1971). For him it is the product of a hegemonic project through which the ruling power bloc secures the consent of subordinate classes. To be effective this common sense necessarily has to be meditated through the specific life experience of the subordinate in the economic corporate moment. As a result contradictions emerge in hegemonic discourse if and when the socioeconomic order generates dissonance between the claims of hegemonic discourse and the everyday life experience. It is on the terrain of this dissonance that the counterhegemonic struggle over the definition of the common sense operates (Simon, 1982).

For Gramsci (1971) the economic corporate level is highly relevant here as logically prior to the more ideologically transient process of fundamental class and subject formation. His invocation of feeling and passion suggests that, as for Lacan and Bourdieu (1977), it refers to dispositions on an unconscious level. Furthermore he suggests that the class context in which these feelings and passions operate should be carefully disaggregated:

> A tradesman feels *obliged* to stand by another tradesman, a manufacturer by another manufacturer, etc., but the tradesman does not yet feel solidarity with the manufacturer; in other words, the members of the professional group are conscious of its unity and homogeneity ... but in the case of the wider social group this is not yet so. (Gramsci, 1971, p. 181)

Cox's (1987) and Harrod's (1987) concept of 'rationalities' of production operates exactly in this way. First, whilst seeking to ensure comprehensive coverage of the world's workforce they are keen to disaggregate work experience. Very much in line with Bourdieu's conception of *habitus* they then identify the 'doxic' intersubjective framework of distinct forms of social relations of production. These define and legitimate the distinct places of the dominant and the subordinate in the social power relations of production, and they provide the motivational inputs for production. On the other hand, dialectically they also define the antagonism that the subordinate feels – we might call it this class unconsciousness, or as Harrod puts it, 'basic consciousness' – in the distinct forms:

> [I]t is clear that the effect of working constantly in an industrial enterprise under the watchful eye of the entrepreneur equipped with the power of instant dismissal, or of working in the field desperately

trying to produce for rent payments under the threat of eviction or beating, or begging for work and money daily, or arguing with suppliers over prices, produce a different basic consciousness of work, life and society. (Harrod, 1987, p. 33)

One aspect of basic consciousness is the awareness that arises from the work–life experience about what actions will 'increase and decrease power and thereby affect return' in a given set of social relations of production. This 'material aspect of consciousness' is, in other words, what has traditionally been referred to as 'interest' (ibid., p. 33). There is, however, another distinct aspect to basic consciousness that operates at a deeper level and in which material consciousness may or may not be embedded. Very much in line with Bourdieu's (1977) concept of *habitus*, or Hegel's (1977) conception of the struggle for external and self-recognition, this refers to a disposition that is produced as a result of one's adjustment to social relations. In other words the social relations of production and their divisions, by assigning people to particular positions, *sui generis* produce 'types of people'. This creates an uneven potential for consciousness to transcend the immediate calculation of material interests, and it is on this terrain that broader ideologies and doctrines and the cross-cutting appeals of ethnicity, gender, nationality and nationalism operate. At the same time the broader ideologies must take cognisance of specificities of the 'deeper consciousness arising from the social relations of production' (Harrod, 1987, p. 35).

Economic corporate analysis: its limits and importance

While the 'economic corporate moment' is the focus of this chapter, it should be made clear that it can only make a limited contribution to the critical analysis of world order. A more complete analysis would have to relate the findings here of the configuration of patterns of social relations of production, with their attendant rationalities and basic consciousness at the economic corporate moment, to the broader field of Gramsci's (1971) relations of force. In other words the analysis would have to be related to the practice of conscious subject formation in a broader civil-societal field; that is, in the sociocultural relations of the public sphere and in struggles over the ethicopolitical. For Gramsci, this partly happens in the second relations of force, where the fundamental classes are organized by bodies geared to representing their broader interests in society (trade unions, chambers of commerce, employers' associations). This is for Gramsci (and as post-structuralists suggest) an ideologically contingent composite category, where conflicts caused by the competing dispositions of industrialists and bankers, or of different types of worker, are mediated through a process in which certain factions come to exercise leadership. Most notably it also happens at a third ethicopolitical level where the general interest is forged on behalf of society as a whole in a hegemonic struggle, and under the leadership of a certain class (for example political parties, the mass media, religious institutions or the state) (ibid., p. 181).

The analysis would also have to be related to the prospects of instituting different social structures of accumulation, given the range of available production technological paradigms. This is what Gramsci calls the structural moment of the relations of force, and it refers to the objective forces of production that exist in society 'objectively and independently of human will' (ibid., p. 180). Finally, it should be related to the distribution of coercive power; that is, the military moment of the relations of force, 'which from time to time becomes decisive' (ibid., p. 183).

A limited analysis of the relations of force is nevertheless necessary, as without a clear picture of how the transnational division of labour generates a complex and multifarious matrix of forms of social relations of production and their attendant dispositions, any attempt to analyze the other levels will be confused, partial and distorted.

In this regard one can point to the potential contribution of economic-corporate analysis in relation to other approaches. One of the problems with the 'work-empty', global civil society, constructivist and postcolonialist studies are their exclusive concern with the ethicopolitical moment. This leads to idealist explanations without a systematic consideration of socioeconomic organization. These approaches generally lack a rigorous conception of socioeconomic context and fail to consider how socioeconomic power relations constrain or enable certain ideological tendencies. To some extent this could be excused with reference to an intellectual division of labour. However even when such studies do provide important insights into subject formation they do not connect an analysis of microlevel resistance with a systematic conception of social structures of accumulation at the macro level that are capable of relating agency with emancipatory, alternative social structures of accumulation. In fact they do not even give a sense of the relative significance and extent of the economic relations that are analyzed in the overall social formation (say of the relative importance of industrial wage employment and household relations over other forms of social relation). This inevitably leads to what Marx (1973) called a 'chaotic conception'.

Neo-Gramscian accounts of world order have a tendency to suffer from similar problems. The contribution of these accounts has been to provide a top-down perspective on transnational capitalism and the anatomy of neoliberal hegemony. The analyses proceed carefully from the economic corporate moment of capitalist class 'fractions', through to the ethicopolitical via socialization processes in nation states and private and public multilateral institutions (for example Gill, 1990; Murphy, 1994; van der Pijl, 1998). But when questions of counterhegemony are addressed, often only briefly in conclusions, the analysis tends to move straight to ethicopolitical social movements. Hence there is a failure to refer systematically and theoretically to the economic corporate moment of the various producers of the world economy as one of the crucial relations of force. The same can be said of the chaotic conception of 'the multitude' in Hardt and Negri's (2000) iconic work. In Chapter 2 Harrod pointed to the dangers of this failure to deal with disaggregation. There is no substantial analysis of how, why and in what manner those oppressed by neoliberal hegemony could spark positive political action to redress poverty and promote emancipation.

This case for grounding critical conceptions of international political economy in an analysis of social relations of production is to affirm a case made by Marxists. However Marxist accounts contain very problematic conceptions of workers. They short-circuit an analysis of relations of force by neglecting a systematic theorization of the economic corporate level and by treating fundamental classes as ontologically primary. The crux of the problem lies in their conflation of capital and the economic logic of the commodity as a dominant *tendential and emergent* causal power in the constitution of the social (which can be defended) with a homogeneous capitalist mode of production as a concrete and achieved reality (which cannot be defended). In its concrete form, capitalism is more complex than is implied by an abstract 'mode of production' analysis. This is not least because the self-regulating market can never be fully realized in light of the problem of commodifying the use-value-specific Polanyian 'fictitious commodities' of land, labour and productive organization. Hence commodity economic logic is always intermingled and articulated with the 'socialization' tendencies of deliberate planning and coordination, which are contingent on specific production and organizational technologies (van der Pijl, 1998). It is also articulated with precapitalist legacies, which are thereby reconstituted and reorganized (Rey, 1976).

In the case of workers, Marxist analyses continue to be influenced by the simplistic two-class model of industrial capitalism observed by Marx and Engels in England in the nineteenth century. Whilst Marxist theory, from the work on imperialism onwards, has recognized that the modalities of capitalism are more complex than they are portrayed, the full implications have not been considered in analyses of subordinate classes. The complexities in question are thus treated as a materialist equivalent of the Hegelian 'Idea' in a process of concrete realization whose time has not yet arrived. At most, then, this enables Marxist scholars to include peasants and landlords in their analyses (as remnants of the feudal mode of production). The result of this faulty assumption of homogenization is that they fail to take account of the variety of forms of social relations of production that exist, even in a world economic order that is dominated by capitalist articulations. Marxism has traditionally responded to this by creating residual, purely descriptive categories such as the 'labour aristocracy', the 'petty commodity producers', the 'lumpenproletariat' and the 'urban marginals', which are little more than, as Harrod (1987) puts it, 'conceptual dustbins'. In addition Marxism has contributed to what feminists have called a 'strategic silence' (Bakker, 1994) on reproductive work, and hence has failed to develop an analysis of 'productive consumption' (Marx, 1973). The problem is that Marxism only offers empty negations, which are defined from the outside in terms of what they are not, since they do not fit the simple and abstract mode of production model. What is required is an understanding of the social relations of production that these categories point to, and the attendant dispositions of consciousness.[2]

The economic corporate moment of the contemporary world order

The previous section argued that Cox's (1987) and Harrod's (1987) typology of patterns of social relations of production enables the construction of a matrix of 'fractions' of labour and their attendant dispositions, as suggested by Gramsci's (1971) 'economic corporate moment'. This section uses their framework to sketch the economic corporate moment of the contemporary world order.

According to Cox (1987, p. 34), patterns of social relations of production are usefully understood as Leibnizian 'monads'. A monad is a simple, irreducible and elementary unity, with its own internal principle. This internal principle should be understood as a synchronic and ideal-typical representation of a given set of internal relations that define the *modus operandis*. But contrary to Leibniz, Cox maintains that different monad production relations can, and indeed typically are, articulated together and thus form a complex system of surplus extraction (a social structure of accumulation) and class fractional relations (a social formation) in and through the relations of force among broader historic blocs (Cox, 1981). The irreducible nature of the forms of social relations of production can be captured with reference to Cox's triad of material capabilities, ideas and institutions (ibid.; see also Cox, 1987).

As part of a research project at the International Institute of Labour Studies (IILS), and capitalizing on the research capacity and data gathering on the world labour force by the associated International Labour Office (ILO), Cox (1987) and Harrod (1987) found that twelve distinct monad patterns of social relations of production exist in the world. Four of these date back to precapitalist times, and in some cases even pre-extractive times (the subsistence, peasant, casual and household patterns).[3] They have nevertheless survived as subordinate 'flanking' patterns in contemporary social formations and structures of accumulation, and they are often sites of particularly severe oppression and exploitation. Sociologically and politically the last three of the patterns are of considerable importance because of the proportion of the world's population that works in the context of these social relations. A further three forms were prominent in the competitive phase of industrial capitalist development in the nineteenth century (the self-employment, enterprise[4] and bipartist patterns). These were subsequently displaced during the process of economic concentration and oligopolization, but they continued to play a role in the dual structure of monopoly capitalism, engendering in the latter a degree of flexibility (Piore, 1980). In the monopoly phase, which entailed larger-scale production and a greater degree of societal rationalization, tripartism, the corporate patterns[5] and state corporatism became predominant forms in the world economy. The two remaining forms (central planning and communal) were particularly associated with the socialist systems of the time.

It is important to be precise about the ontological status of these patterns. They are ideal-type heuristic devices that operate as rational abstractions of a complex reality. This reality can change. Patterns can disappear and new ones emerge, for example today's world, as Federici argues in Chapter 5, there is the question of whether slavery has re-emerged in the sex trade. Furthermore they are contrasting models that analytically isolate and separate types of power relations that might be intertwined in real time and space. For example there is no one-to-one correspondence between the patterns and a particular economic organization or type of profession, for example prostitutes may be self-employed or be in the primitive labour market; farmers can operate in the subsistence, peasant–lord or self-employment forms. Indeed individuals can move between forms of social relations of production, as in the case of the double burden of many working women, who perform household work alongside, for example, industrial work in the enterprise, tripartite or corporate pattern. Hence the analysis delineates the multiple contexts and sources of dispositions of subject formation. (Chapter 4 will discuss how subjectivities are formed through movement between patterns and the attendant production of public spheres).

Space constraints do not permit an exhaustive overview of the monad patterns (for these, see Cox, 1987, pp. 35–109), so we shall consider them as they appear in contemporary social structures of accumulation and world order.

The capitalist core

The contemporary capitalist core is divided into three distinct regions: North America, Western Europe and East Asia, which are connected in a triadic relationship. The three regions have distinct autocentric, or potentially autocentric, production systems that, as Amoore suggested in Chapter 1, are increasingly shaped by the practices of transnational corporations. The lion's share of commodity exchange and foreign direct investment takes place in these regions (Dicken, 1998), and on the whole they are self-sufficient, or potentially self-sufficient, social structures of accumulation. Furthermore, partly in response to the Fordist crisis the regions have developed distinct transnational regional superstructures (the EU, NAFTA and ASEAN), which to varying extents coordinate state action in capitalist regulation (Jessop, 1997).

The relationships between the regions are also important. For example most of the remaining shares of global foreign direct investment go between the core regions. In addition, because of their commercial financial market transactions their financial structures are intimately related to one another. These interregional triadic relations have become critical in determining the qualitative nature of capital accumulation in the regions. The West European and East Asian regions have become dependent on the 'locomotive effect' of the North American region. They depend on loan-based expansion in North America, which in turn depends on access to savings from the accumulated assets in the other regions. Consequently North America is the dominant region in the triad and the US is the hegemonic state. This is also because of the status of the dollar in the world economy and the strength, size and cohesion of the American financial system, not to mention US military dominance. *Inter alia* this gives this region the unique capacity to transform debt into capital (Seabrooke, 2001).

During the Fordist/Keynesian period tripartism (Europe) or a mixture of bipartism and the corporate pattern (North America) were the dominant patterns (Cox, 1987). They were flanked by a small self-employment and secondary enterprise sector (Piore, 1980) and by the household pattern, which in essence provided free labour for reproduction (McDowell, 1991). Whereas for the purposes of this chapter we can operate with commonsensical notions of what the latter pattern entailed (see Chapter 4 for a thorough elaboration), the distinction between tripartism, bipartism and the corporate pattern requires some elaboration. These patterns emerged as a result of the rationalization of large-scale enterprises. Whereas other patterns are based on arbitrary power (whether in the form of non-discursively thematized tradition, direct coercion, or charisma), authority is to varying degrees rationalized in these patterns, and this also provides a measure of protection for direct producers (Selznick, 1969). The patterns are essentially competing ways to integrate the established core labour force into the incorporated enterprise. Tripartism and bipartism are products of the early class struggle, when workers in enterprise labour market relations organized themselves into trade unions in order to fight against the exploitative and anomic conditions of proletarianization (Cox, 1987). After an initially repressive response, the liberal state eventually conceded the right of trade unions to organize and represent workers in wage negotiations, and introduced employment legislation to govern industrial relations. The difference between bi- and tripartism is that in the former case the state does not interfere in detailed and substantive aspects of wage negotiation but only provides a legal framework. In tripartism the state sees wage negotiations as a part of the day-to-day policy tools of economic management, and unions and employers' organizations serve explicit public policy functions as 'factors of order' (ibid.).

The corporate pattern is a less politicized mode of integration of the core workforce of a corporation that represents business interests in a more transparent way (ibid.). However relations must be decommodified to some extent because economies of scale and the attendant bureaucratization require loyalty to the corporation by the core workforce. This is achieved by providing protection against contingencies in the form of company insurance schemes, training and career opportunities. In addition to these measures, the corporate pattern also involves psychological human relations strategies such as integrating workers into the corporate project as individual team members. A recent manifestation of this was discussed in Chapter 1 in terms of the conditions of work for 'insiders' of the corporate chain. Whereas bi- and tripartism, in the interest of conflict avoidance, acknowledge and seek to manage the structurally uneven balance between employers and employees, enterprise corporatism denies the existence of different interests and advances the vision of a harmonious 'productive community'. Furthermore, whereas the two other forms depend on substantive regulation by the state, the classical liberal separation between the state and the economy is upheld by enterprise corporatist rationality, or at least with regard to labour relations.

When Fordism was undermined in the 1970s a set of transformations in the capitalist core resulted in a new constellation. The causal patterns of this complex transformation are neither straightforward nor uncontroversial, and it is beyond the scope of this chapter to clarify them. Nevertheless some of the central effects of recasting the social relations of production and accumulation can be identified. On the level of corporate organization, the 1970s were characterized by a severe squeeze on profitability (Lipietz, 1985). Corporate responses to this included cost cutting and innovations in products and corporate organization. The result was a new industrial paradigm, which has been variously called flexible specialization, post-Fordism or flexible accumulation (Amin, 1994). At the most abstract level this paradigm is based on cybernetic automation of industrial processes and the removal of information bottlenecks. This facilitates increased capital intensity, corporate organization over a larger geographical area, and economies of 'networking and skill to adjust volume to demand without productivity losses' (ibid., pp. 20–1). The latter is made possible by computer-assisted general purpose machines.

In this context, bipartism and tripartism have been challenged as dominant forms of social relations of production in a process led by the corporate search for flexibility and lean production. In essence corporations have used individual contracts, incentives, threats and flexible employment to reduce tripartism in corporate and enterprise relations. They seek to bind their skilled and loyal core workers to the corporation through contracts (Amoore's 'insiders', see Chapter 1 of this book) and to ensure the flexible and cost-efficient deployment of a peripheral workforce through flexible employment, not the least by means of outsourcing and subcontracting arrangements (Amoore's 'outsiders'). It is important not to view these developments too deterministically, however. It has been demonstrated that post-Fordist economies can be generated by bi- and tripartite relations, which apart from providing networking possibilities through codetermination practices also is superior in developing a highly skilled core workforce. Alternative bipartite and tripartite strategies have also been pursued. However moves away from demand management and countercyclical policy in macroeconomic regimes, which account for part of Europe's subordination to the US in global financial networks (Cafruny, 2003), are not conducive to such solutions. Tripartite post-Fordism is not conducive to labour shedding and cost cutting when aggregate demand suddenly slumps, and it seems to be dependent on Kaldor–Verdoorn effects, that is, growth in productivity through a stable climate of learning by doing provided by stable and expansive demand conditions (cf. Boyer, 1997).

Thus whilst varieties of capitalism still exist, the prevailing dynamics have tended to hollow out tripartite relations in Europe and to shift (albeit unevenly and partially) actual practices away from the tripartite to the corporate ideal type, not least in the wake of the procyclical developments in the 1990s.[6]

In this context one must also point to the implications of the failure of the Christian Democratic welfare state to deal with the breakdown of the traditional patriarchal norms that have underpinned the household pattern – the effect of the general tendency towards rationalization of rationalities in the core in the Fordist phase (Habermas, 1975). The absence of supportive measures for women entering the labour market is resulting in falling fertility rates and an ageing population. This and mass unemployment are dramatically increasing the age-dependency ratio, and the emerging fiscal crisis in the social insurance and pension systems is necessitating pension and labour market reforms (Esping-Andersen, 1996), that is, at least insofar as neoliberal macroeconomics and finance pre-empt the alternative of a social democratic expansion of the public service sector and taxation on capital in order to finance increased pension needs, which would represent a tripartization of the political economy of reproduction (see Ryner, 2002).

The Anglo-Saxon heartland of neoliberalism, by contrast, is experiencing an upsurge of the casual pattern following the breakdown of household productive relations. This is the corollary of a rise in the number of female professionals who will not or cannot continue to carry their 'double burden'. In the absence of affordable public childcare and other such facilities, professional middle-class people are increasingly recruiting (often illegal immigrant) workers to take care of their children and homes. This is the outcome of the need to deal with one of the central deficits of neoconservative policy, which like Christian Democracy continues to be based on an anachronistic image of traditional family values (Young, 2001).

The hollowing out of tripartism and the move towards enterprise corporatist relations are likely to enhance 'civic privatism' in the core. This term is borrowed from Habermas (1975, p. 75), who uses it to refer to a retreat from any active part in the deliberations of public life, and more generally the processes of legitimization, while maintaining an interest in the allocation of outputs and the output performance of the public administrative system. Politics is thus reduced to passive consumption in a 'political market'.

We can understand this development by placing it against the backdrop of an everyday dialectic between all four patterns of social relations of production involving waged labour. The transition from the enterprise pattern to the other forms is associated with the contradictions inherent in its 'basic consciousness', which Harrod (1987, pp. 190–6) calls the 'iron law or worker organisation formation'. Following the cue of classical Marxism, Harrod argues that gathering of workers in one physical space and making them produce collectively in a specialized division of labour where the interdependence of their tasks are apparent, provides the basis of a rudimentary sense of togetherness. This results in a sense of collective solidarity, defined in relation to a concrete 'other' (the owner) and enforced by the distinction between those with and without power. This generates an impetus to restrain power, which has provided fertile ground for trade union organization and the transition to bi- and tripartism. In the latter forms of social relations, unions build, elaborate and formalize a 'moral economy' of solidarity and an internal structure of representation (through union officials from shop stewards upwards). Where these relations have stabilized they are usually elaborated in everyday life in working-class neighbourhoods through, for example, working-class sporting associations, adult education institutions and consumption networks such as consumer cooperatives. Lash and Urry (1987, pp. 91–3) call these 'collectivities in struggle'.

On the other hand the Fordist era generated a civic privatist countertendency in the everyday life of waged workers. This countertendency first operated on the level of mass consumption, and was in part the paradoxical result of the success of union organization. In time mass consumption led to an attenuation of communities in struggle as leisure time was increasingly associated with a retreat into the home, promoted, for example, by the spread of televized entertainment and suburbanization. With the attendant increase in the influence of mass media advertisements, the 'semiotics of everyday life' – the discursive form of Harrod's macrorationalities – became even more based on the subliminal manipulation of instincts, as opposed to rational discourse (ibid.). As Habermas (1989) argued, where unions retained a strong position in the workplace they potentially provided a 'discourse ethical' countertendency to this commodification of public spheres. But the disposition of tripartism was Janus-faced. Since it gave unions a measure of power to influence the state, it could at times produce a highly politicized form of collective class consciousness, with industrial grievances, through the representative organs and negotiations, being translated into viable political alternatives (Higgins, 1985). On the other hand union leaders could also be captured by the bureaucratic politics of interest intermediation in the state, and in these circumstances unions ran the risk of becoming transmitters of state discipline, which would alienate the membership and increase civic privatism beyond the sphere of consumption in the core workforce. The latter aspect of tripartism was more prevalent in times of weakness, and it tended to weaken the unions further due to crises of representation (Panitch, 1985). Arguably such developments contributed to the hollowing out of tripartism in Western Europe in the 1980s and the 1990s (for the case of Germany see Deppe, 1998; Beck and Scherrer, 2003), the effect of which was often a move towards a bifurcation of corporate and enterprise relations.

In this context the corporate pattern represents an extension and strengthening of civic privatism from the sphere of consumption to the sphere of production as it depoliticizes production and encourages a conception of working life as a contractual relation between private individuals. It tends to emerge in civil societies where ideological countertendencies to working-class organizations are strong (such as free enterprise ideology, the myth of the working boss and sometimes cross-class discourses of ethnic, national and religious communities). The extension of civic privatism notably operates through the encouragement of a careerist biography and the institutionalization of bonus systems, stock options and actuarial pension systems (for pensions see Harmes, 1998). This changes both the interest of workers and the broader civilizational sense of what and who they are. To the extent that these benefits can be maintained for the core workforce, this can become the foundation of a powerful rationality that pre-empts antagonism in the workplace. It is of course possible that they cannot be maintained (for example serious questions have recently been raised about the future viability of pension plans) and antagonism is generated, but this is likely to resemble the civic privatist reaction of the dissatisfied consumer rather than the reaction of the organized working-class movement of the early part of the twentieth century.

The semiperiphery

As outlined in Chapter 1, the semiperiphery is increasingly connected to the core, and is partially shaped by the transnational corporate strategies of outsourcing and subcontracting. The advantage of outsourcing for the corporation is that it can swiftly terminate or establish contracts and orders in response to market fluctuations. The subcontractors carry the cost of this so are increasingly organizing their work practices around unprotected work. (In this context one needs to consider the resurgence of the enterprise pattern in core regions.) However the new production chain has also provided the basis for the industrialization, transformation and sometimes expansion of the capitalist semiperiphery. This has taken place against the backdrop of the shift from import substitution strategies to export promotion, facilitated by the IMF structural adjustment programmes that followed the debt crisis management strategy outlined in the Baker Plan. One result of this has been the virtual disappearance of what Cox (1987) calls state corporatism.[7]

There has been a lot of hubris about the positive implications of outsourcing for economic development, with early studies announcing a 'new international division of labour'. Evidence suggests, though, that 'flexible accumulation' clusters are also being established in the core, because of agglomeration economies associated with research and development, marketing and close proximity to core customers and the suppliers of inputs (Dicken, 1998). Nevertheless, corporations' outsourcing strategies in parts of the developing world have led to enterprise-pattern industrialization. Paradigmatic examples include the *maquiladoras* in Mexico and the information technology sector in Bangalore, India. While outsourcing strategies have also diffused capitalist production to Western border areas and major urban centres in Central and Eastern Europe (Petrakos *et al.*, 2000), South East Asia has been the main beneficiary. Semiperipheral development depends on the decline of peasant productive activities, thus releasing workers to the outsourcing industries, and on the support of household production and subsistence farming and the circulation of workers between them.[8] This form of production is associated with a feminization of work as women are a cheaper source of labour power (see Chapters 1 and 8 of this volume).

Intensive academic attention notwithstanding, it is important stress the limited extent of this development. Even in countries such as Mexico and Malaysia, manufacturing employs no more than one fifth of the economically active population (ILO, 2000b). The popular image of a rapidly growing female industrial proletariat must also be kept in perspective. Twenty per cent of the female Mexican labour force works in manufacturing, compared with 70 per cent in services (where patterns of social relations are likely to be more heterogeneous). The figures for Malaysia are about 30 per cent and 60 per cent respectively (UNDP, 2002a). This is not to trivialize what is still an impressive increase in industrial employment (in Malaysia from 7 per cent in 1980 to 30 per cent in 2000, and in Mexico from 12 per cent to 20 per cent in the same period ILO, 1990). It continues to be of interest to study the dynamics of worker antagonisms that are generated in this context and their interrelationship with gendered relations and discourses, as well as union strategies. However these developments should be put into context, and for the sake of balance more research should be devoted to other types of production relations in the periphery

The prospect of peripheral countries drawing on the benefits of outsourcing to 'upgrade' to the core of the world economy seemed bleaker after the 1997 Asian financial crisis. The so-called East-Asian tigers seemed to have found a highly effective export-oriented mercantile strategy whereby the authoritarian state provided a skilled and highly disciplined workforce in exchange for technology transfers to state-controlled conglomerates (Evans, 1987). However it seems that this strategy was vulnerable to wage competition as the integration of mass production and consumption never happened. The subsequent opening of global financial markets and the dismantling of the mercantile complexes made the prospect of this even less likely. The Asian crisis resulted in workers being laid off without a welfare safety net (with the partial exception of South Korea), which forced many workers to return to the countryside to try 'to eke out a living' (Anderson and Cavenagh, 2000, p. 1). Nonetheless, the rapid development of the most populous countries of the world – China and to a lesser extent India – is sufficient reason to reassess this verdict in future research.

The periphery

Underdevelopment in the periphery, where there is little diffusion of investment, remains the context in which a majority of the world's population takes part (or not) in the global economy. This is the case in most of Africa and large parts of Latin America, South and Central Asia and the Middle East. Mineral extraction and cash crop agriculture are common, as in the classical international division of labour (for Africa see Saul and Leys, 1999). Moreover indebtedness resulting from failed development strategies has led to the imposition of neoliberal structural adjustment programmes, coordinated and enforced by the World Bank and the IMF. These programmes are reinforcing countries' dependence on low value added specialization, and deteriorating terms of trade are necessitating further borrowing in the 'vicious cycle of the debt trap' (Cheru, 1989, p. 7).

The unequal exchange between the modern sector and traditional peasant agriculture in social relations remains a significant feature in many parts of the periphery, especially in Latin America and South Asia.

However the proportion of the population engaged in agriculture has decreased dramatically since the 1960s. In recent years the structural adjustment programmes have attenuated the already meagre social safety nets as well as the traditional support provided by subsistence agriculture and other types of peasant production. In the absence of increased industrialization an ever larger proportion of the population has to make a living in the precarious informal service sector, in some cases through self-employment but in most cases through casual production relations. With regard to Sub-Saharan Africa, Saul and Leys (1999, p. 15) note that:

> Growing pressure of population means a constantly expanding landless labour force, partly working for subsistence wages on other people's land, partly unemployed or underemployed in the cities, sometimes migrating to neighbouring countries (e.g. from Burkina Faso to Côte d'Ivoire), living on marginal incomes and with minimal state services including education and health.

Unfortunately official statistics (to the extent that they are reliable) are not designed to shed light on this dynamic, nor to verify or falsify it. Especially lacking are reliable and comparative time-series data. Nevertheless some idea can be gained indirectly by juxtaposing the imperfect information that is available. As pointed out above, in developing countries a strong trend since 1960 has been a decline in the proportion of the population engaged in agriculture without a corresponding increase in industrial employment. In Sub-Saharan Africa the proportion of the labour force working in agriculture fell from 81 per cent in 1960 to 66 per cent in 1990, while industrial employment remained more or less constant at 7–9 per cent. In many Latin American countries, such as Peru and Ecuador, the corresponding decrease was from 50 per cent to about 33 per cent, while industrial employment stagnated or increased only marginally (UNDP, 1996:). Since the peasant pattern in Asia and Latin America and the subsistence pattern in Africa have predominated, and since these are quintessentially agrarian, we can take these as proxy data that verify the relative decline of these patterns.[9] The difficult task is to disentangle the highly aggregated and in many respects misleading category of services, which can entail anything from investment banking to shoe shining. ILO (1990, 2000) labour statistics help us somewhat as they enable some disaggregation. What is particularly striking is the emergence and marked increase over time of inadequately described activities and statistical residues.[10] Even more revealing about the nature of the growing service sector are recent ILO (2002) data on the non-agricultural informal sector. These indicate that the lion's share of the growth of service sector employment is associated not with formal employer–employee relations but with self-employment or casual work. The latter is most likely to account for the statistical residues and unaccounted activities.[11]

It is even more difficult to differentiate between those who are self-employed and those who work casually because the term 'own account' does not adequately distinguish between the two forms (self-employment requires a stable and continuous relationship with suppliers and customers that not all own account workers have). Nevertheless ILO statistics on microenterprises in Latin America strongly indicate that roughly half the labour force in South America was self-employed in 1997 (ibid.). Similarly it is estimated that about 56 per cent of India's workforce are self-employed. This excludes one third of the Indian population with no assets at all (Harriss-White and Goopty, 2001) and therefore likely to have to eke out an existence through casual social relations of production. Similarly, in the absence of a thriving cottage industry in Africa casual employment is likely to be the dominant social relations of production of services on that continent.

The situation is less severe in the Maghreb and the Arab world in terms of absolute destitution (UNDP, 2002b). Nevertheless the growth of the working population, combined with reduced employment opportunities in the public sector and a reduction of agricultural employment from about 50 per cent to 15 per cent in 1960–90 (UNDP, 1996), has resulted in a growing body of unabsorbed labour. This is affecting not only the lowest strata of society but also the children of people employed or previously employed by the state, who after completing their education cannot find jobs. Despite some growth in manufacturing, non-waged employment in the informal sector absorbs most of these surplus workers (Farsakh, 2000).

Given the growing importance of self-employment and casual work it is appropriate to conclude this section by outlining their defining features and dispositions. Self-employed people tend to be small-scale commodity producers such as family farmers, shopkeepers and artisans. Survival depends on the ability to sustain profits and remain competitive through 'self-exploitation' and the purchase of inputs at a sufficiently low price. This form of production relation is inherently precarious and operating margins are tight (if they were not the self-employed would expand production, take on employees and the production relation would be transformed). The self-employed are disposed to antistatism, as taxes are a threat to their profit margins. But this does not necessarily lead to radical individualism. To stabilize their market relations the self-employed tend to organize cartels and marketing and credit societies. Their individualist self-image and sense of living under the threat of the bureaucratized world, combined with the compulsion to organize (such as forming cartels), has at times caused them to turn into right-wing populist movements (Cox, 1987).

The defining feature of casual work is that earnings are based on one-off transactions that are not cumulative or continuous. In addition the transactions are not encoded by formal authority and are therefore extralegal. This form of work encompasses a wide range of activities that are typically undertaken by urban marginals, such as shoe shining, car watching, domestic household work, hawking and prostitution. Given the extralegal character of the activities, which causes a relationship of 'violence and deception' in relation to 'established society', the casual worker typically stands in a subordinate relation to a protector (such as a pimp). Alternatively some urban marginals form informal social welfare and self-help networks, based on family, kinship, ethnicity or religious persuasion. This ensures access to earning opportunities and to the purchasers of services (Cox, 1987, pp. 44–8).

Whilst the nature of these social relations has not been well researched, according to Harrod (1987) there is evidence to suggest that they result in a disposition that oscillates between extreme instrumentalism, driven by the compulsion to survive, and millenarianism and populism. The latter involves a 'vague promise of future salvation from the existing conditions', which are associated with individual leaders and persons that 'address themselves to the lowest status and poorest sections of society' (ibid., p. 156):

> The vague and diffuse nature of the targets or causes of poverty in both millenarianism and populism corresponds to the fragmented nature of primitive labour market relations; the social relations of production do not precipitate a collective consciousness that is immediately directed towards redressing power within production or securing an immediate amelioration of conditions of work. The absence of an immediately identifiable target ... and the socially fragmented way in which work is done prevents a continuous relationship of solidarity or companionship in the workplace. (Ibid.)

According to Harrod, these relational characteristics combine with a psychological tendency for fatalism and anomie. This is related to poor diet and squalid living conditions (including malnutrition, lack of sanitation, and disease), a sense of uprootedness, a lack of belonging, unfamiliarity with values and social signs in new circumstances, and the shame that comes from being a perpetual servant. (Urban marginals tend to have been uprooted from disintegrating social relations of production, such as subsistence and peasant farming.) It is not that urban marginals are passive victims, as in their very struggle for survival they constantly have to show creativity. Rather their fatalism is related to their political disposition and the fragmented nature of their one-off social relations, which do not allow easy identification of enemies or prospective beneficiaries. By contrast millenarianism and populism provide a 'psychological palliative' for their condition. 'They offer total, imminent, and collective salvation from the horrors of the existing world' as well as 'a sense of identity, a touchstone for the psyche and a reason for living' (ibid., pp. 157–60). 'Significantly the elements of doctrines are usually a fierce rejection of the prevailing lifestyle of nonadherents, the damnation of established society, and exhortation to clean and uncorrupted living' (ibid., p. 160).[12]

Conclusion

After a theoretical defence of the claims entailed in Cox and Harrod's concept of patterns of social relations of production, and linking it to Gramsci's 'economic corporate moment', this chapter has provided an outline of the composition of patterns of social relations of production in the contemporary world order (Gramsci, 1971; Cox, 1987; Harrod, 1987). In addition an attempt has been made to derive the dispositions of 'basic consciousness' attendant to this composition, constellation or matrix of social relations of production.

It should be emphasized that this has been a preliminary exercise aimed at setting the stage for more rigorous research. Such research will require a much more detailed investigation of the dynamics and patterns in specific locales, which will then need to be aggregated to create a more global picture. In the process, what has been presented here could be viewed as a 'structure of hypotheses' to help orient the research, but it should be tested through a critical empirical investigation. Ideally such research should include a considerable effort to reconstruct data to conceptualize power relations in production, as the existing labour force statistics are not designed to capture these. This chapter has inevitably had to rely on rather circumstantial interpretations of less than perfect proxy data from the UNDP, ILO and other organizations.

Nevertheless, even on the basis of as rough an empirical account as the one presented here, one can conclude that bipartism and tripartism are either declining in the capitalist core in favour of the corporate pattern, or that tripartism is being hollowed out in such a way that its power relations of production are coming to resemble the corporate pattern. The likely effect of this is an increased disposition towards civic privatism among the workers in these relations, which in turn will reinforce the 'macro-rationality' that Habermas (1975) identified for the postwar period. In many instances this tendency is related to and given impetus by a crisis of the household pattern that flanked tripartism in the Fordist period, resulting in a tendency in the core to resolve the problems of social reproduction by deploying domestic workers in the casual pattern.

In addition, not the least because of the outsourcing processes discussed by Amoore in Chapter 1, in the semiperiphery (as many works on the 'new international division of labour' have intimated) there has been a rapid increase in the enterprise pattern and a decline of state corporatism. This raises the question of whether or not the environment is favourable for the establishment of trade unions to organize the proletariat in these increasingly liberal societies, or whether repressive legislation and global competition would prohibit such an effort.

Whilst the importance of the increase of people employed in the enterprise pattern in the semiperiphery due to outsourcing cannot be denied, it should be put into an appropriate context. On a global scale it is still a relatively limited but often precarious phenomenon, as the East Asian crisis of the late 1990s has shown. A quantitatively more significant phenomenon that has received much less attention in IPE is the huge reduction of the proportion of Third World populations involved in agriculture without a concomitant rise in the proportion employed in the enterprise pattern or other formal patterns of employment. This chapter has interpreted this as a dramatic decline of the subsistence and peasant patterns and a corresponding increase in the self-employment and, especially, casual patterns. According to Cox (1987) and Harrod (1987) the former tends to combine a radical individualism with collective organization for self-defence, which sometimes lends itself to right-wing populism. The disposition of workers in the casual pattern oscillates between extreme instrumentalism in the interest of survival and a millenarianist populism. The latter correlates well with the rise of fundamentalist Islam or Christianity in the Middle East, parts of South Asia, Latin America and Africa.

On the basis of this analysis it can be concluded that the contemporary world order is characterized by an ominous polarization of *habitus*

(Bourdieu, 1977) between, on the one hand, a civic privatism in the core, with an affluent, politically disengaged but instrumental public that is susceptible to a crude politics that relies on market techniques, and on the other a populism with strong millenarianist dimensions among the desperately poor in the periphery. This is far from conducive to the benign associative and deliberative liberal-democratic cosmopolitanism projected in much of the global civil society literature.

Of course dispositions imply uneven potential, as opposed to achieved actualities. It would be to fall into the trap of economic reductionism to infer a mechanical automaticity between patterns of social relations of production and political outcomes. In Gramsci's (1971) parlance, concrete political subjects are not formed in the 'economic corporate moment'. Rather they serve as the backdrop for the moment of 'fundamental class' (subject) formation and the 'ethicopolitical moment' of hegemonic struggle between subjects. Islamic fundamentalism has not emerged spontaneously from the slums of the Middle East, North Africa and South Asia. Rather it has been forged politically through societal entities such as mosques and other Islamic institutions (Volpi, 2003). The proclamations of these societal entities – as also is the case with Christian fundamentalist churches, or for that matter the populist cult of Evita Perón in Argentina in the middle of the twentieth century – find fertile ground among social groups shaped by the casual pattern of social relations. Similarly the evolution of party competition in Western Europe and other parts of the capitalist core has shown that the use of marketing techniques, as opposed to the traditional mobilizational techniques used by mass parties, is a winning strategy in an era of hollowed-out tripartism and the rise of the corporate pattern.

A question of vital importance is the degree of contingency of such a societal terrain. Writing on the rise of Pentecostalism in Africa, Corten and Marshall-Fratani (2001) suggest that in this context religion might serve as an 'integrative force' of democracy in the way that Christian democracy did in twentieth-century Europe. As in Victor Hugo's *Les Miserables* the casual pattern can produce a wide range of subjects, ranging from the criminal villain Thenardier to his son, the street urchin Gavroche, who dies a heroic death in the struggle for a democratic France. Scandinavian democratization in the late nineteenth century shows how the rise of a free-church movement among the destitute can provide the foundations for a hegemonic social democratic labour movement (Ryner, 2002). It should be noted, however, that in times when millenarianist fervour served as a social force for modernity and democracy the casual pattern was a transitory phenomenon and populations were progressively absorbed into other patterns of social relations. It is doubtful that this is generally the case in the contemporary global political economy.

Notes

1. I thank Jeffrey Harrod for his thorough review and comments on a previous version of this chapter. Thanks also to Matt Davies, Marlea Clarke, Robert Imam, Mustapha Kamal Pasha, Karim Knio and Mark Neocleous for their very helpful comments and suggestions.
2. This is not to say that there have been no sophisticated Marxists who have appreciated the problems of deploying such a mechanical conception of modes of production in the concrete analysis of workers. The historian E. P. Thompson (1963) is a case in point in respect of the transition from capitalism to feudalism. However even he failed to develop systematically a set of differentiated and context-sensitive categories to capture the making of the working class, and the result was a tendency to revert to description. (This is not detrimental to his analysis since it focuses empirically on the British case, from which Marx and Engels also extrapolated.) More recently, microsociologists who have drawn on both the Marxist and the Weberian traditions (Piore, 1980; Sabel, 1982; Burawoy, 1985) have gone further by developing contrasting models that capture the segmentation of groups in the industrial production process. These are important contributions and have been recognized by Cox (1987) and Harrod (1987) in the distinction between 'enterprise labour market', 'enterprise corporatist' and 'tripartist' social relations. However from a global perspective these contributions are limited in that they focus exclusively on social relations in industrial manufacturing. In contrast Wright (1989) has broken away from the industrial paradigm and, taking a cue from Weber, developed a conception of class differentiation that also takes into account the distribution of benefits and surpluses through bureaucratic rationalization. While this extends the analysis to the service sector it leaves out at least 40 per cent of the world's work that is done in agriculture and the informal economy in the Third World. In other words no account is taken of the capitalist periphery.
3. The peasant pattern was initially called 'peasant-lord' and the casual pattern was called the primitive labour market in Cox and Harrod's 1987 books. However, given Harrod's dissatisfaction with these formulations, as expressed in Chapter 2, we shall use the terminology he has proposed in this book.
4. Called the enterprise labour market in the 1987 books.
5. Called enterprise corporatism in the 1987 books.
6. One proxy indicator in Europe is the fairly uniform decrease of the unionization rates in 1985–95 (47.4 per cent in France, 16.8 per cent in West Germany and 27.2 per cent in the UK). In the corporatist states of Belgium, the Netherlands, Switzerland and Austria the decreases were 6.7 per cent, 9.2 per cent, 21.2 per cent and 29.2 per cent respectively, whilst that in Scandinavia remained more or less stable (ILO, 1998b). Of course one has to be careful when drawing conclusions from this, since employment laws and social insurance legislation in many countries generalize the conditions of collective agreements to the entire workforce. Hence the coverage rates often continue

to be 80–90 per cent. Furthermore, central macroeconomic accords have recently had a renaissance as they offer a quick and efficient way to contain macro wage increases (Schulten and Stueckler, 2000). At the same time these broad framework agreements tend to assign ever more discretion to individual corporations with regard to productivity, absenteeism, the duration and flexibility of working time, new forms of work organization and even the concrete implementation of wage policy (including exemptions from centrally negotiated norms) (Marginson and Schulten, 1999). The latter can be viewed as enterprise corporatist developments within an increasingly hollow shell of tripartism.

7. This is the authoritarian form of corporatism that was pioneered during fascist attempts to control industrial development, but it was also typical of bureaucratic authoritarian state strategies of dependent development in the postwar era, which sought to incorporate strategically important sections of workers into the modernized sectors. This was an extreme case of external bureaucratization, where official representatives of labour carried out coercive as well as doctrinal state functions *vis-à-vis* their members. Peaceful labour relations were closely articulated with the national interest, and if unrest occurred it was generally brutally repressed. This left little scope for the institutional forging of an organized, collective, industrial working-class consciousness. At the same time employment in this form provided a measure of social protection and security. A vivid indication of the decline of state corporatism was the dramatic fall in union membership between the mid 1980s and the 1990s in countries such as Argentina (−48 per cent), Colombia (−37 per cent), Mexico (−43 per cent), Uruguay (−41 per cent), and Egypt (−24 per cent) (ILO, 1998).

8. One often neglected aspect of East Asian development is the extent to which 'self-exploitation' in subsistence farming (providing a supplementary source of food) operates as a mechanism to suppress market wages and provide a buffer when the demand for labour is low (*see inter alia* Barkin, 1990; Evans, 1987).

9. The decline is probably underestimated as the figures include casual agrarian waged labour.

10. For example an increase from 3 per cent to 25 per cent in Egypt 1960–99 and from 4 per cent to 21 per cent in Colombia in 1960. In Malaysia the increase was only from 1 per cent to 12 per cent, but there was an increase of manufacturing employment to 22 per cent, reflecting some absorption of the labour force through semiperipheral industrialization.

11. In the 1990s the informal sector accounted for 50–75 per cent of employment in Ethiopia, 89 per cent in Ghana, 94 per cent in Mali, 56 per cent in India, 31 per cent in South Africa and 32 per cent in Mexico. However these percentages understate the extent of these patterns of social relations. With many more employers or own account workers than employees, what the ILO (1990, 2000b) calls the commerce sector also contains many in self-employed or primitive labour market relations. In 1960–99 the commerce sector employed 8 per cent of Colombia's economically active population, and in Egypt and Bangladesh employment in the sector rose from 8 per cent to 11 per cent and from 3 per cent to 11 per cent respectively.

12. The rise of millenarianism in slums in the Middle East has been examined in the case of the Mahdi Army in Iraq, by ICG (2004); for a discussion of

Morocco see Belaala (2004). There is also a large body of literature on the rise of (mainly) Christian fundamentalism in the wake of globalization in Africa and Latin America, which emphasizes its role in people's response to alienation and poverty in the slums. For a resourceful review of the prolific literature on the rise of mainly Christian fundamentalism see Peterson *et al.* (2001), Corten and Marshall-Fratani (2001), Hopkins *et al.* (2001), Greenfield and Droogers (2001) and Garrard-Burnett (2004).

4
The Public Spheres of Unprotected Workers[1]

Matt Davies

The previous chapters highlighted how 'work-empty' discourses produce thin and problematic concepts and analyses in the fields of international political economy and international relations. In Chapter 1 Amoore demonstrated how work and the restructuring of work are political processes that need to be taken up by these fields. Harrod (Chapter 2) outlined and extended the approach that he (Harrod, 1987) and Robert Cox (1987) introduced in their linked but free-standing volumes on power and production, and carried forward the arguments in Chapter 1 by presenting a 'neomaterialist' analysis of the nexus between power and production. In Chapter 3 Ryner deepened the critique of the 'work-empty' discourses of the fields and provided an analysis of the 'economic corporate moment' in the formation of the poor as social subjects. Together these chapters have put firmly before us the question of the political capacity of dominated people to challenge their status and influence global politics.

The aim of the present chapter is to examine how the global poor can become political subjects, or to put it in slightly different terms, to explore the 'ethicopolitical moment' in their formation as subjects. Can subordinate people's struggle against social power relations challenge the dominant forces in the world order? In particular, can the political, economic and social transformations associated with neoliberalism create the conditions for new forms of political subjectivity that will be capable of transforming the social relations underpinning the global order? As Chapter 1 demonstrated, global political economic restructuring under the banner of neoliberalism is political precisely because it increases the risk and precariousness of employment. Thus unprotected workers seem an unlikely source of antagonistic political subjectivity since their very lack of institutional protection means that articulating political demands is risky. This problem is felt doubly by those involved in the pattern of unprotected labour examined in this chapter – the household pattern – since the family is one of the key institutions that underwrite the division of political economic life into public and private spheres; furthermore, the family has been the site of the global ideological backlash against both women's rights and the idea of state responsibility for welfare.

At the same time there is an urgent need to conceptualize the manner in which women – who work in the household both within the framework of the family and as employees, and also work under other conditions beyond the household – become political subjects. The United Nations (Marcoux, 1997; Cagatay, 1998) has noted with growing concern the 'feminization of poverty' that is accompanying neoliberal restructuring in the developing world. As Bakker (2003) points out, neoliberalism's erosion of the welfare state has reprivatized the provision of care. At the same time women who were previously assumed to be compliant workers in the *maquiladoras* of Mexico and assembly plants of Asia have increasingly become combative labour organizers and protagonists in the resistance to neoliberalism.

The political antagonism that exists in these and other parts of the global political economy has emerged from the counterpublic spheres that unprotected workers create as they move between different patterns of social relations of production. While conflicts within these patterns are important for the transformation or sustenance of the patterns, and therefore may have structural effects on the world order, it is by moving between the patterns that subordinates produce counterpublic spheres.

This argument rests on concepts that have not been well developed in international relations theory. We begin with the question of how to conceptualize the subjectivity of the global poor. We do so by reviewing Harrod's (1987) conception of and methodology for studying unprotected workers, and by articulating a conception of the public sphere that is relevant to this form of political subjectivity. The argument then proceeds to the position of the household in the global political economy, and building on the conceptions of counterpublic spheres and unprotected workers it examines how women move between the patterns of production relations that characterize households and the 'proximate' patterns that draw upon their skills, their availability for the labour market, and the characteristics that are ideologically ascribed to women in the demand for their labour. It is through this movement that unprotected workers produce the counterpublic spheres needed to challenge the dominant forces in the world order.

Of ghosts and laying ghosts to rest: how do subjects make themselves?

The 'work-empty' conceptualizations addressed in the previous chapters and Harrod's (1987) analysis of the prevailing approaches to the underclass, tend to portray the poor as an empty screen onto which theorists can project their wishes or fears. Drainville (2004) echoes this critique, arguing that despite the emergence of a rich and varied body of literature that examines global power as a contingent, relational and situated arrangement, these studies have contributed little to our understanding of the making of transnational subjects. Drainville stresses the need to examine concretely the emergence of political subjects, rather than deriving their emergence from theoretical assumptions about global power. He refers to the subjects derived from these assumptions as 'ghosts'.[2]

Drainville's 'ghosts' haunt much of the international relations literature on the globalization of governance and civil society.[3] Feminist international theory has explicitly addressed this problem.[4] For example, arguing from the collective agency of social movements, Moghadam (2000) traces the emergence of transnational feminist networks that have given supranational form to feminist movements rooted in local conditions and contexts. Eschle's (2001) discussion of feminist social movements highlights debates within feminism that have progressively underscored the need to be analytically sensitive to the specificities of women's social conditions, rather than subsuming women's political struggles into homogenized conceptualizations of patriarchy or sexual oppression. This leads her to a 'transversal' democratic politics rooted in location and the particular connections that can be made between discrete women's struggles.

However, while Eschle is correct to insist on disaggregating the forms of struggle in order to avoid economistic reductionism, the equation of historical materialism with economism is too harsh. Power conceptualized in terms of the social relations of production need not be an economistic conception. Production is not reducible to the economy. Forms of political subjectivity are also produced – though not, or at least not merely, as commodities but as specific patterns of social power relations. Finally, the goods and services produced in the household are not necessarily part of the capitalist economy: they are not produced for exchange or consumption outside the household and the producers are not compensated with a wage; rather their products are extracted directly. Extraction of services and goods from the household is certainly necessary for capital accumulation, as Silvia Federici discusses in Chapter 5 of this volume, but it is sustained by extra-economic means that enable externalization of the costs of social reproduction.

Thus contrary to the intention of feminist analyses of social power, severing the analysis of the politics of women's social movements from the material conditions in which women produce obscures the concrete operations of power. Transnational feminist studies show great analytical sensitivity to the varying conditions of the different segments of the international or transnational women's movement, but by not connecting the differences between identities or political aims to the material conditions of women's lives, their analyses run the risk of arguing a ghost-like subjectivity for women from deracinated concepts of power.

Another important approach to the emergence of new forms of international political subjectivity draws on the notion of public spheres. The concept of public spheres can begin to correct the tendency to assume forms of subjectivity based solely on analytical deductions from concepts of global power, because the public sphere is a space in which subjects form themselves through the articulation of political demands. However the notion of the public sphere has typically been used in ways that reinforce the dominant, state-centric conceptions of global politics. International Relations theorists have turned to critical theory in instances where the call for a 'dialogue of civilizations' is predicated on states or state actors conducting the dialogue.[5] The critical content of the concept of the public sphere is vitiated by the adherence to state-centric conceptualizations of international politics. Studies conducted in this vein have been criticized for their focus on agents who have already been enabled by the public sphere to engage in transnational dialogue, for not paying sufficient attention to bottom-up processes (Cochran, 2002), for not examining how particularistic interests shape the international public sphere (Cheah, 1997), and for neglecting the historical and class bases of public spheres (Davies, 2001).

Each of these concepts – international civil society, transnational feminist networks and international public spheres – opens promising lines of investigation by indicating the production of a space for international political subjectivity by political subjects themselves. But they do not fully dispel Drainville's (2004) ghosts because they neglect the concrete power relations in which subordinate political subjects forge themselves. Addressing these problems requires both a disaggregated account of global power relations, such as that proposed and developed by Harrod in Chapter 2 and Ryner in Chapter 3, and a theory of how political subjects make themselves in the context of concrete patterns of power relations.

Harrod and Ryner both argue the need to approach the analysis of social formations with tools that are sensitive enough to account for the different patterns of power in production relations. Harrod's theory of social power provides a crucial tool for understanding the linkages between different patterns of social power in the production relations that provide the context for subject formation. Unlike the reified concept of power that is prevalent in international relations analyses, and in contrast to the often undifferentiated concept of power found in many structuralist and post-structuralist accounts, Harrod's is a materialist approach to power: it is rooted in concrete social relations of production and therefore responds analytically to the differing social circumstances that power produces and that in turn produce power. The power that a male head of household has over the production of cooking, cleaning and child care by women workers in the household stems from a long ideological tradition of women's subordination within the household and the structure of finance and social opportunities it has created. In a practical sense, patriarchy is present to some degree wherever household relations of production exist (Harrod, 1987). Such power is clearly different in form, origin and structure from that exercised by a landowner extracting rent from a tenant farming family, the power of an employer to dismiss non-unionized employees, and the power a union has over its members and in relation to corporate managers or enterprise owners (ibid.).

In Harrod's conception, power operates at four analytically distinct levels: the dominant–subordinate relations in the production process; the accrued social power of the dominant groups; the political power of states or institutions with the ability to affect distribution; and world power – that is, the ability to exert power on a global scale (ibid.). Relations of domination and subordination order the social relations of production not only within the individual patterns but also between them. 'The relationship of dominance and subordination in the hierarchy of social relations, as with other power relations also means that the groups in one form knowingly or unknowingly extract from the groups in the subordinate forms' (ibid., pp. 20–1). This is the mechanism by which power in production is linked to social and world-ordering power.

This approach to global power as social power can be combined with a conception of how concrete political subjects fashion themselves in the context of specific patterns of power relations, which is the second requirement for a theory of the production of transnational political subjects. This involves the way in which political subjects make themselves through the public spheres that are produced in the lived contexts of social power relations.

Habermas's influential book, *The Structural Transformation of the Public Sphere* (1991), has provoked lively debates on how groups and classes become political subjects and how the public sphere enables some while obstructing others from political subjectivity. As a historical category linked to the formation of bourgeois society under liberalism and capitalism, Habermas's notion of the public sphere refers to a new space for political subjectivity that is separate from the state – whose power the public is supposed to check – as well as from the private realms of the market and the family. Habermas specifically investigated the bourgeois public sphere, 'the sphere of private individuals assembled into a public body, which almost immediately laid claim to the officially regulated "intellectual newspapers" for use against the public authority itself' (ibid., p. 199). The public sphere is a 'realm of private individuals assembled into a public body who as citizens transmit the needs of bourgeois society to the state' (ibid.).

As Negt and Kluge (1993) point out, the notion of the public sphere has a double meaning that highlights its role in shaping the public:

> The public sphere denotes specific *institutions*, agencies, practices (e.g., those connected with law enforcement, the press, public opinion, the public, public sphere work, streets, and public squares); however, it is also a general social *horizon of experience* in which everything that is actually or ostensibly relevant for all members of society is integrated. (Ibid., pp. 1–2, emphasis in original)

The public sphere is a site of production: the site where the capacity of individuals to be in public is produced, together with the 'horizon of experience' or the limits of the possible. The public sphere is thus a site of structural power.

This power of the public sphere to shape the horizon of experience also prevents certain experiences from becoming public. In the case of the specific concerns of this chapter, the experience of labouring and the experience of living and working in the household are specifically blocked from public life. As Negt and Kluge put it:

> What is striking about the prevailing interpretations of the concept of the public sphere is that they attempt to bring together a multitude of phenomena and yet exclude the two most important areas of life: *the whole of the industrial apparatus and socialization in the family. According to these interpretations, the public sphere derives its substance from an intermediate realm that does not specifically express any particular*

life context (Lebenszusammenhang), even though this public sphere allegedly represents the totality of society. (Ibid., p. xlvi, emphasis in original)

How, then, can household workers have a public sphere in which to form their political subjectivity?

Counterpublic spheres and unprotected workers

Public spheres are areas of social life where matters of common concern are expressed and deliberated and political subjectivity is produced, albeit in diverse ways. In her examination of salon and literary societies, Landes (1998) points out that Habermas's work seems to point to multiple spheres of deliberation, even though only one becomes politically dominant.[6] The bourgeois public sphere dominates by controlling the perception of what counts as social life, but at the same time public spheres are necessary for social life:

As long as the contradiction between the growing socialization of human beings and the attenuated forms of their private life persists, the public sphere is simultaneously a genuine articulation of a fundamental social need. It is the only form of expression that links the members of society to one another by integrating their developing social characteristics. (Negt and Kluge, 1993, p. 2)

The concept of the bourgeois public sphere is historically and class specific so we must also investigate the other types of public – or counterpublic – sphere that emerge in conflict with the dominant forms.

Reconsidering the public in terms of opposition to its dominant forms raises the question of how and through which media other groups and classes circulate their struggles. If the bourgeois public sphere has increasingly taken on the character of an area of social life where a public that is capable of holding relevant opinions is formed – that is, an instrument of civil society where consent is articulated and maintained – and if publicity has increasingly taken on the task of advertising as public space is privatized (as Ryner argues with regard to civic privatism in Chapter 3) then it should not be surprising if agents without access to this sphere find other ways of asserting their concerns, whether through residual cultural forms such as *marianismo* in Mexico, or through emergent cultural forms, as in the theatrical protests by antiglobalization campaigners and antiwar protesters.

Such alternative forms of publicity are politically important in two senses. First, they indicate the formation of other kinds of public, based on other rationalities and capacities, and thus alternative forms of subjectivity and agency to those produced in the bourgeois public sphere. Second, as groups form themselves into classes that are antagonistic to the dominant order they create counterpublic spheres: public spheres constituted against the forces of domination and alienation in the (ideological) spaces of representation, in the spaces of consciousness formation, and in the lived spaces of everyday life. Counterpublic spheres must therefore be studied in terms of important elements of everyday life that are usually excluded from both dominant conceptions of the public sphere and from dominant conceptions of international relations, namely the private realms constituted by family relations and the world of work (Fraser, 1997).

However there is no guarantee that alternative forms of publicity, much less mere changes in economic conditions, will transform themselves into counterpublic spheres. To grasp the manner and circumstances of such transformations the cultural analysis of social groups must be supplemented by a political analysis of the groups in their patterns of social relations of production.

As noted in the previous chapters, Harrod's (1987) work provides a framework to think about antagonism in global politics from the perspective of the social relations of production. The two most prevalent concepts used to describe the mass of workers who labour outside the protection of established, formally contracted production relations are the Marxist notion of a reserve army of labour and the notion (more common in mainstream literature) of informal sector labour. The reserve army is presumed to have the economic effect of creating an oversupply of labour, thus depressing wages, and the political effect of dividing the working class into a sector that for fear of unemployment is dependent on the employer and therefore does not identify with the sector outside the security of the labour contract. The informal sector of the economy is an unregulated and untaxed sector in which marginal or excluded workers rely on their entrepreneurial skills to compensate for the lack of steady employment. Such entrepreneurship can take the form of emergency survival activities for petty accumulation in extra-legal relations, such as small-scale artisan workshops or very small enterprises operating outside state surveillance and regulation, or of illegal activities such as prostitution, drug manufacture and dealing, or theft.

Harrod is sceptical of both conceptual frameworks, not because the activities or effects they describe do not take place, but because both tend to conflate very different kinds of social relations and forms of power into overly uniform conceptions. The notion of the informal sector, for example, does not distinguish between the woman who bakes cakes to sell from a market stall while retaining the burden of household labour, and the woman who installs four sewing machines in her front room and hires local girls to assemble garments on a piece rate. Making such a distinction is important to understanding the role of unprotected labour in the global political economy as well as the effects that globalization is having on unprotected workers. It is also important for comprehending the forms of public and political subjectivity that emerge from the movement of people between different patterns of social relations of production, differences that are ignored by the dominant conceptual frameworks.

Harrod criticizes the Marxist notion of the reserve army of labour on similar grounds. However he acknowledges that certain functions of the reserve army are relevant to the understanding of household relations of production: unemployed and partially employed women ensure the cheap reproduction of labour when they have babies; and they provide a 'buffer stock' of labour that can be absorbed or expelled as the demand for labour shifts. Nonetheless, because power relations in the household differ dramatically from those in other social relations of production, the forms of political subjectivity – including the needs, goals, rational-ities, capabilities and resources that can be articulated in counterpublic spheres – cannot be reduced to a one-dimensional imperative derived from the social category. They must be understood in terms of the various power relations in production. Just as in the case of the informal sector, the notion of a reserve army precludes consideration of these differences.

What is the role of the unprotected worker in global politicoeco-nomic change? International migrants are typically subject to unpro-tected working conditions, and their remittances may be crucial to their home nations. From the perspective of the reorganization of production, the flexibilization of labour markets – in the form of reduc-ing the protection workers enjoy under more traditional patterns of social relations of production such as bipartism, enterprise corporatism or tripartism, and moving workers to 'purer' types of labour market – has been a key feature of global and national politicoeconomic reform under neoliberalism.

Furthermore, as Amoore argued in Chapter 1, restructuring has changed power relations in the workplace itself. Summing up the changes in doctrine that followed the retrenchment of the welfare state in the 1970s, Cox (1987, p. 283) argues that:

> While applauding wage restraint and state budget cutbacks, business also demanded a strengthening of managerial authority over the organization of work, an authority that had been weakened by worker power on the shop floor, and the freedom to restructure production so as to be able to make greater use of technology-intensive processes and flexible employment of temporary and part-time non-established workers and support services.

What was at stake in this restructuring of employment relations was not merely the ability to drive down wages or expand the section of workers available for temporary and part-time employment, but the reorganization of the dominant form of production and of political power itself. Thus economic restructuring – as patterns of social relations that characterized of established workers declined and were replaced by patterns that were more characteristic of unprotected labour – also undermined the social foundations of traditional working-class counter-public spheres such as trade unions. In one of the more extreme examples of this sort of restructuring, under the neoliberal reforms of the 1970s and 1980s Chilean legislation established the employment contract as a contract between individual employer and individual employee in an effort to remove employment conditions from the public sphere altogether.[7]

The variety of patterns of social relations of production demanded by flexible accumulation strategies also suggests that globalization is relying on more immediate, even more intimate forms of coercion and control. Self-employed workers must offer themselves individually to clients; workers in subcontracting small enterprises must offer themselves individually to their employers; workers in casual labour markets must deal with potential employers on an individual basis. In none of these cases does the worker enjoy collective protection.[8]

The household in the global political economy

Of the patterns of social relations of production that Harrod (1987) discusses, the household is typically subordinate to the proximate patterns found in almost any other social formation. The household pattern of social relations of production is characterized by, among other things, production for immediate consumption rather than for markets. While some things may be produced in a household for exchange in markets – baked goods or packaged herbs for sale in street markets for example – such production will take place under the patterns of social relations of production that usually characterize families: that is, as extensions of the patriarchically organized household labour of reproduction.

Given that the household sphere is at some remove from international economic policy and planning and represents the private realm in its most obvious form, why discuss the household in the context of the global political economy? It might be useful to begin to answer this question by considering why it is usually not examined in this context. As feminists have argued, this may be party due to the elitist bias in the dominant forms of theorizing international relations. The agents of international systems whose practice appears to have the most direct and immediate force in international relations and the world order are bankers, diplomats, generals and bureaucrats in international organizations. Thanks in part to the efforts of feminist scholars, the capacity of such agents to act has been shown to lie not in their inherent qualities but in their social relations, and particularly in their reliance on the 'invisible' work of the women (and others) who make the social relations of the elite materially possible (Enloe, 1989). Thus it no longer seems strange to think of international relations as including social relations among non-elites. Nevertheless political economy as a discipline is to a large degree an effort to conceptualize the ways we have of ordering our lives between the public and private spheres. Even for those who accept that 'the personal is political', the household remains a sphere of personal, intimate and private relations – even when these relations are ones of exploitation and alienation. The conceptual gap between intimate, private experience and global political and economic relations remains difficult to bridge.

In the following passage Harrod describes the work done in the household and for social reproduction, and how that work itself creates obstacles to understanding its role in global political and economic contexts:

> Throughout the world women may be seen in street markets, supermarkets, and shops and shopping centers, holding children, carrying shopping baskets, or pushing supermarket carts, as they inspect, select, and discuss the food and other items they buy for their children and husbands, and others, who comprise their household. Shopping, as one of the major services women provide for the household, is exceptional inasmuch as it is public, for most of the household work

is done in the seclusion of the house, apartment, room, shanty, or hut. It is there that housewives work to provide the full range of services for the household, including childrearing, food preparation, repairing, cleaning, and management of the household budget with money they earn or is passed to them from the wages of other members of the family. (Harrod, 1987, p. 291)

Feminist economists have contributed to our understanding of the value of such labour to the economy, and have begun to explore possible policy instruments to address unpaid labour at the macroeconomic level (see Bakker, 1998; Elson, 1998). A different line of inquiry explores the contribution of household work by means of the concept of global commodity chains (Dunaway, 2001). Most relevant for the present argument, however, are studies that examine household labour in terms of the coping strategies adopted by poor people in times of economic recession or crisis, or under conditions of economic restructuring, including privatization (Geldstein, 1997), and labour market flexibilization and the loss of state support (González de la Rocha, 2000; Montali, 2000; Bakker, 2003). This body of research links changes in economic policy and accumulation strategies to the way work is done in the household and the attendant strains on and changes in the family.

   In her meticulous examination of the relationship between changes in the labour market in the metropolitan region of São Paulo, Brazil, and family arrangements to insert different family members into the labour market, Montali (2000) argues that the model of the family with the male head of household as the sole provider has become 'concretely impossible'.[9] Montali shows how economic restructuring in Brazil in the 1990s increased the participation of women in the labour market, which in turn made labour relations more precarious and caused a deterioration of family income:

To make matters worse, for the first time since the beginning of the stabilization plan, [in 1998] the deterioration of the real family income was accompanied by a deterioration of the labor market. The reduction of the income of employed people also affected the spouses of heads of households, the only members of families who showed an increase in real income up till 1997. (Ibid., p. 67)

The increased precariousness of family income occurred in the political context of the absence or removal of employment legislation and social protection. The changes were part of the package of policies associated with the neoliberal project of reorienting the state so as to improve the climate for foreign investment and privatization, including privatization of the provision of social services. The policies were implemented unevenly in Latin America – as early as 1975 in Chile but not until the 1990s in Brazil – but they uniformly shifted the burden of social protection and reproduction on to families.

Such a shift was made possible by the fact that the household was, as Cox (1987, p. 50) has put it, the producer of the last resort: 'when unemployment rises, production functions are forced back upon the household. It becomes the buffer for economic crisis to the extent that its emotional resilience can stand the strain.' Similarly Britto da Motta and Moreira de Carvalho (1993, pp. 76–7) argue that increasing pauperization has led to:

> a severe contraction in consumption patterns, leading to the degradation of the quality of life of working-class families, to the point of depriving them of basic necessities such as food and clean water; [and has] caused a corresponding increase in the number of working hours needed to meet the rising cost of the subsistence needs of workers and their families. This has demanded that the working day of those who act as household heads (mainly men, but increasingly women as well) be extended, either through putting in extra working hours in their regular jobs, or by doing odd jobs on the side. Yet, since there are obvious limits to the working day – including biological limits, of course – increasing pauperization has progressively demanded the incorporation of other members of the household into the labour force as the only other means of offsetting the diminishing value of the principal provider's wages.

These descriptions of the household echo Harrod's (1987) observation that the patterns of social relations of production form a hierarchy in which the dominant patterns knowingly or unknowingly extract from the subordinate patterns. Such links must be explored because it is the ongoing transformations of everyday life that make the transitions in global order possible. Lefebvre (1991b) has shown how urbanization and the creation of workplaces outside the home have transformed both work itself and family life. In the social relations of production such as subsistence patterns, for example, work and family are bound together almost seamlessly: the labour of farming, animal husbandry and so on flow easily into cooking and eating, in terms of both place and practice. This is not to say that hierarchies or divisions of labour do not exist in subsistence relations, only that they have an organic character. With urbanization and waged labour, however, work becomes an alienating activity outside the home. Lefebvre shows how everyday life becomes divided between alienating work, the (also alienating) compensatory pursuit of leisure, and the demands of family life.

Looked at from a different perspective, the reproductive labour of the household is:

> assigned low status and consequently allocated to subordinate work-ers. Because these latter are, almost everywhere, women, the origin of the pattern of relations is also associated with the general subordina-tion of women, the creation of a family household with dominant male heads, and the emergence of the concept of 'women's work' used to describe household tasks. (Harrod, 1987, p. 296)

Household labour is viewed as without value and uncompensated, family relations become the means of enforcing the social relations that rely on this devalued labour, and leisure serves not only as compensa-tion for alienating work but also to evade of household labour.

While changes in politicoeconomic structures affect the household, the division of labour within the household and the work that is done there, the household is still a site of production, reproduction and trans-formation. The labour of social reproduction is typically conceptualized in terms of housework, and the household is the site for this labour. Bakker (2003), for example, defines the labour of social reproduction in terms of biological reproduction, reproduction of the labour force and the reproduction of provisioning and caring needs. To this one might add, following Lefebvre (1976), the reproduction of social relations of production. Lefebvre views the household not as a consequence or copy of capitalist relations, but as the 'central location where global relations are produced and reproduced' (Lefebvre, 1976, p. 49). This notion implic-itly informs the view that the 'concrete impossibility' (under conditions of economic crisis and restructuring), of the continuation of households with a sole breadwinner and male head offers the possibility, in the medium term, of more equitable gender relations (Montali, 2000, p. 67).

In contemporary transformations of the global political economy, neoliberal policies have shifted the structure of production relations in such a way that unprotected workers are having to work as self-employed subcontractors, in jobs in the enterprise labour market or as casual labourers. Neoliberalism has not merely restructured the labour market to increase the participation or availability of unprotected workers, but also changed the nature of the power exercised over them. Examples abound, ranging from mandatory pregnancy tests for young women applying for work in *maquiladoras* and monthly checks of female workers' sanitary towels, to timed lavatory breaks and so on (Light, 1999; Salzinger, 2001). In other words, power relations in these patterns of social relations of production are increasingly resembling some of the intimate ways in which power is exercised within the family.[10]

At the same time the household pattern of social relations of production is a 'proximate pattern' (Harrod, 1987) to these other subordinate patterns of social relations. This means that people move between these patterns: workers hired as casual labourers who develop skills or become more regular employees may come to enjoy the slightly higher degree of protection of the enterprise, and laid-off skilled workers may offer their services 'off the books' in the casual labour market. More directly relevant to the present argument, employers in casual or enterprise labour markets may prefer to hire young women for *maquila* work because young women are considered to be more docile than male workers, thanks to their socialization in the family and their perceived dependence on men and elders (see Chapter 8 of this volume). Women also utilize their household skills as domestic workers, and this can make them vulnerable if they live in the house where they work (Britto da Motta, 1999). They also lack access to unions other collective forms of protection (Chaney and García Castro, 1989), and may be vulnerable in terms of citizenship (Anderson, 2000).

The movement of women between subordinate patterns of social relations of production

How does the movement of women between subordinate patterns of social relations of production outside the household affect family life? The double shift, as Harrod (1987) points out, is neither a recent development nor uncommon. Indeed the 'ideal' nuclear family, in which the woman has no need to work outside the home, is exceptional. Nevertheless in times of transition the balance of power relations in households may shift: Harrod cites as examples *marianismo* in Mexico and women's control over the family budget in Japan. But changes are more likely to derive from outside the household, from the movement of women into proximate patterns of social relations of production:

> Women household workers, unlike the self-employed, are nearly always in other forms of social relations at the same time. The

mixture of consciousness produced by household social relations (and its supporting ideology of patriarchy) and the consciousness derived from being a worker at the same time in other social relations is sufficient in itself to override any social similarities arising from the mere structure of the work. (Ibid., p. 245)

According to Britto da Motta (1999, pp. 125–6) the growth of the number of non-resident domestic workers in Brazil has led to women sharing their experiences with other workers during long bus rides to and from work:

Everything is discussed while waiting long hours and traveling together: the irregular service and high cost of public transportation, the often violent popular reaction to the lack of basic services, the 'garbage in front of my door that they haven't collected for six days,' strikes, the low value of the minimum wage, who does or does not have the right to receive it, and other workers' rights. This discourse guarantees a continuous comparison and sharing of experiences.

The shift from resident to non-resident domestic service has also made it possible for women to participate in social spheres such as squatters' movements, racial and ethnic movements, neighbourhood associations and the like.

Elsewhere Britto da Motta and Moreira de Carvalho (1993) show how 'getting out of the house' enables female political participation, even though the women themselves may not perceive it as political. When women engage with friends and neighbours to improve living conditions and public services, they create or join neighbourhood associations to negotiate with state agencies on matters such as education and welfare, and in some cases they also renegotiated their domestic arrangements so that their husbands share the domestic work, freeing time for the women to participate in public activities. This getting out of the home is linked both to pauperization – because support and cooperation are needed if women are to meet even their traditional roles in production – and to the movement of women into the labour market.

When women begin to earn their own wages they may also gain a measure of autonomy from the family. Automated teller machines (ATMs) have been installed in some enterprise zone factories so that workers can deposit or cash their pay cheques. This gives them the opportunity to determine for themselves what portion of their wage to turn over to their families, fathers or husbands for the household or the men's consumption needs, and what portion to retain for their own needs. However women's movement between the household and the factory can also have a negative side in that it increases the risks they face. For example in 1995 at least 150 young women were kidnapped, raped and murdered in Juárez, Mexico; and as many as 400 such crimes have been reported in Juárez since the murders began (Amnesty International, 2003). The targeted women were primarily workers in the *maquiladoras* and they were frequently kidnapped from bars or discos, as they were beginning to assert their economic and social autonomy by going out unaccompanied or with partners of their own choosing. The nature and brutality of the crimes prompted a resurgence of masculine dominance at a time when many of the men in Juárez were unemployed or attempting to secure work as casual labourers across the border.[11] The foot-dragging and unwillingness by the Mexican police to investigate the crimes reflected a particular set of priorities in respect of gender relations, as well as labour relations on the part of Mexican officials. It was left to the families of the murdered women to protest about the crimes, and about the negligence and indifference – and possibly the complicity – of the police.[12]

Thus the movement of women between patterns of social relations of production, especially between the household and proximate patterns of waged labour, are putting pressure on power relations in the household. As the 'producer of last resort', the household has thus become an arena of intense political and ideological struggle, not only internally and culturally but also in terms of national policies (as illustrated by George W. Bush's reinstitution of Reagan's policy of withdrawing US funding from family planning agencies). But can these struggles be extended to challenge the dominant forms of world order? Is neoliberalism producing its own gravediggers?

Do household workers have public spheres?

To address the question of the public spheres of household workers, we must return to the concept of political economy as the study of the ways in which people organize their lives into public and private areas. Housework is part of the private sphere, not only because it is unremunerated and aimed at for immediate, non-market consumption, but also because it relies on secluding the houseworker in a private realm where people cannot, as Habermas (1979, p. 199) puts it, 'confer in an unrestricted fashion – that is, with the guarantee of freedom of assembly and association and the freedom to express and publish their opinions – about matters of general interest'.

However in the lived spaces of everyday life, including that of the household, challenges to the seclusion of the private realm are made and met. This lived space cannot be fully discussed in the abstract. To understand it one would have to study concrete situations in some detail: the architecture of houses and neighbourhoods, as these define public and private areas; the spaces where the collective activities of house-workers are conducted; how knowledge and information are shared, and by what means.[13] Gossip, the collective viewing and analysis of soap operas, shopping – all are spaces where the moral critique of household power relations and strategies for addressing them are carried out.

But as Harrod (1987) has shown, most of the women who are bound up in subordinate relations in the household also work outside the home. The wage is not the only means by which working women gain some autonomy – the latter also develops from struggles against exploitative bosses in factories or small enterprises, against police who chase them from public areas where they are trying to sell things, against abusive home owners who hire them as domestic servants. The lessons learned when engaged in subordinate relations of production such as self-employment, the enterprise labour market and casual labour markets circulate with the women themselves among the different social relations, and this circulation creates the conditions for people to con-struct counterpublic spheres.

One example of how the movement of women outside the home can create counterpublic spheres is the recent struggle over unionization and female identity in *maquiladoras* (see Chapter 8 of this volume). More pertinent to the present argument, however, is the earlier experience of domestic workers in Latin America. The proportion of women who worked in domestic service in the region in the 1980s is difficult to gauge, but it may have been as much as one third (Chaney and García Castro, 1989). These women went through a long and difficult process of organizing themselves into unions and their experiences in many ways prefigured the struggles for unionization in the factories of the export processing zones.[14]

More recently the demand for maids and nannies in North America and Europe has increased (Young, 2001; Ehrenreich, 2003), stretching the distance of women's migration and thus their movement between different patterns of social relations. The reprivatization of the labour of reproduction (Bakker, 2003) has contributed to the commodification of household labour and permitted the penetration of households by employees of national and multinational cleaning services (Ehrenreich, 2003). These service workers risk dismissal if they attempt to organize themselves, but the commodification of their labour has increased their opportunities to interact with one another, and it also has linked their work with that of other service sector workers, such as caretakers and hotel and restaurant employees, whose unions have been among the most militant in recent years. Today the absence of housework from the dominant public sphere (ibid.) is being contested in the counterpublic spheres of workers moving between different types of experience and different patterns of social relations of production.

These counterpublic spheres are not the static, codified and enclosed space of the bourgeois public sphere; rather they are characterized by dynamic flows because of the movement of the people who constitute them. The importance of these places as sites of antagonism will increase as globalization intensifies the immediacy and intimacy of systems of control in the relations of power between dominant and subordinate agents.

Conclusions

The household pattern of social relations of production is shaped both by forces in the social formation at large that rely on the labour of social reproduction, and by the struggle over power relations in the household. This struggle originates both within the pattern and from the movement of women into proximate patterns. Louise Amoore has made a similar observation in respect of the firm in Chapter 1. In her analysis of the firm as a socially embedded but contested institution, she warns against reifying the firm by treating it as a container, and shows how the firm is contested within the social relations of those who work in the firm and across the social and political relations in which the firm is embedded, through its association with other firms, the state and society. Although the firm is a very different social institution from the family, Amoore's argument that 'embeddedness' can mask contestations indicates that antagonism should be at the core of the analysis of the social relations of production, which makes her framework highly relevant to the analysis of the household. Thus to grasp the changing role of the household pattern of production and its potential role as a site of contestation, we must analyze power relations within the household, between the household and proximate patterns of social relations of production, and the relations of the household and the family with the state.

The institution of the family and the rationality produced by living within these relations establish strong barriers to negotiating new patterns of relations or new means of mediating conflicts in this private sphere. As mentioned earlier, Harrod (1987) points to potential patterns of subordinate power in household relations, such as the Japanese example of housewives having control over the household budget, but by itself this is not likely to change the household relations of power. Indeed as Bernard (2000) points out, the stereotype of the Japanese woman with traditional responsibility for household maintenance has provided an excuse for the underemployment of women in Japanese firms, just as women's role in reproduction has often been used to justify the gap between men's and women's pay and employment opportunities in North America and elsewhere. Indeed this pattern of subordinate power in the household can have profoundly conservative effects, giving women a reason to defend the limited power they enjoy over the household budget, for example, rather than to seek a way of transforming the power relations that subordinate them.

However the basic ethic of the family that governs household production is vulnerable because, as we have seen, the restructuring of employment in industry and other sectors of the economy has exerted tremendous pressure on the family and the household. The increasing precariousness of employment and the intensification of power relations in the proximate patterns of social relations of production have put pressure on the household as the producer of last resort. Furthermore, as Bakker (2003) has argued, the restructuring of the state under neoliberalism and the privatization of public services has added to the pressure on the family and household by reprivatizing the labour of reproduction. This has been accompanied by a growing demand for female workers outside the household, thus women are moving between the household and proximate patterns of social relations of production and increasing their potential for social and economic autonomy.

Transforming the power exercised in subordinate patterns, even intimate patterns in the family, into forms of world power rests on the ability of dominant agents to stabilize and codify their power to extract labour and wealth from subordinates. Seen in this light, neoliberalism has not only been a global strategy to expand the role of the market as a means of organizing the world order, in which workers are increasingly unprotected in 'pure' labour markets and the costs of social reproduction are disproportionately borne by unwaged workers. It is also, as Caffentzis (1993) and Federici (1993), have argued, a political strategy of primitive accumulation,[15] extracting labour from unwaged workers through the exercise of power relations within and between patterns of social relations of production. This is sustained at the global level by the protection of private property rights: by enclosing the public sphere and prohibiting the contestation of property rights, resulting in what Gill (1998) calls 'new constitutionalism'.

As a strategy for managing the costs of social reproduction, however, neoliberalism may be reaching its limits. Montali (2000, p. 67) points out that:

> for the poorest families as well as in the middle sectors of society, increasing unemployment and the continuing precariousness of the relations of work began to make the possibilities found until then for confronting situations of economic crisis and scarcity of resources collapse ... [resulting in what González de la Rocha (2000) calls] 'erosion of the model of survival'.

Montali reports that in Brazil in 1990–94 the poverty rate in São Paulo increased from 39 per cent to 48 per cent of families; that is, nearly half the families in the metropolitan region of São Paulo did not have sufficient income to meet their basic needs, reducing the capacity of families to provide the services needed for social reproduction. The Brazilian working class's shift to unprotected patterns of social relations of production has apparently changed it from a reserve army of labour to a surplus population.

The impoverishment of workers has been a universal, if not uniform, development since the 1970s, and the now obvious limits to neoliberal restructuring are making transformation increasingly urgent. Transformations in the patterns of power relations in social relations of production result from conflicts, from antagonism between dominant and subordinate actors. Such conflicts can occur both within these patterns and between them, but transformation is more likely to occur through the latter. This is most evident in the case of the household pattern, where the circulation of women between proximate patterns of social relations of production facilitates the migration of struggles between these patterns. It enables dominated and excluded subjects to produce new rationalities in counterpublic spheres and develop strategies to transform the dominant orders. In order for such alternatives to become politically practical, emergent political subjects must find ways to realize the new rationalities in more or less stable counterpublic spheres; that is, in areas of social life where the common concerns of subordinates can be discussed and further circulated. Such counterpublic spheres not only allow new ways of communicating, incorporating subjects excluded from the dominant public sphere, but also create new ways of organizing the inchoate experiences of dominated subjects and thus the emergent political subjectivities.

Power operating in the processes of production accrues to dominant social groups, who exercise control over the organization of these processes and the distribution of benefits. The power of dominant groups is in part institutionalized in states, which have the ability to affect distribution and project power externally: in the case of dominant states, they can project power to the level of world order. Power is therefore an interconnected, internally differentiated totality. Its very pervasiveness – from the world order down through the hierarchies of patterns of social relations of production – highlights the breadth of social antagonism. The existence of counterpublic spheres of unprotected workers is therefore necessary for global transformation. The counterpublic spheres involved in the household pattern of social relations of production not only help to transform the gendered hierarchies of the household, but also broaden participation in other political struggles by giving poor women access to social space hitherto denied them.

But counterpublic spheres are also as fragile and precarious as the political and economic conditions of the political subjects they enable. Furthermore the consciousness of these subordinate subjects, while materially determined, does not necessarily take a political form. There are also serious obstacles to the internationalization of counterpublic spheres that emerge from the household, despite the common social and politoeconomic problems that households in both core and periphery economies face as the burden of social reproduction is reprivatized.

Hence there is an urgent need for a research agenda in global political economy that takes as its starting point the social forces emerging from the various patterns of social relations of production. The prevailing approaches to the global political economy, such as those which focus on the politics of international economic relations either by reifying states and markets or by concentrating on global trade and high finance, are blind to the political subjectivities that develop amongst ordinary people in their daily lives. Similarly structuralist approaches, including most versions of world-systems theory, conceptualize everyday life as overdetermined and resistant to change, rather than the process by which world power and world order are produced. Power must be studied in terms of the antagonism it encounters or provokes in different patterns of social relations. By disaggregating the social categories used to cover the broad and fluid experiences of unprotected workers, and by identifying the ways in which these experiences are organized and begin to take institutional form as counterpublic spheres, the possibilities for transformation can be brought into sharper focus.

Notes

1. This chapter is a modified and shortened version of an article that appeared in *Global Society*, vol. 19, no. 2. The permission granted by the editors of the journal to reproduce the article here is gratefully acknowledged. The chapter has been through numerous drafts and has benefited from criticisms and comments by many people. In particular I wish to thank Magnus Ryner and Jeffrey Harrod for their careful readings and insightful criticisms. I also thank Isabella Bakker, Véronique Bertrand-Bourget, Silvia Federici, Stephen Gill, Gigi Herbert and David McNally for their thoughtful responses to earlier efforts as well as the present one. I am, of course, responsible for any faults that remain.

2. In Chapter 9 Dimitris Stevis and Terry Boswell use a similar term, 'phantoms', to refer to social entities that have neither voice nor choice, nor anyone to speak on their behalf. At certain points in history, women and slaves have been such entities. The difference between 'phantoms' and 'ghosts' is that the former are worldly and can conceivably gain subjectivity or agency, while the latter are only the product of the wishful thinking or 'cosmopolitan condescension' of theorists.

3. The literature on global civil society is too extensive to be listed here. For important critiques of the concept and summaries of the debates, see Pasha and Blaney (1998) and Amoore and Langley (2004).

4. For a critique of the limitations of some of the feminist approaches, see Chapter 5 of this volume.

5. The notion of an international public sphere has developed in relation not only to Habermas's work, but has also built on Held's (2003) thoughts on cosmopolitan democracy and Bohman's (1997) work on deliberative democracy and public spheres. For an overview from an international relations perspective see Lynch (2000).

6. Habermas (1992) acknowledges the importance of the distinctiveness of a plebeian public sphere. The now extensive body of literature on the plebeian public has highlighted the formation of publics that different from the bourgeois public; see especially Thompson (1963, 1993) and Linebaugh (1992). See also the work of the Subaltern Studies Group, collected in Guha and Spivak (1988), and Ahmad's (1997) withering critique of the Subaltern Studies approach.

7. Chile's employment laws have been reformed under civilian governments, but as Barrett (2001) points out, workers have only enjoyed marginal improvements and the labour movement as a whole remains weak and disorganized. Indeed during the first ten years of civilian rule (1989–98) the rate of unionization declined. Employers continue to have a fairly free hand to dismiss workers. Certain measures have been taken to improve workers' rights in individual employment contracts, and special contracts are now required for certain categories of employee, notably household employees. See also Taylor (2004).

8. 'Each of these different circumstances and different forms of social relations of production produces different material conditions and different levels and types of consciousness, but they all have a common element; in each the woman in question is basically unprotected against the power of employers, customers, controllers of markets, husbands or family. No organization, state agency, or group of individuals intervenes effectively on her behalf to protect

her from even the harshest and most arbitrary exercises of power. She has little chance of altering the conditions of work within any of the patterns of power relations although she may, as has been shown, move from one to another and acquire some positive change in material benefits' (Harrod, 1987, p. 125).

9. While unemployment has affected both men and women in Brazil, male unemployment has increased due to a reduction in the total number of jobs, while the rise in female unemployment is due to an increase in the number of women seeking to join the labour force (Brandão and Montangner, cited in Montali, 2000, p. 63).

10. Chang and Ling (2000, p. 27) identify the 'regime of labor intimacy' with the 'more explicitly sexualized, racialized, and class-based' dimension of global restructuring that 'concentrates on low-wage, low-skilled [*sic*] menial service provided by mostly female migrant workers'. Salzinger (2001) also identifies intimate forms of surveillance in *maquiladoras* where, she argues, the femininity so sought after by employers in these industries is itself produced.

11. It should be noted that none of the perpetrators of these crimes has been arrested, so it cannot be concluded that they were committed by unemployed men, nor even that, given the proximity of Juárez to the US border, they were all committed by Mexican men.

12. The rape and murder in the women in Juárez are discussed in Nathan (1997) and Salzinger (2001). See also Bowden (1998).

13. See Niemann (2003) and Chapter 6 of this volume for a more detailed analysis.

14. See for example the testimonials in Part 5 of Chaney and García Castro (1989).

15. Caffentzis (1993) and Federici (1993) argue that strategies that deny workers access to means of subsistence are instances of primitive accumulation, which both see as a political response to politically and economically driven accumulation crises.

5
Prostitution and Globalization: Notes on a Feminist Debate

Silvia Federici

Introduction

A discussion of prostitution in the context of the current phase of globalization is important for many reasons. First, globalization has produced broad changes in the organization of prostitution, providing crucial mirrors for the effects of globalization on the social position of women and the reproduction of the workforce. Second, prostitution is a key example of 'unprotected work', as defined in this volume. Thus it is a paradigmatic case for understanding how globalization is affecting the growing number of workers who are excluded from contractual relations and of the ways in which they intervene in the shaping of the world economy and contemporary political debates.

This chapter analyzes the dynamics of this intervention while discussing the controversy that has developed in international feminist circles over the politics of prostitution in the global economy, not least with reference to appropriate actions to be taken by governments, NGOs and the United Nations.

Since the early 1980s, networks of radical feminists have formed in several countries in response to the global expansion of the sex industry[1] and reports of a new trafficking in women. They insist that international law should sanction these phenomena more strictly, and some argue that prostitution should be declared a violation of women's rights. However feminist advocates of sex workers' rights have denounced these efforts as part of a campaign to abolish prostitution, and they have charged that the identification of sex work with 'sex trafficking' and 'sexual slavery' makes sex workers more vulnerable to institutional repression by reinforcing the connection between prostitution and crime in the public imagination (Kempadoo and Doezema, 1998).

This conflict peaked in 1995 at the UN Beijing Conference on Women, where a compromise was reached to keep 'abolitionist language out of the final document'. It was agreed that only 'forced' prostitution would be classified as 'violence against women' (Doezema, 1998, p. 34). The conflict, however, has continued and reached a stalemate that revolves around opposed ideological and political assumptions about the meaning of work, the possibility of individual choice and the conditions for women's liberation.

In this context, the aim of this chapter is to reframe the debate in such a way as to help us to transcend the proposed alternatives and to demonstrate that it is in the interest of feminists to mobilize in support of the struggle of sex workers. If we analyze prostitution in terms of the power relations that structure unprotected work in today's global economy, we can see that neither more severe sanctions against sex trafficking nor the free market model of prostitution advocated by some sex workers' organizations give women and prostitutes in particular more social power, in view of the shift that globalization has produced in the power relations between workers and employers and the power structures that dominate the sex trade in the global marketplace (international financial institutions, state apparatuses, transnational corporations and organized criminal networks). We can also see that sex workers are presently the object of an attack that negatively affects all women.

Feminists have a role to play connecting the struggle of sex workers with that of other workers and with the social movements that are resisting globalization. The success of this struggle and the possibility of constructing a world beyond the commodification of life depend to a large extent on the degree to which the globalization process can be reversed.

To provide evidence for these arguments we shall reconsider the theoretical model proposed by Jeffrey Harrod (1987) to conceptualize the position, consciousness and potential for struggle of unprotected workers in the sex trade. The changes that have occurred in the structure of the sex industry and sex work require us to modify some of his assumptions. For example prostitution should not be seen as an activity that necessarily pertains to the realm of a casual employment pattern of production relations. New forms of prostitution organized in terms of indentured labour and other forms of coerced work emerged in the 1990s. Furthermore, while in some parts of the world sex workers are drawn from the ranks of a displaced peasantry, in Western Europe they include migrant women who in their home countries, prior to their integration in the global economy, had waged jobs or other forms of income (as teachers, factory workers, market vendors) or they are students trying to pay school fees, or unsupported mothers stranded by welfare cuts. As Davies argued in Chapter 4, the experiences of differing patterns of power relations shape the consciousness and sense of possibilities of prostitutes and do not always conform to those that Harrod attributed to sex workers in his 1987 volume. Finally, Harrod's insistence that power relations at the point of production are key determinants in the formation of workers' consciousness (see Chapter 2 of this volume) must be commended, at a time when social subjects are idealistically defined as products of discursive practices. Nevertheless we must be alert to the dangers of reductionist readings, as Ryner (Chapter 3) and Harrod (Chapter 2) indicate. Power relations in the workplace can be affected by political activity and the presence of social movements in respect of redefining the main categories of social reproduction. The power that the rise of feminist movements in Europe and the US gave to prostitutes in the 1970s to challenge their marginalization is exemplary in this respect. It shows how a social movement can bring about political recomposition among different sectors of the workforce. In this case the movement unified the prostitutes' struggle with that of women working in factories, offices and homes. By the same token the decline of feminist activism and the divisions that have emerged among feminists concerning the social meaning of prostitution have contributed to the difficulties faced in the struggle for prostitutes' rights.

This chapter is divided into three sections. The first examines the rise of the prostitutes' rights movement in Europe and the US in the 1970s and its connection with the contemporary women's liberation movement, focusing on Western Europe and the US. The second section examines the new forms of sex work that have developed in Western Europe since the late 1980s as a consequence of the internationalization of the world political economy. This is not to suggest that the sex workers' movement is strongest in Europe or the US or that we can draw conclusions about the global sex workers' movement from the trends in these regions, even though commonalities can be found. However in several countries of Western Europe, Italy being the most outstanding example, prostitution is presently a hotly debated issue that also has serious implications for immigrants' rights.

The first two sections serve as the analytical backdrop for an examination of the debate between 'abolitionist' feminists and feminists who take a free market stand on sex workers' rights. Both strategies are insufficient to confront the new realities that have developed in the world of prostitution and are thus bound to fail even in their own terms.

Polarization of the feminist movement on questions of prostitution and sex trafficking has become part of the problem, as it has arguably had a freezing effect on feminist initiatives on behalf of sex workers at a time when such initiatives are most needed.

Out of the shadows: from prostitute to sex worker – the prostitutes' rights movement of the 1970s

In the 1970s a movement to win for prostitutes the same rights as those extended to other workers emerged in Europe and the US. It was triggered by the famous occupation in June 1975 of the Church of St Nizier in Lyons, France, by a group of about 200 sex workers. Now viewed as the 'Stonewall' of the prostitutes' rights movement (Bell, 1994, p. 104), this occupation was soon followed by similar initiatives in other French towns and other countries. By the late 1970s the movement had gained momentum, producing not only an international campaign for prostitutes' rights but also the beginning of what appeared to be a historic change in the social position of sex workers.

The occupation of the Church of St Nizier occurred in the wake of a series of physical assaults that took place after the introduction of a more restrictive law forced sex workers to work in isolated areas to avoid police harassment (Jenness, 1993; *New York Times*, 7 June 1975). The rapidity with which the movement spread and was radicalized shows that it responded to broader social currents. Indeed the rise of the prostitutes' rights movement must be understood in the context of the profound legitimation crisis that permeated every aspect of social and cultural life in Europe and the US in the 1960s and 1970s, finding its most direct expression in the resurgence of social radicalism. As Bell (1994) writes, the movement emerged at the intersection of feminism and gay liberation, both of which originated from the struggle for civil rights, which had secured for all oppressed groups greater power to challenge the dominant order and normative values.

One crucial dimension of this challenge was the feminists' revolt against the gender hierarchies underpinning the sexual division of labour – the very premise of capitalist organization of work, especially in the Fordist era (McDowell, 1991). By challenging women's confinement to unpaid domestic labour and analyzing housework as an economic activity that catered to the reproduction of the workforce, feminists opened the way to redefining female sexuality as work (Dalla Costa, 1975; James, 1975; Federici, 1975; Federici and Cox, 1975; Fortunati, 1981).

Prostitution was also redefined, practically and theoretically, as an aspect of reproductive work. Thus as more women rejected the unequal exchange at the heart of the nuclear family and proclaimed their determination to reclaim their bodies and their sexuality, the stigma attached to prostitution began to lose its power, appearing as an instrument by which a patriarchal society divided women and disciplined them to accept unpaid labour. Prostitutes thus 'came out of the shadow' to which they had been confined by the criminalization of prostitution, and established themselves as a 'new political subject' (Bell, 1994, p. 102), speaking for the first time in their own voice.

Within a few years organizations proliferated on both sides of the Atlantic to demand the end of police harassment, amnesty for all, the removal of criminal records and, crucially, the recognition of prostitution as work (Corbin, 1990; Jenness, 1993; Bindman and Doezema, 1997; Pheterson, 1989). From the start the prostitutes' rights movement called for a set of policy reforms that lay at the heart of their programme, including the decriminalization of prostitution or, in the case of the English Collective of Prostitutes, the abolition of all laws against prostitution, with legalization being rejected as a form of 'state control of the trade' (Chapkis, 1997, p. 155). The movement thus opposed the introduction or maintenance of brothels and 'Eros Centres', such as the ones operating in Nevada and introduced in the 1970s in Germany and the Netherlands, charging that they prevented sex workers from controlling their earnings, working hours and the number of clients they served.[2] In the same spirit the movement opposed confining sex work to red-light districts, arguing that zoning was a tool of police control and that prostitutes should have the right to work wherever they wished, without restrictions on the organization of their work (Jaget, 1980; Chapkis, 1997). Sex workers called instead for standard labour laws to be extended their work, enabling them to form unions and engage in collective bargaining. They also supported a self-employment model of prostitution, claiming it would allow them to keep a higher percentage of their earnings, refuse unwanted clients and better protect themselves.

The prostitutes' rights movement made the public more aware of the reality of sex workers' lives. A number of international gatherings, such as the World Whores Congresses held in Amsterdam in 1985 and Brussels in 1986, the first of which produced the first World Charter for Prostitute Rights (Delacoste and Alexander, 1998; Bell, 1994), were particularly significant. The launching of so-called hookers' publications (journals, newsletters, pamphlets) and widely publicized events such as the Hookers' Balls, organized by COYOTE[3] in San Francisco starting in

1976, were equally important. In addition sex workers began to hold press conferences, have meetings with political authorities and stage demonstrations, effectively placing the question of prostitution on the political agenda and making demands (for example for day care) that marked the continuity of their struggle with that of other women.

Like feminist and lesbian movements, the prostitutes' rights movement became the site for a critique of capitalist sexuality and the divisions created among women on the basis of sexual behaviour. Against the mother/whore dichotomy and the attempt to make of the prostitute the quintessential symbol of the evil woman, sex workers insisted that servicing men sexually was a task that had been socially imposed on every woman and that the main difference between the prostitute and the wife was that the wife worked for no pay. They also questioned the stereotype of the prostitute as a victim of necessity or abuse, daring to proclaim that prostitution was a legitimate labour market choice that should compare favourably with other jobs available to women in terms of pay, control over working conditions and power relations with men. This was not just an ideological stand. As the women's movement opened new economic opportunities for women, fewer turned to prostitution out of economic indigence, so that earnings for sex work increased and working conditions improved (Danna, 2004).

The new organizational bonds that sex workers established among themselves further enabled them to raise the price of their services. Anecdotal accounts tell us that after the occupation in Lyons, some prostitutes began to inform their clients about their demands (Jaget, 1980). Stricter rules were adopted with respect to the duration, cost and types of sexual service provided. Among prostitutes working in the streets, a spatial and social reconfiguration developed that not only delimited the work areas for each prostitute but also instituted systems of mutual support against client and police abuse. By the late 1970s, in some European countries prostitutes were leaving the streets and moving into apartments, seeking higher earnings and more independence (Danna, 2004b). On a practical level, however, the most important achievement of the prostitutes' rights movement was the creation of sex workers' organizations that many authorities recognized and cooperated with, for instance in the planning of information campaigns about HIV infection.

As Outshoorn (2004) has shown, the institutional response to the prostitutes' rights movement was slower and more uneven than it might have been expected. In France a report commissioned by the government after the occupation in Lyons never saw the light of day, while in

Germany and the Netherlands prostitution was legalized. In all abolitionist countries – for example France, Italy and Sweden – prostitution was decriminalized but prostitution-related activities continued to be penalized under obscenity laws and laws punishing third parties. Only in Spain (in 1995) was prostitution in closed places completely decriminalized.

Nevertheless the prostitutes' rights movement forced politicians and legislators to confront the discriminatory character of prostitution laws and treat prostitution as a gender issue, rather than a moral sin or crime (ibid.). Support by feminist organizations and the increased presence of women in public offices facilitated this process. In 1977 in Boston, Massachusetts, the first female judge was appointed to the state's Supreme Judicial Court on the morning in which three arrested sex workers, in an unprecedented move, 'put the Commonwealth's prostitution statutes on trial', declaring that they 'derive[d] from a "man-made code " ' (*Boston Phoenix*, 15 February 1977). The readiness of the courts and the police to prosecute male clients from the 1980s onwards can also be seen as an effect of the gendering of prostitution. Similarly the cultural climate created by the feminist movement enabled prostitutes in the US to make the private morals of public officers a national issue: in response to police harassment they began to reveal that men 'who made and enforced the laws against prostitution' were among their customers (*New York Times*, 10 November 1979).

In sum, by the late 1970s prostitution was being redefined socially, culturally and sometimes legally as 'sex work'; that is, as a form of reproductive labour that was not qualitatively different from massage, entertainment, psychotherapy and other forms of healthcare. As for sex workers themselves, their rewards went beyond material gains. More crucial was their new sense of legitimacy, their refusal to remain invisible and be victimized, and the shift they produced in the public's perception of their social role. This change was reflected in the pride with which some prostitutes flaunted their identity as 'hookers' and 'whores' – terms once considered badges of shame – while at the same time refusing to 'fit the role'.

However in the women's movement this positive revaluation of prostitution was not a general rule. Anticipating the later debate, part of the movement condemned prostitution as a typical expression of patriarchal dominance and patriarchal relations (Outshoorn, 2004). But for many feminists (for example McElroy, 2004), and to some extent for the public in general, by the late 1970s the prostitute was becoming the symbol of a new type of woman: more free, more in control of her sexuality, more apt to demystify the mercenary character of capitalist society and to challenge the main ground of the exploitation of women – namely unpaid labour in the home, including sexual work, which was now redefined as an aspect of the physical and emotional reproduction of the workforce.

None of these developments can be attributed to changes in the power relations that characterized sex work in the countries where the movement took off. What enabled sex workers to go public, despite the risks involved in the disclosure of their identities, was the social revolution provoked by the feminist movement, which gave women more power in their relations with men and placed the sexual norm on trial. The emergence of sex workers' and transexuals' movements in Africa, Asia, Latin America and Australia in the 1980s and 1990s (Kempadoo and Doezema, 1998) in conjunction with the rise of feminist movements in these regions confirms the importance of this connection.

The debt crisis, structural adjustment and the globalization of sex work

The social expectations raised by the prostitutes' movement in the 1970s have never been met, although some of its accomplishments – for example the formation of prostitutes' organizations – have been consolidated. With few exceptions, neither in Europe nor in the US has prostitution been legally recognized as work. Moreover, while a small class of prostitutes working from private apartments and serving a more affluent clientele may have enjoyed the earnings and independence that sex workers fought for, for the majority of sex workers working conditions have deteriorated. Most importantly, the hope that the prostitutes' struggle might have a transformative character and the capacity to subvert the mechanism of the capitalist exploitation of women's labour has suffered a setback. The very fact that the question of prostitution has been framed in terms of 'sex trafficking' in feminist and institutional circles since the 1980s demonstrates how much the terrain on which sex workers organize has changed.

Multiple factors have been responsible for this situation. Among them was the political shift to the right with Reaganism and Thatcherism, which reframed social questions as law and order questions. In the US this shift can be dated to the late 1970s, when in response to the increased visibility of street sex workers a moral crusade was mounted to bring about more restrictive measures against prostitution. Between 1976 and 1979 a media campaign highlighting citizens' initiatives to keep their neighbourhoods 'clean' and the problem of run-away teenagers 'turning tricks' gave the green light to a coast-to-coast crackdown on streetwalkers (*New York Times*, 4 May 1976).[4] The crackdown intensified with the institution of a policy of mass incarceration, which imposed stiffer penalties and mandatory sentences for consensual crimes (Parenti, 1999), increasing the number of women in prison by 573 per cent in less than two decades (between 1980 and 1997) (Boyes-Watson, 2003). Later the threat of AIDS and the so-called crack epidemics further weakened the prostitutes' bargaining power by intensifying the public's suspicion of commercial sex and consolidating the image of the sex worker as a cause of social contamination (Jenness, 1993). The 1980s also saw a growing division within the feminist movement that affected its support for the prostitutes' struggle, with some feminists redefining prostitution as a form of violence against women (ibid.).

Workers' resistance to the neoliberal agenda in much of Western Europe was more intense than in the US and the political context in which the prostitutes' rights movement developed was more complicated. In Europe in the 1980s the sex workers' movement was still expanding. The first political organization of prostitutes – the Committee for Prostitutes' Civil Rights – was formed in Italy in 1982, triggered by 'the unpunished violence inflicted on sex workers by American soldiers of the Aviano military base' (Danna, 2004b, p. 41). But here too the threat of AIDS soon put the prostitutes' movement on the defensive.

However the developments that have most radically changed the organization of prostitution as a business and form of employment have been the neoliberal turn in international economic policy and the process of economic globalization. The structural adjustment programmes imposed by the World Bank and the International Monetary Fund (IMF) on the indebted countries of the South – centred as they have been on debt repayment, fiscal austerity and the shift to export-oriented forms of production – have led governments to disinvest in public spending, to encourage labour migration and to sponsor development schemes based on tourism and the commercialization of sex. These policies have combined to boost the sex industry, restructuring it as a global business and one of the main sources of capitalist accumulation, with entire regions being turned into sites for sex tourism and the mass recruitment of sex workers for international export.[5]

The high levels of unemployment and pauperization that economic liberalization has produced have caused millions of women from the South to migrate to more affluent countries where their employment alternatives have generally been restricted to domestic work or prostitution

(Federici, 1999; Young, 2001; Ehrenreich and Hochschild, 2003; Danna, 2004b). In the UK the dismantling of social support programmes and the shift from welfare to workfare have hit women with dependent children especially hard, leading to an increase in the number of sex workers (Phoenix, 1999).

The currency and banking deregulations promoted by the World Bank and IMF have facilitated the formation of transnational criminal networks operating like multinational corporations. These are mostly involved in the smuggling of immigrants and/or the sexual exploitation of women and children (Mittelman, 2000). The fact that many young men now seek to enrich themselves by trafficking people and pimping women must be attributed to their loss of other forms of income and the breakdown of social cohesion, produced by mass impoverishment and the many wars that have accompanied the internationalization of economic relations. The plunder of public assets by the elite, encouraged by privatization, has contributed to this process.[6]

Have these developments been automatic consequences of an autonomous globalization process, or are they part of a planned restructuring of the exploitation of labour, as some writers have suggested (Federici, 1999; Agathangelou, 2004)? The phenomena described are so pervasive and structurally inscribed in international economic policy that we may surmise that they are not unintended. A growing body of literature testifies that governments, corporations and international financial agencies have not only benefited from but have also assisted and promoted the large-scale exportation and migration of female labour from the South to the North. Remittances sent by migrant women have helped to pay foreign debts (Oppermann, 1998), keeping rivers of money flowing into the coffers of the IMF and World Bank. These institutions have never questioned the source of the payments but have continued to promote adjustment and, predictably, more female migration. Similarly sex tourism has become a development scheme for some developing countries as well as a cash cow for international airlines, hotel chains and banks (Truong, 1990).

Meanwhile importing female immigrant labour has enabled governments in the developed countries to resolve the housework crisis opened by the women's movement (Enloe, 1989). As in the case of sex tourism, there has been a remarkable fit between female pauperization in the South, women's refusal to engage in unpaid labour in Europe, the US and Japan, and the need of governments and corporations to ensure the reproduction of the male workforce. A new international division of reproductive labour has emerged as a consequence of structural adjustment and globalization, whereby large quotas of the reproduction of labour power in Europe and North America (to name the main beneficiaries) have been unloaded onto the shoulders of women from the adjusted countries of the South and Eastern Europe, with a consequent cheapening of the cost of labour (Federici, 1999). Watanabe (2000), in her study of Thai female migrants to Japan, has found the same trend operating there. Thai women now provide the same reproductive services that Japanese women have refused to perform for no pay. In other words governments and employers in Europe, Japan and the US have profited from the fact that immigrant women from Thailand, the Philippines or the Caribbean now walk children or the elderly to parks in New York (or Paris or Tokyo), clean the homes of other women, who are thus 'liberated' to do salaried work, or provide men, whose wages have been falling, with a steady supply of 'fast sex' (Federici, 1999). In almost every country of the North, a large proportion of the workforce now consists of low-paid and undocumented immigrant labourers who cannot afford to bring their families with them or form a family where they work. This has made the provision of cheap sexual services even more essential for governments. Indeed as precariousness is becoming a general working-class condition, we are entering a phase similar to that which characterized the beginning of industrialization, when the prostitute played a key role in the reproduction of the working class – in some cases more crucial than that of the wife (see Federici, 2004).

The internationalization and expansion of the sex industry in the 1980s and 1990s – now estimated to be one of the main sources of capital accumulation and the third most important non-legal form of revenue after the drug and arms trades – should be viewed as an essential part of the global restructuring of the sexual division of labour and of the reproduction of labour power, of which sex work is one of the pillars. This development has procured billions of dollars for its operators but has not improved the conditions of sex work.

Focusing again on Western Europe, we find similar patterns to those found in other cases of unprotected work. The changes that have taken place in the working conditions of the majority of sex workers can be described as follows: competition has intensified, earnings have fallen, risks have increased and it has become far more difficult for sex workers to struggle effectively or even organize.

Increased competition is only part of the problem. Since the late 1980s the majority of sex workers in Western Europe, especially streetwalkers, have been foreign immigrants.[7] They come mainly from Africa (Nigeria, Ghana, Ivory Coast), Eastern Europe (Albania, Romania, Moldova,

Ukraine, Russia) and to a lesser extent Asia (the Philippines) and Latin America (Colombia, Peru). Thus a larger section of the sex workforce in Western Europe is more vulnerable to exploitation and abuse than ever before. In addition to the risks and violence to which sex workers are exposed by the nature of their work, they now face higher levels of police brutality, the threat of deportation and the ostracism of local communities that make them the target of their resentment of foreign workers and their racial biases. Many sex workers are also subject to the control and violence exercised by the criminal organizations upon which they have had to rely in order to migrate. These organizations demand heavy sums in compensation for their services, keeping migrants in bondage until their 'debt' is paid and beyond.

As this phenomenon has been the target of much feminist antitrafficking campaigning, it must be stressed that dependence on and bondage to intermediaries, including criminal networks, have become common experiences for immigrant workers, male as well as female. They are structural features of a global economy that promotes the transnational movement of capital but severely restricts the movement of labour to fit market needs.

Just how extensive trafficking and bondage are among immigrant prostitutes, and the extent to which their situation can be described as sexual slavery (as some feminists have done), are matters of intense debate (Danna, 2004b). This is complicated by the fact that until recently in international law the definition of trafficking was very broad, referring to the illegal transportation of people across national borders without specifying if it involved coercion or entrapment. Since the UN Conference on Transnational Crime in Palermo in 2000 the term has been given a more specific definition, including deception and forced captivity. But its application is still a difficult matter and the potential for confusion between consensual cross-border smuggling and kidnapping is very high.

However if we take the case of Italy – which along with Greece and France is the main destination for immigrants from Eastern Europe and Africa – there can be no doubt that coercion among sex workers is extensive. A study completed in 2001 (Carchedi, 2004) concluded that the two main groups of immigrant women working as prostitutes in the country were in bondage for at least part of their stay.

African women generally work under the control of a madam – often a conational and a former prostitute – to whom they are bonded until they pay their debt. Often in these cases, although various forms of psychological and physical intimidation are used to enforce compliance (including voodoo rituals threatening death to those who rebel), 'violence is not the dominant relation' (Danna, 2004b, pp. 87–9; see also Carchedi, 2004). Presumably the tie between these sex workers and their exploiters is to some degree consensual and the working relationship is structured as a form of indentured labour. This fact was stressed by several of the Nigerian prostitutes who Kennedy and Nicotri interviewed in Turin in 1999: while acknowledging their bondage they insisted that nobody had forced them to emigrate and that they had arrived at their decision after consulting their friends, families or other members of their communities. The same women added that they had known what to expect upon arrival, although they had underestimated the magnitude of the debt they would have to repay and how harsh and repulsive their working conditions would be. They also declared that, despite the disgust they felt for this work, they were proud of contributing to their families' well-being and of being able to buy their parents a house or, more commonly, to put their brothers through school. Far from being resigned to their situation or ashamed of it, almost all saw it as an opportunity to better their lives and an acceptable price to pay for the possibility of going home with some savings to start a new life (Kennedy and Nicotri, 1999). Nevertheless they left no doubt that their working relations were abusive and that they had to defend themselves at all times from violence from their bosses, their clients and the police.

Today, however, these women's expectations of the future seem not to have been realistic. The number of people preying on the earnings of African sex workers has increased, as many are now controlled by two madams and the sum they have to pay for their transport has skyrocketed (Carchedi, 2004). African sex workers also face stiffer competition, further cutting their incomes and forcing them to work in more isolated and dangerous spots. In part this is due to the arrival of younger African women who are willing to take more risks (for example sex without condoms). As one woman put it: 'it used to be that the women who came to Italy from Africa were older ones – mothers who needed money for their children, married and with some experience. Now it is children who come' (Kennedy and Nicotri, 1999, p. 13).

But the main competition African sex workers face is from women from the former socialist countries of Eastern Europe, whose economies have been wrecked by privatization and war. The most severe instances of abuse have been reported in the case of these women, particularly those from Albania and Kosovo. According to the testimonies collected by health authorities and rescue organizations, these women are enticed to migrate by male friends or relations with the promise of a job and are transported to Italy, Germany or Greece. After their arrival they may be sold to other traffickers more than once and be forced to prostitute by violent means, often being tortured until they comply (Castiglioni, 2001). Other means to force women to prostitute include the confiscation of their passports and the threat that they and their families will be hurt, or that their families will be informed about the nature of their activity, which would prevent many women from returning home. These are not idle threats. In Italy alone scores of prostitutes were murdered in the 1990s, prompting a journalist to speak of a creeping 'genocide' (Moroli and Sibona, 1999, p. 187).

However for the majority of East European migrants we should resist the image of complete victimization. Sex workers' organizations remind us that the accounts of enslavement that prostitutes give to the police may be a defensive response by women who wish to deny responsibility for their situation (Murray, 1998). Carchedi (2004) also indicates that the situation of sex workers has been evolving. Cases of entrapment diminished in the 1990s, as women in Albania and other parts of Eastern Europe were becoming more aware of the destiny awaiting them if they migrated and they could no longer be easily deceived with the promise of a job. It also appears that more prostitutes are now coming from Ukraine, Russia and Moldova, where women have more social power than in Albania and can decide the terms of their work, even in prostitution (Corso and Trifiró, 2003; Carchedi, 2004). Carchedi further argues that an Italian law passed in 1998 giving trafficked prostitutes a permanent residence permit on condition that they testify against their captors has made it necessary for the latter to acquire the cooperation of the women they transport. Thus a more negotiated arrangement has developed, whereby women can keep more of the money they earn and have more mobility and the promise of freedom.[8]

Furthermore, just to migrate is a struggle. It signifies rejection of the poverty and hopelessness imposed by the policies of international financial institutions or the dangers of war. Many sex workers recognize this fact and analyze their situation in terms of the economic and political crises wrecking their countries, or in the case of African sex workers the legacy of colonialism.[9] Consequently they do not display the self-deprecation and fatalism often attributed to sex workers (Harrod, 1987). Instead they often exhibit a sense of the injustice their communities have suffered and a determination to make the best of their situation, which they evaluate by comparing it with the other alternatives available to them. The attitude of the Colombian prostitutes interviewed by Corso and Trifiró (2003) is typical. They said they had come to Italy on their own and had turned to prostitution after taking several jobs and realizing they would never derive substantial income from them. Like the African sex workers in Turin, they insisted they did not see themselves as victims but admitted that their attempt to improve their situation faced great constraints.

The main obstacles sex workers meet in their effort to improve their lives derive from the continuing pauperization of their home countries, which constantly fuels migratory movements and subjects those who have migrated to more competition and new demands. The position of sex workers has also suffered because of the policy of the European Union (EU) towards immigrant communities, which have been increasingly treated as national security threats (Agathangelou, 2004) in the wake of the terrorist attacks in the US on September 11.

In the climate generated by the 'war on terror', as well as in response to complaints by local residents, in 2002 the local councils in several French towns took action against prostitutes and homeless people, especially targeting foreign sex workers (CABIRIA, 2002). As part of a package of measures on internal security, the Sarkozy Law was passed in 2003. This restrictive legislation allowed for the immediate deportation of prostitutes from countries outside the EU and made passive soliciting a crime. In Italy, despite the introduction of a law giving trafficked prostitutes a residence permit if they denounce their exploiters, arrests and deportations have escalated. This has been justified in the name of internal security and the combatting of illegal immigration.

Prostitutes are not the only targets of this crackdown. As international economic policies produce new diasporas and authorities are increasingly incapable of controlling migratory flows, the measures adopted in the Schengen Treaty (1995) to secure the external borders of 'fortress Europe' are applied with a vengeance. Detention centres for immigrants have proliferated in several countries, while off the coast of Southern Italy the Mediterranean has become a graveyard, with boats carrying clandestine immigrants being shipwrecked in the attempt to elude coastguard patrols. But while all immigrants have come under attack, sex workers have been penalized most as they are most visible and most vulnerable to police brutality and institutional repression. Deportation can be particularly tragic for them, for those in bondage still have to pay their debts and the communities to which they return often ostracize them, even though they may have benefited from their earnings.[10]

In conclusion, like other non-contractual workers in the new globalized economy, sex workers operate in a battlefield in which the possibility of achieving legitimacy and autonomy has been seriously jeopardized. Immigrant prostitutes have not ceased to struggle. In a few Italian towns some have had meetings with local residents to negotiate terms for a peaceful coexistence (Danna, 2004b). Others have come forward to denounce their exploiters. For most, everyday life is a struggle to avoid arrest, maintain their health and sense of dignity, and to set some money aside for their families and themselves. In some cases their efforts have paid off. The resources sex workers send home to their communities keep children in school in Africa and Colombia, keep families from falling apart, buy houses and prevent the sale of land (Corso and Trifiró, 2003). But the cost for the women is high and the gains to be made from sex work are diminishing. Some former prostitutes told Corso and Trifiró that in the 1990s their earnings dropped by half, which is why, as Danna (2004b) has noted, sex workers in Western Europe constantly move from country to country, seeking more advantageous working conditions. Moreover compared with the situation in the late 1970s the social stigma attached to prostitution has grown.

The publicity the media have given to the phenomenon of sex trafficking,[11] the consistent association that is made between prostitution and criminal organizations, and the nightly television images of sex workers being arrested or forced onto planes to be deported have erased the image of the prostitute as a more liberated woman and recreated that of the criminal or victim. Thus while in terms of their physical presence in the streets sex workers are more visible today than they were in the 1970s, they have become more isolated in other ways, especially from other women. This situation is summed up by the words of a Nigerian prostitute in Turin:

> our madam always tells us ... every day ... we should not talk about ourselves with our clients, nor with the police and even less with journalists ... [b]ecause here in Italy we Nigerians have many enemies: Italians hate us, the police persecute us, and there are clients who beat us up; thus we keep our mouths shut. (Kennedy and Nicotri, 1999, p. 149)

The feminist debate on prostitution and sex trafficking

The new forms of prostitution that have emerged with the expansion of the global economy have been central to the debate that has unfolded among feminists on trafficking and prostitution. However neither side of the debate has addressed the problems faced by the women who now constitute the bulk of the sex workforce in Europe, nor have they treated these women's situation as the expression of a predicament that all workers face. The objective in this section is to stress the limits of the debate, to reframe it on the basis of the trends that affect unprotected workers in the new global economy, and to substantiate the present author's call for a widespread feminist mobilization on behalf of sex workers and against the exploitation of immigrant women.

The debate emerged in the early 1980s when, in response to reports about the growth of sex tourism and child prostitution in South East Asia, feminist groups with an abolitionist stand in respect of prostitution began to organize. The Coalition Against Trafficking in Women (CATW), a US-based organization founded in 1992, has been at the forefront of the abolitionist camp and the fight against sex trafficking. The CATW argues that prostitution is, under any condition, a coercive activity that is no different from rape, and as such it should be considered a violation of human rights. According to the CATW no woman chooses to become a prostitute. Thus the distinction between voluntary and forced prostitution should be rejected, as should the distinction between child and adult prostitution. The CATW and other abolitionist organizations, such as Women Hurt in Systems of Prostitution Engaged in Revolt (WHISPER) (Wynter, 1998), have condemned the efforts made by sex workers' organizations to have prostitution recognized as a legitimate occupation. They also condemn the use of the term 'sex work', which they claim sanitizes a form of slavery and ignores the high cost paid by the women involved in it. In the abolitionists' view, prostitution amounts to capitulation to male needs and the paradigmatic relation of sexual subordination. Therefore the only acceptable struggle on this terrain is the fight to put an end to it.

The CATW has been engaged an international campaign to convince governments and the United Nations (UN) to impose more stringent sanctions on sex trafficking while at the same time insisting that prostitutes should not be penalized. The organization has been relatively successful in these efforts. Although its attempts to have the UN declare prostitution a violation of human rights have twice failed, the CATW can take credit for placing sex trafficking on the international political agenda in both institutional and feminist circles. For the same reasons, however, it has come under intense criticism by advocates of sex workers' rights, who have accused it of dismissing the wishes and experiences of the very women whose dignity it claims to defend (Jaggar, 1997). Critics also consider that by associating prostitution with sexual slavery the CATW has helped to devalue and marginalize sex workers, denying them any agency and reinforcing the identification of prostitution with crime.

Sex workers' advocates further point out that characterizing prostitution as a uniquely degrading and dangerous occupation is arbitrary since, given the state of the world labour market, the alternatives open to women (domestic work or work in a sweatshop) are no less dangerous or humiliating, nor do they spare women from sexual assault. The numerous cases of migrant domestic workers who have been enslaved by their employers and severely abused sexually and otherwise have been extensively documented (McClintock, 1993; Chang, 2000).

Furthermore the methodology abolitionists employ to acquire their data on trafficking and coercion has been challenged. McElroy (2004) notes that the evidence abolitionists use consists mostly of testimonies given by women under arrest, seeking treatment for drug use or enrolled in programmes to get them off the street – all of whom are plausibly interested in dissociating themselves from prostitution.

In sum, critics of abolition argue that the experience of sex workers cannot be dismissed, especially by women who enjoy a greater degree of power than sex workers and are not likely to bear the consequences of their recommendations; that sex trafficking may not be as extensive as is claimed and that sex work is not always coerced labour; and that the concept of 'choice' should be relativized or dismissed as it assumes that free individuals choose without the structural constraints of sex, race and class.

There are also legitimate misgivings about the demand for more severe antitrafficking legislation. What most matters, however, is that abolitionists deny any rationality to the practice of prostitution, which they portray as a product of female blindness and male manipulation. This position precludes any understanding of the meaning of prostitution, especially in the present international context, and of the social forces by which it is structured.

Feminist abolitionists therefore have little to offer to the immigrant women discussed above or to any other sex worker, other than to recommend that they quit their work and denounce their traffickers. Abolitionists assume that banning the forms of female exploitation that have traditionally been considered most degrading is the best way to protect the status of women. This viewpoint can be compared to that of the craft workers who defended their social position by excluding those workers whose presence could devalue them. Fear of devaluation has been an important, though unthematized, issue in the feminist movement. In the 1970s it surfaced in relation to the question of whether housework could provide a common ground for the feminist struggle (Malos, 1995). Thirty years later, with female participation in the workforce averaging more than 50 per cent, the fear of devaluation is no longer generated by the spectre of the housewife but by that of the sex worker, who embodies all that middle-class, professional women wish to deny in their quest for self-valorization. In the eyes of many feminists today, the prostitute represents a 'fate worse than death', the identity that most reminds them of the historical degradation of female labour and women's subordination to men. This explains their insistence on disassociating women from prostitution in the assumption that the status of women can be improved by enforcing a closed shop policy.

However this strategy is inadequate in any historical period and is especially myopic at present. In a world economic context in which millions of people are daily deprived of their most basic means of subsistence, the pressure on women to take risks is bound to continue and grow. New laws against trafficking cannot stop this trend. Indeed it is already widely recognized that more restrictive laws on border crossing would only make immigrant women more dependent on the services of traffickers and criminal organizations (Danna, 2004a; Carchedi, 2004; Guillemaut, 2005) and intensify the class bias of international law. Thus just as law enforcement agents arrest and penalize the most proletarian prostitutes – immigrants, streetwalkers, often women of colour – it is the 'lower-class' traffickers who are penalized while the true beneficiaries of the sexual exploitation of women operate under the cover of respected business organizations – travel agencies, hotel chains, banks, airlines – or the offices of governments, police departments and international financial institutions.

Given the limits of the abolitionist position, it is not surprising that in recent years the feminist literature in defence of sex workers' rights has expanded. Advocates of sex workers' rights and sex workers' organizations are more diverse than abolitionist organizations and cannot be reduced to one position. These comments refer particularly to libertarian advocates of a free market model of prostitution, who view commercial sex work as a pinnacle social service rather than a degrading activity (Jaggar, 1997; Platt, 2001).

While abolitionists refuse to qualify prostitution as work – surprisingly assuming that work cannot be a form of coercion – libertarian sex workers' rights advocates see this legal step as decisive for the prostitutes' struggle, as if work could not be a form of exploitation. Indeed libertarian advocates of sex workers' rights assume that the recognition of prostitution as work would confer autonomy and control that no dependent workers currently enjoy in capitalist society. Undoubtedly the insistence with which they pursue this objective is justified. It is an incontrovertible fact that many of the abuses perpetrated against sex workers stem from the lack of legal recognition of their work. Prostitutes cannot denounce those who rob or assault them; they cannot use the money they earn as they wish as they cannot open a bank account or rent an apartment without revealing the source of their income; nor can they live with other women or men who could give them protection because the latter could be accused of profiting from prostitution. Immigrant prostitutes would also benefit from legal recognition, which in principle would give them the possibility of obtaining a residence permit (Corso and Trifiró, 2003). Moreover the recognition of prostitution as work would constitute a true cultural revolution. These advocates do not sufficiently recognize, however, that work in dependent conditions is subject to the kind of restrictive regulation that sex workers' organizations have rejected, and that as a consequence of globalization even the limited entitlements available to the unionized working class are in jeopardy.

Furthermore self-employment has historically proven to be deceptive in its promise of freedom, and it is practicable only in those professions where the employed have the power to control entry (Harrod, 1987) – a difficult feat for sex workers and achievable only through the use of force. As we have seen, competition is already a serious problem for immigrant prostitutes, providing justification for the involvement of 'protectors' in the organization of sex work. How this problem would be solved once decriminalization was achieved and how prostitutes with less social power would cope with it remains to be explained.

Another problematic tendency in the libertarian/free market position stems from an inversion of the error made by the abolitionists, who see violence and coercion everywhere in the sex trade. Libertarian advocates of sex workers' rights often reduce the significance of violence and coercion, despite what the evidence shows, and to the extent that they do recognize the presence of violence and coercion in prostitution their only response is to call for penalization. This inability to confront such a crucial issue as the existence of violence and unfree labour in the sex industry – an undeniable reality as we have seen – constitutes a serious limit to their position. In the eyes of many other women, reports of abuse are frequent and horrific enough to require some action to be taken.

Furthermore the frequency of violence and bondage in sex work is symptomatic of the structural social transformations that are resulting from the globalization process and should be a major concern for all feminists – and indeed for all women. Violence and bondage in sex work should not be ignored for the sake of protecting the image of sex workers. Instead the causes should be exposed and traced to their roots in the macroeconomic policies adopted by international financial institutions such as the IMF and World Bank – policies whose documented effect is that all workers are increasingly unprotected.

Another social fact of historic significance is that with globalization illegality has become a mass working-class condition. Indeed it is so widespread as to amount to a *de facto* criminalization of large sectors of the workforce, reminiscent of the formation of an *ex-lege* proletariat at the dawn of capitalism, as described by Marx. Domestic workers, workers in sweatshops and the informal economy, smugglers, traffickers, street children and undocumented immigrants of all types: a vast swathe of humanity has been plunged into illegal status as the price of survival or the cost of refusing to accept the misery with which they are surrounded. The new phase of globalization has caused a massive expansion of unfree labour that affects, according to statistics recently released by the UN, 12.3 million people worldwide (*New York Times*, 12 May 2005). The immigration policies adopted by the EU have also placed workers in bondage by making the loss of a work contract cause for deportation – a stipulation that prevents workers from negotiating better working conditions and provides an incentive to employers to neglect their obligations.

These developments and figures should be a major concern for both sex workers' advocates and antitrafficking organizations, as they are evidence that globalization is undermining a wide range of work-related contracts. Even in the so-called affluent countries, established workers are experiencing a 'race to the bottom', undermining the possibility of secure employment and access to social entitlements such as a pension, health and unemployment benefit and union representation – all rights that sex workers' organizations assume they would obtain if prostitution were recognized as work. Hence this recognition – necessary as it is – would not be sufficient to guarantee sex workers the safety and benefits they desired unless the present economic trends were reversed.[12]

Conclusion: reframing the debate

What, then, are the alternatives? Despite the profound differences between their respective positions, both abolitionist and libertarian feminists have one thing in common: they do not recognize a fundamental fact concerning the possibility for social struggle in the present international context. Economic globalization has so deeply undermined the reproduction of the global workforce, especially in the South, that the guarantees workers once had are under attack. It is increasingly difficult for workers to expand their rights or to defend existing ones. Recognition of this reality has to enter and reframe the debate on prostitution. The value of women cannot be defended by a policy of exclusion, nor would recognition of prostitution as work give sex workers the rights that this should guarantee. What is needed is a new social contract: communities affected by globalization have been deprived of resources that must be restored, and the structural racism that characterizes international economic relations must be eliminated. This has been recognized by feminist organizations such as the Philippines-based GABRIELA network, which argues that the best strategy for transforming the lives of women, beginning with sex workers, is to democratize political life and create the necessary conditions for dependent countries to 'delink' from the global economy.

This would certainly be a daunting task, but one that would be less difficult if feminists were not polarized on the question of prostitution. The progress made in the 1970s provides an example of how a strong women's movement challenging conventional norms can transform the public view of sex workers and prepare the ground for a world beyond prostitution and the commodification of human life. In the 1980s and 1990s, as Outshoorn (2004) has documented, whenever feminist organizations were sufficiently united to make their voices heard, the institutional debates on prostitution responded to their demands. Outshoorn concludes, however, that with few exceptions – most evidently the activities of antitrafficking organizations and the English Collective of Prostitutes in the UK – the question of prostitutes' rights has not been a priority for feminists for more than two decades in Western Europe and the US. Nor have sex workers' rights been taken up as an issue by the growing antiglobalization movement, although this may soon change, as the inclusion of an essay by Kamala Kempadoo, 'Globalizing Sex Workers' Rights', in Louise Amoore's edited volume *Global Resistance Reader* (2005) suggests.

Placing the prostitution question in the context of the growing pauperization and criminalization of a large section of the working class is essential if this stalemate is to be overcome. The stakes are certainly high, for as McClintock (1993, p. 1) puts it: '[e]mpowering sex workers empowers all women'. This is not only because the 'whore stigma' is a tool for disciplining women (ibid.), but also because it is thanks to the struggles of foreign sex workers that many otherwise completely demonized communities across the world are now able to survive. Mies (1998) and other subsistence-work theoreticians have powerfully demonstrated the vital role that women's access to land and female farming are playing in the global reproduction of life (Beanholdt-Thomsen *et al.*, 2001). It must be added that often it also because of the money sex workers have sent home that the land available for subsistence farming has not been lost, despite the efforts by international financial institutions to impose a world regime of land privatization.

The alternative some feminists have proposed – more restrictive laws against sex trafficking – is a minefield. For as Ruggiero (2000) has shown, in a world where attempting to escape impoverishment often comes at the price of criminalization, the boundaries between crime and resistance and between victim and victimizer are extremely blurred.

Notes

1. I prefer the term 'sex industry' (Barry, 1981, 1992; Barry *et al.*, 1984; Raymond, 1998) to other proposed options – such as 'sex business' (Hanochi, 2002) or 'desire industry' (Agathangelou, 2004) – because I wish to emphasize the homogeneity and coordination of the constituent economic activities across international borders and their integration with international economic policies. I also question Agathangelou's use of 'desire' to characterize the sex industry as it defines desiring activities in an arbitrary way. Why, for example, should the food industry not be defined as a 'desire industry'?
2. Sex workers in the brothels of Nevada have to live on the premises, accept any client and forfeit 50 per cent of their earnings, in addition to paying fees for room and board. (www.bayswan.org/Laura.html, May 2002). For a description of working conditions in German Eros Centres see Jaget (1980, p. 165ff).
3. COYOTE is the main sex workers' organization in the US. For its history and social significance see Jenness (1993).
4. A crackdown on prostitution was staged in San Francisco in 1976–77 (*San Francisco Chronicle* 28 November 1976, 4 January 1977, 5 January 1977, 7 January 1977). In New York a bill was passed in 1976 outlawing 'loitering for the purpose of prostitution' (*New York Times*, 11 June 1976). Nationwide the crucial years were 1979–81. The following are some newspaper headings that reflect the climate in this period: 'Neighbors Take to the Streets over Women of the Streets' (*The Phoenix* (Brooklyn), 23 August 1979); 'City Prostitutes Invade Residential Communities' (*New York Times*, 15 August 1981).
5. For the relationship between structural adjustment, globalization and the rise of the sex industry see Petras and Wongchaisuwan (1993), GABRIELA (1997), Kempadoo (1998), Oppermann (1998) and Agathangelou (2004). For the relationship between structural adjustment and labour migration see Mittelman (2000) and Colatrella (2001).
6. For an analysis of the social and economic dynamics triggered by privatization in Albania see Maida and Mazzonis (2004).
7. In France foreign prostitutes account for more than 60 per cent of all prostitutes (CABIRIA, 2002); 'in Greece, the Netherlands and Austria it is reported to

be 70%; in Spain, Germany and Italy at least half of the persons who prostitute are foreigners' (Danna, 2004b, p. 185).
 8. Carchedi (2004) may be overly optimistic as the conditions set for acquisition of the permit – that sex workers must denounce their exploiters and enrol in programmes to help them quit prostitution – have been severely criticized as jeopardizing women's safety and right to choose.
 9. Complaints about the Italians' 'colonial mentality' and racism were commonplace among the women interviewed by Kennedy and Nicotri (1999).
10. Many deported prostitutes, however, return after a brief period of time, particularly those from Albania.
11. Starting in the late 1980s, more than 90 per cent of media references to prostitution concerned cases of enslavement or of punitive expeditions by the police and local residents. Typical headlines in Italian papers were as follows: 'Night of fear in Val D'Aosta: 200 people threaten women who were coming down the train ... blitz conducted by the mayor, Nigerian women saved by the police' (*Stampa*, 8 April 1990); 'Death contract for Albanian women: ... if I don't keep my word they will cut me up' (*Corriere della Sera*, 18 July 1996); '50,000 on the road of slavery' (*Manifesto*, 23 April 1998); 'Nigerian women controlled by a "voodoo priest" ' (*Manifesto*, 29 April 1998).
12. This view is also held by an organization that occupies a third position in the debate: the Global Alliance Against Trafficking in Women (GAAT), which distinguishes between 'voluntary' and 'forced' prostitution and proposes that the laws prescribed for other immigrant workers be extended to voluntary prostitutes.

6
Migration and Unprotected Work in Southern Africa: The Case of the Mining Sector

Michael Niemann

This chapter draws and elaborates on Harrod's (1987) analytical framework in an analysis of the political economy of unprotected work in the specific context of the mining sector in southern Africa. It builds on a previous work on migration (Niemann, 2003) that incorporated the concepts of social space developed by Lefebvre (1991a). The main argument of that article was that by paying attention to the social spaces and lived experiences of migrant workers in southern Africa, international relations (IR) theory would gain a broader understanding of the international relations of southern Africa and begin to ask questions that might allow it to move from describing the politics of the region to challenging power structures in ways that matter in the everyday lives of people there.

Harrod's sophisticated analysis of the social relations of production offers important insights that can usefully be adapted to understand the everyday work experiences of migrants, not just at the current juncture but also as part of an understanding of the historical trajectory of southern Africa. It complements the work of Lefebvre in that it provides concrete examples of how social relations of production emerge in specific spatial forms and contribute to the emergence of new spatial forms. The intention here is to show that the changing nature of the social space we call southern Africa has been intricately related to the changing forms of migrant work, particularly in the mining sector, and that these relations have produced a specific postapartheid IR in the region.

Following what Harrod (1987) calls the subsistence pattern of social relations of production, which prevailed prior to the widespread use of migrant labour, we can identify the steady emergence of multiple patterns of paid labour for migrants, ranging from occasional waged work to extended work under trade union contracts. Since the formal end of apartheid there has been a significant move towards subcontracting, with an attendant undermining of trade union power. As social space has become increasingly marked by market relations, many migrants have had to take up unprotected work, with all the attendant shifts from formally organized to informal migration. In short the international relations of southern Africa in the postapartheid era have been characterized in part by the contradiction between flows of people driven by market forces and the assertion of territorial control to limit such flows.

The next section provides an outline of Lefebvre's (1991a, 1991b) approach to everyday life and social space. This will be followed by a short introduction to Harrod's various patterns of social relations of production. The remaining three sections analyze the contradictions of social space and the manifestations of these contradictions in the social relations of production for migrants in southern Africa. Finally, the conclusion will discuss the relevance of these analyses for our understanding of IR in the region.

Social spaces and everyday life in IR

Just as it has ignored the topic of work, IR theory has on the whole been silent on the question of space, in part because this question is assumed to have already been settled. IR practitioners and analysts have been happy to adopt a dominant view of 'space as container' in their treatment of the state and the global system. Even if it has been problematized in terms of power relations rather than in institutional terms, the state continues to be seen as a fixed unit 'of secure sovereign space' (Agnew, 1994, p. 106) and thus as a container of society (Taylor, 1994b). Taylor (1994a, p. 1918) has shown that this 'embedded statism' did not occur accidentally as the evolution of the social sciences has mirrored the evolution of the modern territorial state – the two emerged as 'state sciences' as it were. However, while the social sciences cannot be faulted for the fact that their 'spatial ontology was ... materially based upon a very real spatial congruence of social activities' (ibid., p. 1919), their failure to problematize statism begs the question '[was] it error or [was] it ideology? The latter is more than likely. If so, who promotes it? Who exploits it? And why and how do they do so' (Lefebvre, 1991a, p. 94)?

The answer to this question, according to Lefebvre, lies in a critical analysis of the spaces of everyday life, contested places that are characterized by the mystifications of a hegemonic capitalist system and the struggles to overcome them. He proposes that this critique should focus on the totality of social life – the contradiction between the ideological concept of the autonomous individual and the actual loneliness of the atomized person confronting the machinery of capitalism – rather than on social practices or representations of these practices. One significant aspect of this critical analysis of everyday life is the relationship between work and leisure and the complex articulation of these conflicting but mutually constituted categories. For Lefebvre, the goal of a critical analysis of everyday life is to create opportunities for humanity to face 'a new imperative: the practical, effective transformation of things as they are' (ibid., p. 134).

Lefebvre's critique of everyday life anticipated the emphasis on social space in his later work. In this he aims to transform the traditional dialectic of historicity and sociality into what Soja (1996) calls a trialectic of sociality, historicity and spatiality. In Lefebvre's words, '[s]pace does not eliminate the other materials or resources that play a part in the socio-political arena. ... Rather, it brings them together and in a sense substitutes itself for each factor separately by enveloping it' (Lefebvre, 1991a, pp. 410–11). Work again appears in this analysis both as the force that produces social space and as a reflection of this space. It is, however, embedded in a system of two dialectical movements – the dialectic of spatial terms and the dialectic of spatial history (Dimendberg, 1997) – that define everyday life at any given moment.

The dialectic of spatial terms comprises a 'conceptual triad' that consists of spatial practice, representations of space and spaces of representations (or lived space – *espace vécu*). Spatial practice refers to the manner in which social forces produce the spatial structures through which they organize their practices and which are directly apprehensible by the senses. It 'is thus presented as both the medium and the outcome of human activity, behavior, and experience' (Soja, 1996, p. 66). Representations of space express the manner in which space is conceived in a society by those who participate in the creation of dominant discourses, the imposition of forms of order. 'Such order is constituted via control over knowledge, signs, and codes: over the means of deciphering spatial practice and hence over the production of spatial knowledge' (ibid., p. 67). Spaces of representation, finally, incorporate both of the previous legs of the triad and refer to 'space as directly *lived*, with all its intractability intact, a space that stretches across images and symbols that accompany it, the space of "inhabitants" and "users" '(ibid.). This focus on actual, lived spaces enables us to imagine and find 'counter-spaces, spaces of resistance to the dominant order' (ibid., p. 68).

The working of the dialectic of spatial terms is intricately linked to the dialectic of historical spatial forms, which outlines the various forms of social space that have existed in human history so far and one that may emerge in the future. Lefebvre identifies four historical spatial forms: absolute space, historical space, abstract space and differential space (Dimendberg, 1997). At first glance this categorization may appear to be yet another 'stage theory', especially as Lefebvre considers that these forms appeared in chronological order. But the emergence of a new form of social space does not imply the elimination of previous forms. Rather, true to the dialectical process, earlier forms of social space are both preserved and transcended in later forms. There is also no implicit or explicit teleology that necessitates the development of new spatial forms. The logics of emergence and transcendence are driven by the socioeconomic forces that develop in societies. Social space is produced and is thus subject to the same constraints as all other production processes. As these constraints change over time, so too does the nature of the social space that is being produced. For Lefebvre, abstract space is currently the dominant form of social space. Its primary characteristic is the generalization of abstract labour through universalized commodity exchange. Abstract space is global in nature, subject to expanded market relations and dominated by representations of space that reflect and advocate the neoliberal or Washington consensus (Lefebvre, 1991a, p. 282).

The spaces of social relations of production

Given the central role of labour in both the production of social space and everyday life, it is only logical to link Lefebvre's work to that of Harrod's treatment of work and production. Harrod (1987) begins his analysis of work with a focus on power, which he situates at four levels: power in production, social power, political power and world power. Rather than viewing these levels of power as separate categories, he considers that they are interconnected, with power in production constituting 'the basis for a better comprehension and subsequent discussion of social, political and world power' (ibid., p. 13). In other words the exercise of power in production and the attempts of workers to resist it determine the nature and organization of production, which in turn affect the nature and exercise of power at the social, political and ultimately the global level.

Throughout history the universal human need to engage in productive activity has always been in the context of specific social relations that differ from one historical period to another as well as within the same period (ibid., p. 13). A pattern of social relations of production therefore refers to a very specific and historically contingent arrangement of production relations. In his analysis of production in the contemporary world, Harrod identifies twelve patterns of social relations of production. These range from subsistence to state corporatism to central planning, with subsistence constituting the most dispersed form of power in production and the latter two forms representing the most centralized modes of social relations of production, where power is concentrated in the hands of corporations or the state bureaucracy. Of course these forms are ideal types, and any concrete example of production relations is likely to be more complex.

By now it should be clear that Harrod's patterns of social relations of production represent the interplay of Lefebvre's spatial practice/representations of space/lived spaces at particular moments in the historical trajectory of social space. The key here is to understand production in the broadest sense of a society producing itself. The 'who gets what' (ibid., p. 9) of production reflects not only the power relations between any given worker, employer and the state but also the larger power relations expressed in the trialectic of spatial practice/representations of space/ lived spaces of any given social formation at any given point in history. The organization of any specific production process is limited by existing spatial practices, but at the same time it creates new spatial practices. In the process the representations of space, be they ideological or technical, change to conform to the new practices. The contradictions generated by this interplay are then experienced in the lived spaces.

The next section will consider different moments in the history of southern Africa, in order to demonstrate the utility of embedding Harrod's modes in Lefebvre's spatial framework. Space will not permit an extensive historical analysis. Instead what might be called vignettes should provide a sufficient basis for the final section, which focuses on the postapartheid era. For the purposes of these vignettes, the subsistence, casual, enterprise and self-employment patterns of social relations of production are of interest. In conjunction with Lefebvre's conceptualization of social space, these modes will help shed light on the changing forms of work and everyday life among migrants in southern Africa.

Land and cattle: absolute space and the production of historical space

Absolute space was the space of 'cosanguinity, soil and language' (Lefebvre, 1991a, p. 48). It arose from fragments of nature that were chosen for their inherent qualities of place (often for ritual reasons) but lost their naturalness the moment they were consecrated and thus became occupied by political forces. Absolute space was both 'civil and religious' (ibid.), preserving unmediated relationships while establishing the beginnings of an administrative apparatus. Spatial practice, representations of space and lived spaces were not yet marked by significant internal contradictions. Between the eleventh century and the European incursions of the sixteenth and seventeenth centuries, many segments of southern Africa's social space resembled such absolute space.

Cattle herding resulted not only in status distinctions in these communities but also in the extension of power over a larger areas, leading to sociopolitical agglomerations characterized by 'a substantial central settlement ... surrounded at a distance by several smaller centers, each at the hub of network of smaller villages and hamlets' (Omer-Cooper, 1994, p. 8). Expanded reproduction facilitated larger political communities and more complex political processes. As political communities split, chiefly families migrated and established their rule over new constituencies with less centralized forms of rule. The mixture of herding, hunting and limited agriculture reflected a relationship to nature that was still characterized more by appropriation than by domination, yet these spaces already contained within them the potential for transformation in that cattle herding enabled a process of accumulation that transcended daily life.

The social relations of production resembled in many ways Harrod's subsistence model. Social practices and distinctions were determined as much by extraeconomic as by economic factors, given that the relations to the production process were not highly differentiated. Households engaged in communal relations in which authority structures were not the result of opposing interests (Harrod, 1987).

However, expanding production and technology sowed the seeds of a new form of social space. In his discussion of the Karanga states, Newitt (1995) points out the similarities between the establishment and maintenance of states in Europe and southern Africa, particularly in respect of the manner in which the power of emerging states was underwritten by the separation of labour from the reproduction of the family, where Kiteve peasants, for example, were required to work on the chief's fields for a certain number of days each year.

The addition of peasant social relations of production to the subsistence pattern therefore predated European incursion into the subcontinent and made for a more complex situation than was often assumed. Social status and ownership of resources (often cattle) represented a crucial distinction through which differences in power increasingly reflected differences in interest between producers and appropriators. Nevertheless these two patterns of social relations existed side by side and often overlapped in that any individual could easily experience multiple contexts in his or her daily life.

Increased surplus production in turn facilitated another crucial development in the production of historical space: the deepening of regional trade flows that linked the wealth of East African port cities and the trade of goods produced in the interior along routes that 'criss-crossed the high veldt and linked its communities with neighbors beyond the Limpopo or north of the Zambezi' (ibid., p. 50). In short, while not yet broadly present, certain aspects of historical space had already been created prior to European incursion.

Historical space is the space of the town, which controls its surrounding countryside, the space of accumulation, beginning with but not limited to the primitive accumulation described by Marx. Historical space is characterized by production for exchange, where 'exchange value becomes general through the circulation of gold and silver [and] relational networks of markets and communications' (Dimendberg, 1997, p. 23). For Lefebvre the crucial characteristic of historical space is the separation of productive labour from the 'the process of reproduction which perpetuated social life' (Lefebvre, 1991b, p. 49). European settlement in southern Africa – first in Mozambique and then in the Cape Colony – was an intrusion that greatly sped up the production of historical space and initiated the production of abstract space in southern Africa. While they initially participated in established circuits of exchange, the European settlers' different ambitions quickly brought them into conflict with Africans. Driven by these conflicts, followed by the conflicts between the *voortrekkers* and the British and then between various African states, a new north–south pattern of migration and labour flows emerged in the early part of the nineteenth century and established new links between the Cape and all points north to Lake Tanganyika. These movements in turn led to the establishment of fewer but larger African states that were far more organized and bureaucratized than the small chiefdoms that had coexisted with one another (Martin, 1987; Omer-Cooper, 1994; Thompson, 1995).

European demands for resources, and particularly for labour, added new contradictions to the historical space and set in motion the process that led to the production of abstract space. For Lefebvre, the key contradiction in historical space is the separation of productive labour from the general process of reproduction, which in turn leads to the emergence of abstract labour, labour as a commodity and thus a generalized system of accumulation and abstract space. The three following sections provide vignettes of the manner in which these changes in social space coincided with changes in the pattern of the social reproduction of labour.

Gold and diamonds: the emergence of abstract space

Although labour shortages had caused European employers in Africa to look for workers beyond the fluid boundaries of their respective territories since the mid 1800s, the discovery of diamonds in Kimberley led to a significant increase in the circulation of workers attracted by the higher wages paid at the mines. De Kiewiet (1941) estimated that about 100,000 Africans worked in diamond fields between 1881 and 1895, providing support and livelihood for the 400,000 or so dependents who joined them. While the formal recruitment of labour beyond the borders of the Orange Free State and Natal was organized quickly in response to the increase in demand (Newitt, 1995) a large number of other Africans made their way to the mines along clandestine routes.

Although Harrod (1987) concentrates on the urban context in much of his discussion of the casual pattern of social relations of production, the emerging employment patterns in the early days of mining conformed to a large extent to the casual pattern. Rather than being displaced from rural to urban areas where they served as 'unskilled, undifferentiated, and interchangeable units of labor' (ibid., p. 136), African migrants went to Kimberley in search of casual employment to supplement income from other sources. Harrod describes the primitive labour market as a 'buyers' market', implying a relative abundance of uprooted or landless workers seeking employment in the informal sectors of cities (ibid., p. 134). In southern Africa, in contrast, the shortage of workers permitted labourers to seek out more generous employers. Furthermore work at the mines or other locations was only one aspect of the palette of work opportunities available and African migrants exploited this to the best of their ability, leading to a constant fluctuation and circulation of labour. The power relations implied by Harrod were therefore not yet present in southern Africa.

Because proletarianized labour had no choice but to sell its labour power, migrants resisted the process of proletarianization. Most viewed their migration to the mines in strictly utilitarian terms as a means to acquire resources not available at home. In this sense their view of work was hardly different from that of their employers. Connections to their homes were maintained even though poor transportation made this difficult. In the early years they left the mines when the hunting season came or the cold winter temperatures made life in Kimberley or Johannesburg too miserable. Harvest time was also an important point at which to leave for home (Harries, 1994). However, once the diamond business had been monopolized by de Beers this flexibility was eliminated.

Despite these differences, a casual pattern along the lines suggested by Harrod was created through the coercive and racist policies of both corporations and states. Race permeated the social relations of production in that the dominant groups' attitude towards migrant workers during this period was increasingly characterized by fear and repression (Harrod, 1987). Efforts to limit the mobility of workers, changing pay cycles and the emerging compound housing system all created a situation of artificial abundance that over time became real as alternative means of social reproduction for Africans were eliminated. Fear, repression and the occasional feeling of guilt were assuaged by racist ideologies that located the explanation of the treatment of the dominated group in their very racial nature.

The discovery in 1886 of gold in Witwatersrand closed off alternative modes of labour organization for ever. Gold mining in South Africa involved deep underground work that was both capital- and labour-intensive. Whereas diamond mining had quickly been monopolized by de Beers, gold mining remained a relatively competitive business. The varying quality of the ore posed a problem in that the richer mines had an incentive to improve labour conditions and offer higher wages in order to attract labour while the poorer mines had to pay lower wages in order to remain profitable. With the support of the state the mine owners solved the competition problem by adopting a binding system of labour recruitment, which flooded the market with migrant workers while pushing down wages (Harries, 1994). By 1899, 70,000 Mozambicans worked in the gold mines, or 75 per cent of the total labour force. 'The phenomenal success of management in bringing through and holding a wage reduction of well over 25% while at the same time increasing the workforce by 21% depended on the recruitment of cheap Mozambican labour' (ibid., p. 140). Ultimately the very success of the gold mining industry in South Africa depended on the availability of Mozambican workers, without whom the relatively marginal ores could not have been extracted profitably.

The casual pattern that predominated during the early period was thus replaced by what Harrod (1987) calls the enterprise pattern of social relations of production. Under this the employer had 'complete power to dismiss workers, to fix wage levels, to reject unions and ... to change the pace and conditions of work' (ibid., 1987, p. 183). On the surface this pattern seems little different from the casual pattern since both were characterized by the exercise of unchecked power by the employer. However, whereas the casual pattern did not presuppose the organizational structures of a complex firm, the enterprise pattern did. Within the context of these complex structures the need for specific skills, the regularity of labour and the impact of state influence combined to create a model of social relations of production that imposed some structural limitations on employers' power (ibid., p. 184).

In the employment of migrant workers in South Africa these limitations manifested themselves in ubiquitous fixed-term contracts, the common recruitment of workers, at least in the mineral sector, and increasingly specialized work, which led to fixed patterns of recruitment and the formalization of these through treaties with neighbouring states. While individual workers were still unprotected in that they had no organization to fight for their rights, the process of recruitment and work organization created patterns that were difficult to deviate from, even for employers.

Such changes in the patterns of social relations of production were intricately related to larger changes in social space in the region. The struggle over political space was eventually settled in the proclamation of the Union of South Africa in 1910. Thus while the emergence of the enterprise pattern was driven by conflicts over the profitable exploitation of mineral resources, it can also be linked to changing spatial configurations in the region. Similarly the deeper entrenchment of racism and the ever-stronger policy of exclusion challenged the nationalist representation of social space.

It is here that the link between Harrod's framework of social relations of production and the IR of the region becomes clear. The operation of the enterprise pattern of social relations of production required and generated the following:

- Spatial practices that produced unified but multilayered social spaces in South Africa. The latter was unified in that alternative sources of power were eliminated, but it was multilayered as prior forms of social organization continued to exist.
- Representations of space that depicted these spaces as a national territorial state, despite the fact that the vast majority of the population was not considered to be part of the nation.

- Lived experiences, especially those of migrant workers, that functioned within but also overstepped and undermined these practices and representations. The need for labour combined with the exclusion of the indigenous population set in motion migratory patterns that negated the image of the modern territorial state as a coherent, self-contained entity.

It was therefore not surprising that migrants made every effort to evade the organized recruitment efforts in order to maintain control over their choice of employment location and time period. In the early years of the Kimberley mine, large numbers arrived on their own and then served as informal referees for family members or friends who were interested in working in the mine. Even after the implementation of the large-scale recruitment apparatus of the enterprise market, migrants from southern Mozambique and other areas made every effort to circumvent the formal recruitment mechanisms:

> Clandestine emigration allowed the African miner an element of choice as to where and for how long he worked, and of course enabled him to evade the deferred pay arrangements. In 1967 it was estimated that although only 80,000 Mozambicans were working on official contracts in South African mines, there were altogether 300,000 workers in South Africa. (Newitt, 1995, p. 498)

This clandestine migration has continued to be significant to this day. While the current claims about illegal immigration into South Africa are certainly overblown, there is nevertheless evidence that migrants continue to view South Africa as a place for potential employment and are willing to cross borders, legally or illegally, to seize the opportunities available.

The period between 1880 and 1970 thus witnessed the gradual transition from historical space to abstract space in southern Africa. This transition was driven by the contradictions inherent in the dialectic of spatial terms of that period. These contradictions manifested themselves in the everyday lives of migrants. The spatial practices of both the Chamber of Mines and the migrants built a regional network of flows with a firmly established north–south pattern. At the same time southern African space was increasingly conceived in terms of fixed territorial units containing clearly identifiable societies. Workers' resistance to proletarianization was pronounced and to some extent slowed the formation of abstract space. By the 1970s, however, their labour had indeed become abstract labour.

The end of apartheid and the consolidation of abstract space

A key aspect of Lefebvre's (1991a) dialectic of spatial history is that earlier forms of space do not cease to exist but are subsumed into the later forms. Absolute space, for example, survives in part as the basis for lived spaces, as places of political or religious symbolism. Similarly, in southern Africa aspects of historical space, such as the village embedded in its surrounding countryside, survived in the context abstract space, enabling a limited opportunity to maintain the unity of labour and reproduction. This survival was directly related to the racially stratified nature of southern African space, where the families of migrants were generally not permitted to join them at their place of employment and thus maintained village life, albeit in a form quite different from the premigration era. The racist structures of minority rule also persisted much longer in southern Africa than in the rest of the continent, and it took persistent struggles in the Portuguese colonies, Zimbabwe, Namibia and finally South Africa to bring these to an end by the mid 1990s. Finally, the combination of racist social structures and the linkage between state and capital in the minority-ruled states of the region resulted in a web of regulations, laws and administrative structures that on the surface resembled the Fordist systems of Europe and North America. As a result abstract space as a space predominantly governed by the logic of capital accumulation and commodity exchange was never quite completed. The apartheid years, and particularly between the 1970s and 1994, can therefore be best described as an attempt to consolidate abstract space without ever quite achieving that goal.

As pointed out above, abstract space is one in which spatial practice and lived spaces recede into the background while representations of space dominate. In southern Africa the experiences of migrant workers, especially miners, were therefore increasingly determined by rationalization, planning and bureaucratic control as mining became one of the largest sources of formal employment in South Africa, reaching a level of 534,255 in 1986 (Chamber of Mines, 2000, p. 21). These bureaucratic manipulations were evident in the fluctuating share of foreign workers in mining labour total. As James (1992) has pointed out, the degree to which foreign miners were employed was subject not only to internal dynamics in that they were utilized as a means to blunt the power of South African miners, but also to external dynamics, for example when Zimbabwe and Malawi changed their stand on migration.

Up to the late 1980s the social relations of production in the mining sector morphed into patterns that resembled the tripartite model proposed by Harrod (1987, pp. 16–17) and discussed in some detail by Cox (1987, pp. 74–80). This model recognizes the emergence of worker organizations as a counterbalance to the growing power of employers and the intervention of the state in the resulting conflict. More specifically, it recognizes that the development of workers' organizations changes the dynamic of power relations from one of domination to one of bargaining. The inclusion of state power in the bargaining relationship further complicates this process in that the state plays an active role in shaping labour–capital negotiations and coordinating these along the lines of national economic policy.

In South Africa this process began in 1982 when the Chamber of Mines formally recognized the National Union of Mineworkers (NUM). In only six years the NUM had signed up 360,000 members, or about 60 per cent of the total mining labour force (James, 1992). While the system in South Africa seemed on the surface to be similar to arrangements in Western Europe, the persisting racism that permeated South African society limited the ability of the NUM to achieve many of its objectives. The intervention of the state was never neutral and power relations were such that the workers could never count on their own mobilization to force the hand of the state in their favour. Indeed state repression was often the answer to efforts at mobilization. The institutional arrangements were also stacked against the NUM and '[i]n defending workers' rights to job security, as in protecting their health and well-being, the NUM faced an uphill battle' (ibid., 1992, p. 103).

Nevertheless the NUM made progress in its negotiations with the Chamber of Mines, resulting in larger wage increases than initially offered. However its attempt to procure a massive increase under the 'living wage' slogan ultimately failed and its power waned after the failed strike of 1987. Moreover inflation, particularly during the 1980s, undermined the wage increases and workers' purchasing power was actually lower than it had been before the recognition of the NUM (ibid., pp. 106–8). Nonetheless wages were certainly higher than they would otherwise have been.

The apartheid era, particularly the first 30 years, can therefore usefully be described as characterized by a racist version of Fordism. According to Jessop (1994, p. 252), Fordism is a 'mode of economic regulation' that combines the tripartite pattern of social relations of production with specific monetary and fiscal policies to secure effective demand; that is, 'state sponsored social reproduction oriented to the generalization of norms of mass consumption and the provision of infrastructure and means of collective consumption and ... state involvement in managing the conflicts between capital and labor over both individual and social wage' in order to secure and maintain a virtuous cycle of economic growth. In South Africa the white population was the primary beneficiary of this mode of growth. The struggle of African workers, and migrants in particular, for better living and working conditions in the face of state repression yielded far fewer benefits. Nevertheless the relationship between labour and employers became embedded in a set of bureaucratized rules aimed at managing the economy in such a fashion as to maintain economic growth and its redistribution, some of which did flow to workers and migrants in the mineral sector.

In this system the positions of state and capital were often quite at odds. Their struggle over the colour bar – the job reservation system that formed the basis for white economic advancement – highlights their conflicts. While capital, as represented by the Chamber of Mines, was interested in promoting Africans because it was able to pay them less, white workers resisted what they perceived as the erosion of their privileges. In the initial compromise a significant amount regulatory power was reserved for the state, a position that satisfied white miners since they assumed that racial solidarity would outweigh the demands of capital. The NUM opposed this compromise and thus found itself in agreement with the Chamber of Mines (James, 1992). The final regulation, adopted in 1988, specified competence requirements that while not coded in racial language continued to provide some advantages to white workers. However the long effort to eliminate the official colour bar was accompanied by the promotion of Africans into positions that historically had been off limits (ibid.).

Since the late 1980s the mineral sector has gone through a massive retrenchment which, in the case of gold mining, has brought down employment levels to 176,090 in 2002 (Chamber of Mines, 2002, p. 21). Much of this retrenchment was the result of global competition in gold production and the neoliberal emphasis on non-inflationary monetary policies. The burden of retrenchment was borne more by South African miners than their regional counterparts. Between 1978 and 1984 the share of foreign miners declined from almost 48 per cent to about 42 per cent, but it increased again to almost 50 per cent by 1997 (Chamber of Mines, 1994, 1998).

The dramatic retrenchments in the gold mining sector have been directly related to a relatively new phenomenon, the emergence of subcontractors who employ retrenched miners (as well as novices), often in positions that are no different from the ones they occupied before they were laid off, but at dramatically reduced wages and virtually without benefits (Crush *et al.*, 1999). Foreign miners constitute 33 per cent of total subcontract employees and this is due to the more specialized nature of the jobs that subcontractors are hired to perform. In particular some core production activities require the expertise of experienced workers predominantly from Lesotho and Mozambique (ibid., pp. 16–18).

In Harrod's terminology, the past decade has been marked by a move away from the tripartite pattern of social relations of production and back either to the enterprise or to the casual pattern. The latter has emerged mostly because the reduced availability of employment opportunities through formal migration channels has increased the degree of informal migration, not just to South Africa, the most publicized case, but also to other states in the region (see for example McDermott Hughes, 1999).

A further factor in the decline of mine-worker migration is postapartheid South Africa's changed economic and political roles in the region. The adoption of the GEAR (Growth, Employment and Redistribution) programme in 1996 represented a significant departure from the more radical rhetoric of the pre-1990 ANC. As Ahwireng-Obeng and McGowan (1998) have pointed out, the key principle underlying the GEAR strategy is that the inequalities brought about by the long history of discrimination and apartheid cannot be remedied by internal redistribution but require a strategy of economic growth that is founded on a significant expansion of non-mineral exports to the rest of Africa, and particularly southern Africa.

In line with this goal, the Southern African Development Community (SADC) has become not only a proponent of a regional free trade zone and but also a vehicle by which South African capital, as the springboard of global financial interests, has extended its penetration of the region. While this is not a new phenomenon in that the spatial practices of the past century have always been based on such penetration, as Mlambo (1998, p. 102) points out the 1970s and 1980s were characterized by a significant degree of capital flight from the region in general and South Africa in particular. Since the end of the apartheid era capital flows have increased within the region, thus significantly increasing South African penetration. Hence the region's integration into the global economy is currently being rearticulated according to the abstract logic of neoliberalism.

The effort to regulate and curtail the inflow of migrants, especially in light of the high level of unemployment, will clearly have an impact on the international relations of the region. The debate on the redrafting of the Immigration Act and the 1997 green paper that served as its basis highlighted the contradictory social forces at work. On the one hand the mining companies wanted to retain the preferential position their labour recruitment system supported, while the government and non-mineral businesses were interested in a migration control system that was in line with the labour requirements of the GEAR strategy. However as South Africa dominates regional trade and investment, its neoliberal restructuring policies and the retrenchment of traditional migrants' jobs have led to growing unemployment in the migrants' home countries, so the flow of undocumented migrants into South Africa is likely to increase. 'Put differently, as South Africa closes the main gates ... it unconsciously opens up the back door for undocumented migration' (Matlosa, 1998, p. 37).

In response to the perceived increase (the actual numbers are very much in dispute) in legal and illegal immigration, various sectors of society and the government have called for decisive action to curtail the inflow. Migration has emerged as a crucial area in which domestic concerns clash with regional reality. A gut-level reaction to immigrants has led to increased use of barriers and fences, some of which are electrified. The policy of closed borders is, however, unlikely to have the desired effect since the regional spaces already created through the actions of migrants limit the ability of the government to implement its policy. Even during the apartheid years the efforts to control influx and police the movement of Africans were of limited success. The needs of employers and the desire of women to join their husbands, and of families to visit relatives, were all translated into spatial practices that defeated any attempt to tighten borders. Today such efforts are bound to be even less effective.

Conclusion

This section began with the proposition that Harrod's work on unprotected workers and Lefebvre's conceptualization of social space would complement each other and provide a fruitful set of questions for investigating international relations. Using the example of labour migration in southern Africa, the efficacy of this approach has become evident. From precolonial days to the legal end of apartheid, the changing forms of social space were clearly matched by relevant forms of social relations of production. Although there is a danger of oversimplification, we can detect a connection between absolute space and the subsistence pattern of social relations of production, historical space and the peasant and casual patterns of social relations of production, and abstract space and casual, enterprise and bipartite/tripartite social relations of production. Equally important, Lefebvre's claim that different historical forms of social space exist side by side is supported by Harrod's conceptualization of multiple coexisting forms of social relations of production.

Surprisingly, in the case of southern Africa the highpoint of apartheid rule in South Africa was associated with the most protected form of social relations of production (in the context of capitalist production) for mine-worker migrants – the tripartite pattern. Since the end of apartheid, retrenchments in the mining sector and changing forms of labour organization have turned the clock back to the enterprise labour market form of social relations of production. However this development should not come as a surprise. In Western Europe and to some extent in North America, similar changes have occurred with the post-Fordist restructuring of production structures. This suggests that the years of formal apartheid rule (1948–94), can be characterized as a racist variant of Fordism.

Finally, the international relations of southern Africa were intricately bound up with the changing forms of social relations of production. The racist variant of Fordism required sustained access to regional labour resources in order to protect the status of the white population. The end of apartheid as a legal system therefore constituted a further step towards the deepening of abstract social space. The sad irony is that the achievements of the anti-apartheid struggles also furthered the penetration of abstract space into new spheres of life, both at the level of the individual worker and at the level of regional politics. Postapartheid southern Africa, although now free of racist power politics, is marked by new international relations, driven by market forces rather than the desire to further human development.

7
The Working Poor: Labour Market Reform and Unprotected Workers in the South African Retail Sector

Marlea Clarke

This chapter engages sympathetically, but also critically, with the anti-essentialist and disaggregated conceptualization of unprotected workers presented in previous chapters in this volume (especially in Chapters 2 and 3). It does so in order to offer an analysis of the history of unprotected work and workers' struggles in South Africa, and the processes of labour market restructuring during the first ten years of democracy. As such the chapter seeks to demonstrate the significance of a modified variant of Harrod's (1987) typology of unprotected workers for an analysis of the achievements and limitations of postapartheid labour market reforms, as well for a clarification of the strategic terrain of the continued struggle for emancipatory structural reforms in South Africa.

When the African National Congress (ANC) was elected in South Africa's first democratic election in 1994, high degrees of inequality, exploitation and unemployment characterized the labour market. In response to this, and in order to fulfil promises made to the union movement during the liberation struggle, the new government committed itself to a programme of labour market transformation aimed at removing the last vestiges of the apartheid labour market. Guided by the framework outlined in the Ministry of Labour's five-year programme, the Department of Labour reformed the country's labour market institutions and introduced new employment legislation. The reforms have brought in a new system of industrial relations and improved employment standards for many workers. Overall the new regulatory framework has begun to address the extreme inequality and discrimination that were the effect of apartheid policies and labour market regulation.

However simultaneously with these reforms there has been a steady decline in full-time, permanent employment (standard employment) and a concomitant rise in various forms of non-standard employment and other types of unprotected work. Unemployment – already high at independence – has continued to rise and informal work has grown significantly. The result has been an overall rise in unprotected work and the extension of employment conditions that have characterized non-standard employment into sections of the permanent workforce (Clarke *et al.*, 2002). These employment trends raise serious questions about the appropriateness of the current forms of regulation and protection and the traditional forms of union organizing. The union movement has generally failed to address these changes in the nature of employment and shifts in the structure of the black working class. It has failed to develop new strategies of organizing and representing workers in emerging unprotected occupations and jobs. New patterns of employment, and the slow pace at which the union movement is obtaining an understanding of and addressing these changes, have contributed to growing tensions and divisions among workers. Consequently declining union membership and intraworker dynamics and tensions are intensifying and facilitating neoliberal socioeconomic restructuring and the continued rise of unprotected work.

Despite the extent and widespread impact of employment changes, South African policy makers, government officials, trade unions and scholars have neglected these important developments. Instead attention has generally focused on a narrow range of workplace issues that affect permanent workers in core sectors of the economy. As a result there is a dearth of information on the growth of unprotected work, changes in workers' consciousness and workplace struggles linked to employment changes and growing poverty among the country's working class. This chapter addresses these neglected topics. The first section engages with Jeffrey Harrod's (1987) work on unprotected workers and research that focuses more directly on segmentation and different types of employment relationship. Informed by Harrod's analysis of the political economy of unprotected work and studies of segmentation and employment form, the second section explores the history and recent growth of unprotected work in South Africa. The last section offers a detailed investigation of how these processes are taking place in the retail sector. It exposes the limits and weaknesses of the new regulatory framework, union policies and organizing strategies with regard to unprotected work and unprotected workers.

Segmentation, power and the unprotected worker

Theorists who take a segmentation approach seek to understand labour market structures (including segmentation) by exploring the way in which labour market structures, norms and practices are shaped by the social and political context in which they are embedded. Three dimensions structure labour markets: demand-side (those which structure labour demand and labour processes), supply-side (processes of social reproduction) and state regulation. Demand-side factors determine what jobs are available: the technical requirements of different labour processes, the labour control strategies used by employers, the design of jobs, and industrial structure (Rubery and Wilkinson, 1981; Marsden, 1992). Supply-side factors shape labour market participation, such as the source of labour and its nature and quantity. These include gender divisions of labour in the household; demographic factors and social norms that affect the labour force participation rates of different groups of workers; trade union structures and strategies; and occupational socialization (Freedman, 1976; Humphries, 1977; Rubery, 1978; Cockburn, 1983).

Finally, state and social regulation is to do with labour regulation and a variety of other policies and legislation that affect the labour market. In general these are political apparatuses that both shape and are shaped by the labour process (Burawoy, 1985). For example the state plays a direct regulatory role in the labour market by developing training systems and other educational programmes, and by regulating employment contracts and conditions of employment through legislation (Marsden, 1986; Wilkinson, 1988). Indirectly, state provisions such as childcare and welfare programmes contribute to the structuring of production and the reproduction of labour (Burawoy, 1985).

Despite the richness of this literature, segmentation theory is weak in respect of explaining the decline in full-time employment and the parallel growth of casual work. Recent works on employment trends have filled some of the gaps in this literature. This growing body of literature focuses on the shape, organization and regulation of different types of employment relationship (Deakin and Mückenberger, 1992; Vosko, 2000; Fudge and Vosko, 2001). Drawing on the theoretical contributions of segmentation theory, these scholars have analyzed employment trends and the changing nature of the employment relationship with reference to regulatory developments at the national and international levels (Butchtemann and Quack, 1990; Vosko, 2000). It is argued that a particular employment relationship emerged and was consolidated in Canada and other advanced capitalist welfare states in Europe and North America in the postwar period. Commonly referred to as the standard employment relationship (SER), this relationship was characterized by the presence of a continuous, full-time employment relationship where the worker had one employer and normally worked on the employer's premises or under his or her supervision (Vosko, 2000). Typically the SER included both a standard employment contract (full-time and permanent) negotiated in collective bargaining agreements, and social benefits such as unemployment insurance and a pension scheme.

As Vosko and others have noted, although the SER was numerically dominant a large percentage of workers were excluded from its benefits (ibid.; Pollert, 1988). White male workers, and especially unionized workers in core sectors of the economy, were the main beneficiaries of the SER. Women, immigrants and non-white workers were often excluded from secure employment and had to take jobs with inferior wages and employment conditions, or work in marginalized sectors characterized by low wages and employment insecurity. These non-standard employment relationships included a range of employment forms, all of which differed from the SER in that they were not unionized, full-time, permanent or secure, nor did they carry the social benefits associated with standard employment (Butchtemann and Quack, 1990; Vosko, 2000). Non-standard employment included temporary, seasonal, casual, part-time, self-employment and other forms of employment that were excluded or only partially covered by employment laws and policies. Women and visible minorities were disproportionately found this category of work. As Fudge (1997) notes, while not all non-standard jobs were low-paying and insecure, the majority of them were.

Rather than conflate such a diverse range of non-standard employment relationships, other scholars have focused on issues of vulnerability or precariousness instead of employment form. Drawing on the work of Rogers (1989), Fudge (1997) proposes that researchers should identity and look at the factors that make employment unstable and unprotected. According to her the emphasis should be on understanding workers' protection and vulnerability (levels of precariousness), rather than strictly on employment form. Issues such as employment security, access to benefits, control over work, degree of regulatory protection and income levels are key factors in determining whether or not a particular form of employment is precarious (ibid.).

Despite its important insights and theoretical tools there are significant weaknesses in this literature. First, its explanation of how or why non-standard employment is rising is limited. Apart from outlining changes in employers' hiring practices and new developments in social and employment policies, little attention is paid to national processes of political, economic and industrial restructuring, and the impact these processes have on employment shifts. Second, it is generally silent on the connection between different types of waged work and workers' consciousness. Linked to this, a third weakness is that it tends to overlook or disregard the part played by political struggles and class alliances in shaping and reshaping social relations. Although third- generation segmentation theories do explore trade union structures and strategies, little attention is paid to the relationship between employment and class consciousness.

These weaknesses are particularly apparent in works that concentrate on employment form and the changing nature of the employment relationship. While these works offer important insights into changes in the employment relationship and the degrees of vulnerability associated with different employment forms, workers' agency is generally not taken into account. Thus the terrain of struggle is limited to policy and legislative developments, with appropriate policy reforms presented as the appropriate solution to the growth of unprotected work.

Harrod's (1987) analytical framework on the political economy of unprotected work offers important insights that can help us to address some of the weaknesses in the literature on the changing nature of employment. In contrast to works based on segmentation theory and other studies of different patterns of employment, Harrod's analysis focuses directly on power and the patterns of power relations involved in production. He starts with power in production and then looks outwards from it; thus highlighting power relations as a key factor in conditions of work. While the political struggles and class conflict involved in the control and regulation of work tend to be overlooked in much of the literature on employment trends under contemporary capitalism, for Harrod the power relations in production are the source of the consciousness, contradictions and dynamics that produce change.

Advancing the innovative conceptual framework presented by Cox in *Production, Power and World Order* (1987), Harrod (1987) theorizes and examines power relations in production in terms of six patterns of social relations: subsistence, peasant–lord, primitive labour market, enterprise labour market, self-employed, and household. The power relations that govern the production of established workers are the bipartite, tripartite, enterprise corporatist and state corporatist modes. A full discussion of each of these is beyond the scope of this chapter, but the following sections will refer to them in the context of South Africa. As we shall see, Harrod's conceptualization of the relationship between the various forms of social relations and types of unprotected work is useful in understanding the different degrees of power that individual groups of workers have in postapartheid South Africa.

Harrod differentiates unprotected workers from established workers, and defines the former as relatively more exploited and insecure. As he would acknowledge, this definition is not very precise. He notes that 'the term unprotected worker is one of convenience and is intended to indicate the nonestablished workers or the least powerful of producers in the world labor force' (ibid., p. 38). Some disaggregation is offered. Drawing on more conventional categories, Harrod argues that unprotected workers comprise: subsistence farmers, peasants, urban marginals, unorganized wage workers, the self-employed and housewives. For Harrod, power relations, consciousness and modalities of struggle are central to different types of unprotected work. For example at one end are unionized workers in public sector employment or other work that is protected by state legislation, such as those in bipartite or tripartite social relations. At the other end are unprotected workers in casual and enterprise labour markets.

There are some problems with this definition. Similar to the problems associated with the standard/non-standard dichotomy, the general categories of 'unprotected worker' and 'established worker' do not adequately distinguish between the different degrees of vulnerability and insecurity involved in the various types of unprotected work. Moreover it hides the existence (and in many cases the recent increase) of vulnerability and insecurity among many established workers. Linked to neoliberal restructuring, job insecurity is rife and the gains previously won by labour are now being eroded in many countries, with union membership and power declining *vis-à-vis* growing employer offensives (Moody, 1997, 1998; Munck and Waterman, 1999). Thus even many established workers have limited or declining regulatory protection, employment security, benefits and control over their work. This, as we shall see, is the case in many workplaces in South Africa.

Finally, Harrod's categories of unprotected workers (see above) do not adequately cover the wide variety of workers in unprotected or poorly protected work. This problem, as we shall see, is particularly apparent when trying to understand unprotected work in South Africa, where very diverse power relations and different social formations have existed simultaneously often even in the same workplace. Harrod draws too stark a distinction between unprotected and established workers, and clusters quite diverse groups of workers into the same category. For example a very broad range of workers would fit into Harrod's classification of self-employed, but while some of these may be subject to considerable exploitation and have little stability in and control over their work, others will enjoy high wages and independence from clients.

Nevertheless the importance of Harrod's work is that he draws our attention to issues of power and control over production. And like Fudge (1997) and others, he emphasizes the importance of divisions between workers in respect of vulnerability, employment conditions and control over work. The intensity of employers' power over workers, and possible labour responses to general and specific dynamics of power relations, are at the centre of his work. While his specific categories of unprotected workers are not very applicable in the South African case, his description of how power relations and consciousness are central to unprotected work and the political struggles surrounding work offers a rich and useful contribution to our investigation of precarious work in postapartheid South Africa. In particular his analysis of different power relations between workers and between different economic groups in society offers important insights that can help us to understand unprotected work in the South African retail sector.

The history of unprotected and non-standard work in South Africa

Unprotected work under apartheid

The roots of South Africa's contemporary labour market and distinctive pattern of non-standard and unprotected work lie in the country's history of political and economic development. Specific patterns of industrial development and the consolidation of racist social and economic policies under apartheid resulted in the creation of a large pool of unprotected or poorly protected workers. Deep divisions between full-time, permanent workers and casual and contract workers were created and maintained by apartheid policies, employment legislation and recruitment practices. As indicated in Chapter 6, the apartheid regime codified and extended a coercive system of control and regulation of the African workforce through the migrant labour system, the pass law, the job reservation system and policies aimed at directing and redirecting labour mobility (see also Southall, 1999).

The dual system of labour relations created by the Industrial Conciliation Act of 1924 was entrenched by the Native Labour Act of 1953 and the Industrial Conciliation Act of 1956 (ICA). Aimed at preventing trade unionism among black workers, the ICA excluded Africans from all its provisions, including collective bargaining. In addition formal job reservation was introduced, with race being the defining criterion for employment in many jobs. In general industrial policies, employment legislation and employers' practices facilitated the growth of full-time, permanent, protected employment for white workers but few black workers. As a result employers were generally free to determine the wages and working conditions of most black workers.

Employment legislation and social policies introduced over the subsequent decades reinforced this dualism. National programmes such as the Workmen's Compensation Act (WCA) and the Unemployment Insurance Act (UIA) provided benefits and social security to workers defined as employees, while other groups of workers – such as casual labourers,[1] domestic workers and most agricultural and mining workers – were excluded from coverage. Since black workers were concentrated in the mining, agricultural and domestic sectors, most black workers remained unprotected or barely protected. Moreover the growth and consolidation of the standard employment relationship mainly benefited, white male workers, and despite the employment and social security reforms of the 1960s and 1970s many black workers remained unprotected, either by virtue of their exclusion from protective laws, or by apartheid legislation and employment practices.

During this time labour relations for most black workers in South Africa were characterized by the direct exercises of power by employers. Although the apartheid state intervened widely in the economy, for a large percentage of the workforce labour relations resembled what Harrod calls the 'enterprise labor market'. This mode of social relations of production was structured by the:

> individual labor contract between employer and employed in which the employer is basically dominant ... [T]here is no effective worker organization or state protective agency that intervenes between buyer and seller of labor to redress the power inequality of the parties in any substantial way. The employer's dominance is manifested by

the ability to take alone major decisions about wages and conditions of work, hiring, dismissal, investment, location, products and other factors associated with the management of an enterprise. (Harrod, 1987, p. 184)

Most black workers and a large number of women workers were employed in workplaces where there was no collective bargaining and protective labour and social policies did not apply. In general these workplaces were marked by exploitation and employers had broad power over production. However, although labour legislation prohibited black workers from joining unions, power was not as concentrated among employers as in Harrod's enterprise labour market.

Despite the strong support of the agricultural and mining sectors for this racially exclusive industrial relations system, by the early 1970s it was under challenge. Rapid urbanization, the continued growth of the manufacturing and commercial sectors and the emergence of militant African unions brought the traditional labour framework under review. Reacting against apartheid and the exploitative working conditions, workers became progressively more organized and militant during the 1970s. New, unregistered African unions signalled the beginning of what is often referred to as a period of 'building from below' (Friedman, 1987). Despite resistance from the government and attacks on workers by employers, these new unions grew rapidly. The strategies they adopted were considerably different from past ones. Partly as a result of being excluded from the industrial relations system (and collective bargaining in particular), the new unions concentrated on the individual workplace and on building up a strong shop steward structure (Baskin, 1991). In addition plant-based unionism developed in factories where there was majority union membership.

Political pressure from the militant unions – along with ideological differences between commercial agriculture and mining on the one hand, and manufacturing and commerce on the other – caused the state to rethink the country's industrial relations system and limited reforms were introduced.[2] Importantly the reforms redefined African workers as 'employees', thus African workers were now entitled to join registered unions and participate in official collective bargaining. More extensive reforms were introduced during the 1980s, and some African unions began to participate in the system. Nonetheless, until apartheid ended and more extensive political and labour market reforms were implemented in the 1990s, Harrod's (1987) tripartite model only really existed for unionized, white, established workers.

Unprotected work and labour market reforms under the ANC

Given South Africa's racist history and the delineation of protected and unprotected work, it was no surprise when soon after the country's first democratic election in 1994 the new ANC-led government committed itself to far-reaching labour market reforms aimed at protecting vulnerable workers. The government introduced new tripartite processes and institutions, as well as new employment statutes to increase workers' rights and improve employment standards. Four new statutes were introduced: the Labour Relations Act 65 of 1995 (LRA), the Basic Conditions of Employment Act 75 of 1997 (BCEA), the Employment Equity Act 55 of 1998 (EEA) and the Skills Development Act 97 of 1998 (SDA). The LRA overhauled collective labour relations and extended organizational and collective bargaining rights to all employees. The BCEA set minimum employment standards for workers and created a new body, the Employment Conditions Commission (ECC), which was made responsible for setting wages and working conditions for workers in unorganized sectors. The EEA addressed workplace discrimination, while the SDA introduced a national skills development strategy.

The introduction of the new employment laws ushered in a new system of industrial relations, and stronger regulations have begun to address the extreme inequality and discrimination that characterized the apartheid labour market. The new regulatory regime has brought about some diversification of the labour market. For example social security benefits and employment rights have been formally extended to most workers (and to a far more diverse constituency of workers), and employment equity and other pieces of new legislation have resulted in better representation of women and black workers in professional occupations and in management and supervisory positions. Coverage has also been extended to farm, domestic and many casual workers. While previous legislation specifically excluded casual labourers and workers who were employed for fewer than three days per week, most sections of the BCEA now cover those who work more than 24 hours per month.

However, slow economic growth during the ANC's first two terms in office, combined with the demand by domestic capital and international funding agencies for labour market flexibility, weakened the regulatory effect of the new employment legislation and put pressure on the labour market. As our case study of the retail sector will demonstrate, various forms of unprotected work have survived and even flourished. Weaknesses and loopholes in the new laws, flexibility provisions in the BCEA, officially sanctioned exemptions from legislation, and limitations on the reach and enforcement of laws and collective bargaining agreements have created an environment in which protected (or standard) employment has declined and various forms of unprotected work have thrived. For example, although the BCEA formally includes casual workers, many temporary and fixed-term contract workers[3] are effectively excluded from many provisions in the new Acts (Godfrey and Clarke, 2002). Exemption provisions for small businesses, individual companies and specific groups of workers are also contained in the new legislation, as are provisions for the relaxation of some standards (ibid.).[4]

In addition the legislation has inadvertently created new categories of non-standard and unprotected work. For example a clear division has been created between employees and independent contractors. Those who fit the definition of employee are now covered by legislation, while those defined as independent contractors are not. The traditional reading of 'employee' has restricted the ambit of legal protection to those workers who have employment contracts and excludes those who have a contract of service (a contract regulating work that is not employment) (Cheadle and Clarke, 2000). Thus independent contractors, even those who in reality are dependent workers (such as task-based factory workers), are excluded from employment protection. Other groups of non-employees also remain unprotected. Dependent self-employed workers such as homeworkers, owner-drivers and task-workers all fall outside the definition of employee in the Act, and therefore are not protected by legislation (Clarke *et al.*, 2002).

The politics of trade liberalization, privatization and the encouragement of the small business sector under the ANC have contributed to the expansion of unprotected work, and to the extension of some of the conditions of non-standard employment into sections of the permanent workforce. Indeed in response to more competitive international and domestic markets many companies are outsourcing work to smaller firms that are officially exempt from legislation, or that selectively apply employment laws (Clarke *et al.*, 2003). Informal work has grown significantly, and the poorly regulated temporary employment industry is quickly becoming the fastest growing industry in the country (Clarke *et al.*, 2002, 2003).

Alongside these changes, old forms of casual and contractual employment have continued since the end of apartheid. Still other forms of casual work have been reshaped to conform to the modern, advanced, capitalist (postapartheid) economy. Unprotected work is also growing in sectors and workplaces where unionization is low, the monitoring and enforcement of employment legislation is weak, and exposure to competitive international markets has made it difficult for unionized workers to resist workplace restructuring to reduce labour costs (Clarke *et al.*, 2002, 2003). Formal employment has shrunk, informal and subsistence work has become more prevalent and various forms of unprotected work (such as casual, informal and temporary employment) have grown significantly. The overall result is that, despite the development of the new regulatory framework, many workers continue to be poorly protected.

New contractual arrangements now play a crucial role in shaping employment conditions and protection for different groups of workers. Although race and gender no longer directly determine workers' access to protected employment the employment changes are neither race- nor gender-neutral. Women and black workers are still disproportionately represented in low-income sectors and low-end occupations where a growing number of jobs are being converted into casual or temporary positions. Racial and gender inequality persist in unemployment rates, employment income and in the incidence of low and uncertain wages. Overall the employment changes have created new divisions between workers and widened the existing differentials among them, thus amplifying racial and gender segmentation in the labour market.

The growth of unprotected work: casualization, externalization and informalization

Casualization, externalization and informalization are facilitating unprotected work and a steady increase in the number of unprotected workers in postapartheid South Africa. Casualization is taking place through the reduction of permanent, full-time staff and an increase in part-time, temporary and casual employees who are not entitled to the benefits enjoyed by permanent, full-time employees. For example, according to national statistics temporary labour increased by as much as 42 per cent between 1999 and 2002 in some sectors (Naidoo, 2003). As noted above, although new legislation has extended protection to many casual workers, coverage is only partial (some exclusions to benefits still apply) and is limited to workers with formal employment contracts who work more than 24 hours per month for one employer. Research suggests that employers in most sectors are continuing to hire casual workers as a way of reducing labour costs and increasing flexibility (Theron and Godfrey, 2000; Du Toit and Alley, 2001). In addition casualization has put in downward pressure on full-time workers' wages and working conditions.

The term externalization refers to business practices that make use of external sources of labour. Called 'distancing' by some scholars, this process involves the transfer of labour to homeworkers, subcontractors or temporary workers supplied by temporary employment agencies (Anderson *et al.*, 1994). Externalization can also involve the legal restructuring of a working relationship – from a contract of employment to another legal relationship, usually a commercial contract that provides goods and services to a business. The use of homeworkers to supply retailers or manufacturers with finished garments, and the use of consultants who work continuously on the employers' premises but under a service contract rather than an employment relationship are two examples of externalization (ibid.).

Theron and Godfrey (2000) have applied the term externalization to a range of legal contracts that shift work from an employment relationship to a commercial contract regulated by the rules of contract, such as subcontracting or outsourcing work to a contractor rather than directly employing workers to carry out the work. According to Robinson (2004), as a result of externalization and casualization in the road haulage industry about 27 per cent of jobs (involving 16,000 out of 60,000 workers) are outsourced. Employers are also externalizing work by using a third party to employ their staff, usually a labour broker or a temporary employment agency (Clarke *et al.*, 2002).

Regardless of how externalization takes place, restructuring employment relationships by 'distancing' labour allows employers 'to operate outside the legal constraints that have been developed to protect working conditions and to guarantee certain minimum levels of protection' (Anderson *et al.*, 1994, p. 497). In most cases workers have the legal status of a self-employed person or contractor rather than an employee, even though in practice they are as dependent on the business for their wages as workers in a direct employment relationship. As outlined earlier, weakness and loopholes in the legislation allow the client to transfer both the cost and the risk to the worker.

The third process, informalization, has received some attention by policy-makers in recent years. Over the past decade there has been a dramatic increase in unemployment and informal work. While the ANC claims to have created about two million jobs since 1994, opposition parties, unions and labour market researchers fiercely dispute this figure, arguing that about a million jobs have actually been lost. Job creation has continued to be outstripped by job shedding and the inflow of new entrants to the job market. According to the government's Labour Force Survey, in 1995 there were (using the narrow or 'official' definition)

1,644,000 unemployed people (16.9 per cent) and in 2001 4,525,000 were unemployed (29.5 per cent) (Clarke *et al.*, 2003), while the expanded definition gives rates of 29.2 per cent in 1995 and 41.5 per cent in 2001 (Statistics South Africa, 2002).

Even some of the country's mainstream economists have recently acknowledged the growth in casual and informal work, noting that there was a significant change in the nature of employment between 1999 and 2003 (Bhorat and Hinks, 2006). Drawing on national labour force data, they contend that the share of informal self-employed workers increased from 9.8 per cent to 12.6 per cent during this time period (ibid., p. 9). And, according to their calculations, casual employment[5] as a proportion of total employment increased from 36.6 per cent to 38.3 per cent between 1999 and 2003. Other writers have argued that currently full-time occupations employed little more than 40 per cent the economically active population by 2004, which decreases to approximately one-third for just the economically active African population (Barchiesi, 2004). As will be discussed in the next section, the proportion of informal employment has grown significantly in the wholesale and retail trade, accounting for 60 per cent of the sector's overall growth in employment between 1997 and 2001.

Of course informalization, externalization and casualization are not distinct processes. In many cases they happen simultaneously and intersect each other. For example, since independent contractors are not considered to be employees of temporary employment agencies, research suggests that agencies utilize this legislative loophole to hire temporary workers as independent contractors. Temporary workers also tend to be hired on fixed-term contracts with labour brokers and temporary employment agencies, and these contracts usually correspond to the duration of the contract the broker has signed with the client. In both cases temporary employment agencies are able to arrange their contractual agreements with temporary workers in such a way as to bypass legislation, thus placing workers outside the protective embrace of employment laws.

Unprotected work in the South African retail sector[6]

The wholesale and retail sector is one of the largest employers in South Africa and is the fourth largest contributor to GDP: in 1999 its contribution to GDP was estimated to be 12.4 per cent. It is also frequently described as one of the most rapidly changing sectors in the country

(W&R SETA, 2001). Retail trade has three main subsectors – food, clothing and furniture/household goods – and there is a diversity of retail outlets, ranging from very small corner cafés[7] to large department stores and supermarkets. As in other countries, economic growth and the modernization of the sector in the postwar period resulted in the establishment of large department stores and supermarkets, and a concomitant decline in the number and importance of small corner shops. But unique to South Africa was the fact that employment patterns in the retail industry were shaped by apartheid in terms of employment legislation, social welfare programmes and sectoral wage determinations.

Nonetheless, in contrast to the contract labour system that persisted in the mining and agricultural sectors, various postwar developments in the retail sector resulted in stable, permanent, protected employment for most workers. While the mining and agricultural sectors continued to be characterized by high levels of non-standard employment until the 1980s, full-time, protected employment was increasingly extended to women and black retail employees during the country's postwar growth period. Initially white women were the main beneficiaries of the expansion of full-time, protected employment in retail. However the continued expansion of the sector, and especially the establishment of large supermarkets in African areas, created employment opportunities for black workers. Moreover rising wages and improved employment conditions for all workers meant that many of the benefits associated with the standard employment relationship were extended to African workers. Workplace struggles, the emergence of strong, independent black trade unions, and increased employment opportunities for African workers reduced inequality in the sector. By the end of the 1980s effective union organizing in the sector had resulted in significant wage increases and improved benefits for the lowest-paid workers, thereby reducing segmentation.

While casual and contract workers continued to account for a large percentage of the workforce in most sectors, by the late 1980s a growing majority of retail workers were in full-time, permanent and protected employment. As will be discussed in more detail below, however, trade liberalization, deregulation and pressure from more competitive international markets have prompted the restructuring of employment arrangements in the retail trade. Very much along the lines suggested by Amoore in Chapter 1, this restructuring has largely taken place by means of informalization, casualization and externalization. While the modernization and growth of the retail industry between the mid 1960s and late 1980s resulted in significant employment growth and expansion of the standard employment relationship, restructuring over the last decade or so has eroded secure, full-time employment in the sector and facilitated a dramatic increase in unprotected work.

Casualization

Until the late 1980s retail stores generally hired very few workers on a part-time basis and instead maintained a small (but growing) pool of casual workers to staff their stores during peak hours, holidays, weekends and late night opening times (Clarke and Kenny, 2002). Over the last decade there has been a significant change in this staffing practice, with most employers now using large numbers of casual workers (or newly created 'flexitimers') to staff their stores in the evening, during busy holiday periods, over the weekends and even during regular weekday shifts. In the 1990s all major retailers (food and clothing) reported increased use of casual workers, generally far exceeding the ratios of casual versus full-time permanent workers set by the Wage Determination.[8] According to three large retailers, in the late 1980s at least 70 per cent of store employees were permanent and only 30 per cent were casual, but by the late 1990s these numbers had almost completely reversed (interviews with, human resource managers, November 2002).

The term 'casual' is really a misnomer in most large supermarkets as most casuals have been employed for many years (often more than five), work close to full-time hours on a regular basis, and are treated by management as permanent workers. Thus while in practice they are permanent workers who work part-time hours, their employment status as casuals means that they generally do not have permanent contracts and have less job security and mobility (Clarke and Kenny, 2002). In general casual employment in the retail trade is characterized by a lack of entitlement to the employment benefits and forms of protection that full-time, permanent workers receive. Furthermore, casual workers are often not unionized and are poorly protected by store-based wage agreements. For example in the 1990s casual workers at one large grocery chain were not entitled to benefits such as sick leave, maternity or paternity leave, or an annual bonus (Kenny, 1998). Casual workers at other large supermarkets do not have written employment contracts, and complain of unequal treatment and poorer working conditions than their counterparts in permanent, full-time employment. With a few rare exceptions, casual workers are not entitled to additional training and have limited job mobility.

Downward pressure on the wages and working conditions of all workers and the prevalence of jobs with irregular work schedules are further indications that casualization has taken place in the sector. Job security and benefits have dropped as a growing number of workers – even those with full-time, permanent jobs – are now employed in precarious jobs. For example workers employed in retail growth areas (spaza shops,[9] franchises and convenience stores) tend to receive lower pay, fewer benefits, have less job security and often have 'on-call' working arrangements in comparison with the more regular shifts and better pay enjoyed by their counterparts in large, unionized department stores. According to Kenny (2001), casual workers in one large supermarket chain could be called in at short notice to work unscheduled hours, and if they were unable to work the managers punished them by not scheduling them at all the following week.

Informalization

Alongside casualization there has been a substantial increase in the size of the informal economy in the retail sector. The relaxation of apartheid legislation regulating business development in African homelands and black townships in the 1980s resulted in the rapid growth of black retailing. Spaza shops, generally owned and run by black retailers, became increasingly prevalent in townships and rural areas. By the late 1990s it was estimated that there were approximately 6,000 registered spaza shops, of which about 1,000 were located in Soweto (Cant and Brink, 1999). Spaza shops and informal trade grew rapidly during the 1990s, with informal trade taking a growing share of the sector (Euromonitor, 2003). Although informal retail trade was dominated by unregistered spaza shops, the presence of hawkers and flea markets – selling everything from fruit and vegetables to clothing, jewellery and electrical goods – grew in all neighbourhoods, including residential areas previously reserved for whites.

According to the October 1998 Household Survey the wholesale and retail sector was the second largest informal sector in terms of employment. By the end of the decade it was estimated that there were between 50,000 and 100,000 spaza shops (including both formal and informal traders) in South Africa, with the average-sized spaza shop being operated by the proprietor plus one employee (W&R SETA, 2001). Two thirds of these shops were owned by women (ibid.; Theron and Godfrey, 2000). While men made up 53 per cent of workers in formal retail stores, women workers formed the majority in informal trade (almost 70 per cent).

The actual size of informal trade, the number of informal businesses and the number of employees working for these businesses is difficult to determine with any real accuracy. However national data (Torres *et al.*,

2001; Statistics South Africa, 2002) and sector-specific research (W&R SETA, 2001) reveal a similar trend: the rapid growth of informal trade, and therefore a growing number of employees without formal protection by employment legislation and social policy. According to the *Mesebetsi Labour Force Survey*, Torres *et al.* (2001), almost half the workforce in the retail sector is now in informal trade. Data from the Mesebetsi survey provides a reliable indication of the growing importance of informal trade and is consistent with other research on the sector. For example the *South African Department of Labour's national* Labour Force Survey found that of the estimated 2.3 million persons who were running at least one non-VAT-registered business in March 2001, 69.4 per cent were in the wholesale and retail trade (Statistics South Africa, 2002). In general workers employed by informal retailers are excluded from any form of employment or social protection. Their degree of vulnerability and exploitation is higher than for temporary or casual workers in formal retail enterprises. Given the number of small family-based retail businesses, even if workers in informal businesses were covered by legislation it is unlikely that many of them would have the ability to claim rights and benefits.

Alongside the growth of informal traders has been an increase in informal production and distribution. The emergence of small informal producers in both the food and clothing subsectors and increased competition from imported goods have led to new sourcing arrangements. Importantly, clothing retailers turned away from formal manufacturers and began to buy directly from the homework and informal sectors during the 1990s. Food retailers have also shifted their food packaging and preparation activities to small producers in the informal sector. In 2001 large grocery retailer reported buying about 20 per cent of its delicatessen foods from small businesses, many of which were exempt from employment legislation.[10]

Externalization

Although externalization is less prevalent in the retail sector than in many other sectors, it is steadily growing. For example retailers have begun to outsource what they view as non-core functions: cleaning, transportation and security. Rather than work taking place through an employment contract it is now carried out under a service contract with a contractor or smaller company. In the 1990s there was an increase in the number of contractors and external agents supplying goods and services to the sector. Many retailers have also outsourced warehousing, shelf-stocking and training. Subcontracted workers, particularly merchandisers, are increasingly employed by labour brokers contracted by suppliers.

Since the late 1990s some grocery stores have also relied on labour brokers or temporary help agencies to supply workers during distribution peaks, or on a temporary basis as shelf-packers, stock takers or packers in the warehouses. In order to reduce the wage costs and scheduling problems associated with maintaining a large pool of casual workers, in 2000 one of the largest supermarkets in the country began to use a labour broker to supply cashiers. According to the human resource manager the store was following this strategy on 'a trial basis to see if it is easier than all the headaches of keeping so many casuals on staff.'[11] Surprisingly the manager was not concerned about the effects this might have on work performance and customer service, as the following comment reveals: 'Our cashiers aren't friendly or committed to the company now, but we have to pay them anyway. If we outsource, service cannot get any worse and we will not have the hassle and pay problems.'[12]

As stated earlier, externalization, informalization and casualization are not discrete processes, and they are increasingly overlapping and reinforcing each other. For example stores use the services of labour brokers and other temporary employment agencies to recruit and place casual workers in various jobs. In addition workers in small spaza shops and informal retailers tend to be in an ambiguous or a disguised employment relationship, or are excluded from the provisions of employment legislation due to legal exemptions or weak monitoring and enforcement mechanisms. Informalization is contributing to a rise in the number of workers who are not defined as employees under current legislation. According to the 2001 Labour Force Survey, approximately 94 per cent of people working in the informal part of the industry are not classified as employees (Statistics South Africa, 2002). This is not surprising as many workers in informal businesses are friends or relatives of the owner, and therefore rarely have a clear employment relationship.

The growth in informal trade and the shift in employment from supermarkets to franchise stores and smaller retailers helps to account for the growing polarization of the sector. Work in informal trade is more precarious, vulnerable and unprotected, with workers hired according to very individualized terms that offer no real legal protection under employment legislation and social security programmes. Employees in franchise stores and smaller retail outlets generally receive lower wages and fewer benefits than workers in larger unionized retail outlets. Polarization in wages and working conditions is also evident in large department stores, where casual workers receive fewer benefits and less employment security than their full-time colleagues.

Although the racialized and gendered characteristics of employment carried over from the apartheid era is changing, the labour market remains highly segmented. Even though whites no longer have privileged access to protected employment, women and black workers dominate the service sector and jobs at the bottom end of the job market. Women and black retail workers are disproportionately found in jobs in which casualization and externalization are common. For example blacks make up the majority of employees in low-skilled occupational categories, and women workers (especially black women) are generally employed in jobs that have been reduced to casual or temporary positions, such as service, shop and market sales jobs. In the early 2000s Africans accounted for 57 per cent of those employed in these jobs (W&R SETA, 2001), of whom 31 per cent were women and 26 per cent were men. In contrast, white workers held 45 per cent of managerial positions in the retail sector. Research shows that the employment changes to date have had little impact on employment patterns at the managerial level.

Hence while the legislative reforms have eradicated the wage differentials between the racial groups and new legislation has improved workers' employment conditions, externalization and informalization have contributed to the growth of unprotected work. As Harrod (1987) argues in respect of unprotected workers in general, South African temporary or casual workers, and those employed by informal traders, have little power over production and working conditions. Thus formal equality between the sexes and between white and black workers under the new regulatory framework has gone hand in hand with the growth of various forms of unprotected work. Overall, employment norms have deteriorated and segmentation has deepened as more workers are now engaged in casual, informal and other forms of unprotected or non-standard employment with inferior wages and working conditions. In effect reregulation and resegmentation characterized the first decade of labour market restructuring under the ANC government.

Union politics and strategies

The situation described above is the result of two important factors. First, COSATU's ongoing alliance with the ANC has resulted in the labour federation accepting significant concessions in the new legislation and compromises over economic, trade and other policies. Despite not winning some of its central demands during the negotiations over the new legislation, even with COSATU's continued opposition to core sections of the Basic Conditions of Employment Act (BCEA), the union federation accepted that the legislation was the best it could get. Albeit reluctantly, the union movement has acknowledged that the political influence it once had within the ANC has been consistently weakened since the 1994 election. During the negotiations the unions' reduced power *vis-à-vis* business often resulted in their fighting to defend workers' existing rights:

> there are a number of challenges we have faced in the negotiations. Most critically has been the overall policy shift in government at a macro level, which is reducing the space for winning new rights for our members, and in fact has forced us to at times, take a defensive position, seeking to protect the rights we have in the current law. (COSATU, 1996, p. 6)

Despite the fact that the legislation protects only a shrinking core of the workforce, the union federation has continued to promote new laws and address weaknesses in the regulatory framework through legal and technical changes to the legislation.

Second, COSATU has fought for labour market reform and vigorously defended the newly established tripartite labour market institutions. As a result, organized labour's focus has been on its traditional constituency (large formal businesses in core sectors of the economy) and on political processes aimed at reforming the labour market. A growing number of workers in non-standard employment lie outside trade union activities and the tripartite structures.[13] Labour's preoccupation with institutional structures and formal negotiation has created new dynamics and tensions among workers, often intensifying the process of socioeconomic restructuring. In the retail trade and other sectors, organized workers' lack of understanding of the restructuring process has led them to view casual workers, rather than the process of casualizing workers, as the root of their problem.

Further more, in contrast to COSATU's history of mass organizing and community-based protests in the 1970s and 1980s, during the past decade the union movement has increasingly relied on political link with the ANC and participation in formal negotiations with the government and business to press for labour market transformation. Indeed, the participatory democratic structures and mass organizing that shaped the black union movement in the decades following its re-emergence in the late 1970s have radically declined since the early 1990s. COSATU has increasingly concentrated on legal and technical policy negotiations with business and the government, thus placing power and decision-making in the hands of a few leaders and national officials. The trade union federation has continued to rely on tripartite institutions, policy processes and alliance structures to challenge ANC policies and defend the rights of its members. As Bassett (2004, p. 14) notes, this strategy has resulted 'in a politics concentrated in the interventions of leaders rather than in developing the capacities of the membership'.

In contrast to Harrod's (1987) suggestion that casual workers have tendency for millenarianism and populism, working-class communities and groups of casual workers continue to organize collectively (even if within different clusters of the workforce) to challenge working conditions. For example innovative campaigns and mobilizing strategies outside the traditional trade union movement suggest that new forms of organizing and representing marginalized workers are emerging. One new organization, the Men on the Side of the Road Project, is playing an important role in organizing and representing the large and growing number of temporary and day labourers. In addition a new organization for casual farmworkers was formed in March 2004 to mobilize casual farm workers and to improve their working and living conditions. This group – Sikhula Sonke, meaning 'We Grow Together' – is not formally registered as a trade union, although it is performing many of the functions of a traditional trade union. It is committed to organizing beyond the traditional workforce by representing farm dwellers as well as farmworkers. Within three months of its launch, the group already had 2000 signed-up members, most of whom were women (Bell, 2004).

There are hopeful signs that the South African trade union movement is still committed to challenging the patterns of social relations that prevail under the ANC government. Importantly the movement's renewed commitment to reaching out to women and non-standard workers, and to making COSATU 'a home for all working people', suggest that more new forms of organizing may emerge. The recently launched 'organizational renewal process' is another hopeful sign that unions may shift their attention away from alliance politics and begin the difficult process of rebuilding a strong working-class movement that is capable of advancing alternatives to neoliberal government policies.

Conclusion

Casualization, informalization and externalization have resulted in a substantial rise in unprotected work and unprotected workers. This is particularly apparent in the retail sector. Despite the introduction of new employment legislation aimed at reregulating the labour market, the sector has become increasingly unregulated with the growth of informal trade and the increased use of subcontractors and casual and temporary workers. Alongside the proliferation of unprotected workers, employment changes and workplace restructuring have eroded the wages and working conditions of non-standard workers and many permanent workers alike.

Changing forms of employment, and particularly unprotected work, raises serious questions about the appropriateness of the current regulations, employment protection measures and traditional forms of organizing. For the most part the union movement has failed to address changes in the nature of employment and shifts in the structure of the black working class. The slow pace at which the union federation has tried to understand and address the new employment arrangements has caused a decline in its strength, and growing divisions among workers. However socioeconomic restructuring has created new sites of struggle, and new political spaces for different forms of organizing and mobilizing to emerge. Even if hesitantly and fraught with problems, the organizational renewal process and other activities within the labour movement suggest that COSATU is attempting to revive and transform unions, and to extend protection to more workers. Workers' renewed commitment to unionism, and the progress made in linking up with the country's new social movements, also indicate that labour is playing an important role in challenging the neoliberal economic and political reforms.

Notes

1. In general, casual workers were those who worked fewer than three days per week for one employer.
2. When the definition of employee was amended in 1979 to include African workers with permanent urban residence rights while still excluding migrant and contract workers, the unions refused to accept this revised definition and continued to organize migrants and block the growth of compliant parallel unions (Greenberg, 1987). Opposition by unions to the intially limited reforms resulted in the government launching a far more extensive process of reforms.
3. In contrast to indefinite contracts, fixed-term or limited duration contracts are contracts that last for a defined period or until a specific job has been completed.
4. The BCEA's flexibility provisions allow for the variation of some standards (such as working time and overtime pay) for some workers. Consequently different degrees of protection are afforded to different workers.

5. They include those who work in the informal sector and those employed in the formal sector with a casual, temporary, seasonal or part-time contract in their definition of a casual worker. Although this definition is too general and includes a diverse range of workers with differing levels of coverage and protection, their calculations do support the argument advanced in this chapter. In general, this statistic reveals the general growth of non-standard, rather than just casual, employment.

6. This section draws on the extensive fieldwork the author carried out in 1999–2003 for her PhD dissertation.

7. These are small corner grocery stores, often family-run.

8. During the apartheid period, Wage Determinations (set by the Wage Board) regulated wages and working conditions of unorganized workers.

9. Informal retailers in townships and other African areas.

10. Interview with human resource manager, 4 March 2001.

11. Interview with human resource manager, 3 March 2000.

12. Ibid.

13. The country's main tripartite economic and labour policy body is the National Economic Development and Labour Council (NEDLAC). Established in February 1995, it is a statutory body whose task is to consider all proposed employment legislation and all significant changes to social and economic policy. Three of its four policy chambers are organized along essentially corporatist lines, with organized labour, organized business and the government represented in equal numbers. Only the fourth chamber, which considers social and developmental policy, includes representatives of civil society groups.

8
The Condition of Hegemony and Labour Militancy: The Restructuring of Gender and Production Patterns in Mexico

Teresa Healy

In the early 1990s, labour movements in North America were fighting a losing battle to prevent the North American Free Trade Agreement (NAFTA) from being concluded. In Mexico NAFTA was viewed as institutionalizing, extending and deepening the neoliberal strategies imposed by international financial institutions, transnational employers and the Mexican state under the neocolonial leadership of the US. In Mexico the neoliberal ideas, institutions and accumulation strategies we now refer to as 'globalization' have not been easily imposed as they had a specific genesis in the contradictions arising from an earlier corporatist social compromise under conditions of external domination. In fact Mexico has not been able to overcome the deep social crisis that has characterized the country for many years. While powerful social forces try to convince workers, indigenous peoples, peasants and women that they should or must accept the terms of neoliberal globalization, this effort has gone against the lived experience of the communities of people who have been degraded in the process. When social movements resist powerful social relations, their efforts leave their mark on history, even when they are not completely successful.

In this chapter it is proposed that the model of production patterns developed by Harrod (1987) and Cox (1987) can make a strong contribution to our efforts to analyze the context in which Mexican labour movements contest the terms of North American integration. Following the Gramscian conception of relations of force (see Chapter 3), this argument will be pursued by relating patterns of relations of production to Mexican state forms, world order and struggles over hegemony.

The chapter also demonstrates how a gender analysis can be fruitfully integrated into the account.

In the context of neoliberal globalization it is difficult but not impossible to integrate an analysis of both national specificities and world order. It is not necessary to replicate the problems of world systems theory, which has been criticized for being far too ready to 'collapse potentially contradictory state–society relations into an ahistorical, abstract unity' (Rupert, 1995, p. 10). The emphasis on historical changes in the structure of production is the crucial means by which this specificity can be maintained. We shall use the concept of 'pattern of social relations of production' or 'production pattern' as shorthand. As Harrod describes it, one of the benefits of the method employed here is that:

> a map of social relations of production can be produced for any social formation ... Equipped with a view of the groups in different forms, the consciousness of the groups produced by social relations, and the class alliances such a consciousness may produce, a political analysis can be pursued that indicates the direction of change, the form of state, and state action precipitated by such power dynamics. (Harrod, 1987, p. 25)

To explain the contested character of globalization in Mexico, we need an historical perspective and a set of conceptual tools that will enable us to see both general and specific dynamics, including the role played by gender. More generally, it is important to analyze the extent to which gendered inequalities have been constructed within the relations of production so as to link different production patterns to one another over time. It can be argued that the production patterns promoted by dominant national and transnational social forces throughout twentieth-century Mexico were both highly gendered and interrelated. In Mexico patriarchal historical structures, fashioned under colonialism and woven into capitalist society, contributed to what Gramsci (1971) called a passive revolution stabilizing Mexican society in the mid-twentieth century. Moreover a particular form of hegemonic masculinity ensured that landowners and *caudillos* (regional strongmen) supported the passive revolution, as they were incorporated into the hierarchy of the social order. Despite temporary stabilization, the ideas, institutions and material conditions underlying the configuration of production patterns were constantly challenged and subsequently transformed by political and economic struggles. Working-class movements contested the conditions under which they worked and lived throughout the century. Rarely, however, was the gendered character of these patterns challenged by labour. In the current conjuncture, this has not only made it possible for the old official state-corporatist structures to enforce neoliberalism in the workplace, it has also produced divisions that have contributed in a central way to the failure to transform antagonisms into effective counterhegemonic struggle as production patterns in the dominant sectors are feminized in a process that is aptly termed 'maquilization'.

This chapter will not construct a complete map of the hierarchy of productive patterns in Mexico, but it will point out important links between a number of them and make the case that this is a useful approach, not only because it allows us to discuss labour's efforts to contest capitalist hegemonic projects, but also because the significance of social relations other than class can be examined as well.

We shall consider the example of Mexican workers in the automotive industry. The production patterns represented by automotive assembly have never been the most widespread in the Mexican economy. Non-established workers involved in household and peasant production, for example, have had more of an impact on Mexico's economic structure, and have been far larger in number than workers in industrial production. However, throughout the twentieth century the automotive industry was the barometer of how certain patterns were privileged over others. Since the 1917 revolution the state has given priority to three production patterns: the enterprise pattern, the corporate pattern and state corporatism. Most recently the state and international capital have attempted to create a new globalized pattern that has aspects of all three. As a consequence of the post-1968 crisis in Mexico, and despite ten years of concerted economic integration on neoliberal terms, formerly protected workers have lost their acquired rights. A crisis of representation within the unions and the state has not been resolved, and neither has the unemployment crisis been solved. The fact that the 'worker-father' has become more akin to the '*maquila* girl' is cause for serious reflection on the significance of gendered inequalities, both historical and current.

In pursuit of this argument, the chapter begins with a conceptual discussion of the condition of hegemony in order to set the framework for the subsequent section, which examines Mexico's passive revolution and 'organic crisis' in the mid twentieth century. Consistent with a historical structural analysis the sociopolitical dynamics will be analyzed in a broad historical time span, before concluding with the current juncture in an account of increased specificity, with special reference to the automotive sector.

The condition of hegemony

In Gramscian approaches it is often argued that hegemony is established at the centre and becomes weaker at the periphery of world order. There is reason to suppose that hegemony will be difficult to sustain in peripheral countries if no leading class is able to present its interests in universal terms. It is expected that coercion rather than consent will tend to characterize social relations within civil society and the state. If social practices in the core are emulated in the periphery in ways that do not respond to the social problems experienced there, the ability of the leading classes to secure hegemonic order at the national level will be undermined. Instead of constructing a coherent national project, the leading classes will become identified with, and will identify themselves with, the process of internationalization. As described by Cox (1993, p. 61), 'hegemony is more intense and consistent at the core and more laden with contradictions at the periphery'. As a result the hegemonic character of world order may be weakened at the margins, where dominance characterizes the role of the state. There the intellectual and moral leadership of the centre is less compelling.

An openly coercive order verging on crisis, however, does not characterize all marginalized countries at all times. Consequently a dichotomous distinction between hegemony and non-hegemony is insufficient to comprehend societies that have at different times achieved stability, despite their marginalized place in the world order. It is therefore useful to conceptualize the space between hegemony and crisis in terms of the condition of hegemony, rather than its presence or absence. With regard to countries such as Mexico, we might inquire as to the condition of hegemony at the margins. In other words, to what extent is the general interest perceived as being shared, and if it is, how is that perception created? What has been the role of working-class organizations in revealing the unequal and unsupportable aspects of globalization, and thus challenging the hegemonic project?

Consequently it is not the presence or absence of hegemonic historical structures that we look for, but signs of whether hegemony is waxing or waning. With this emphasis on the rise and decline of hegemony it is more likely that shall look for the ways in which subordinated groups continually test the boundaries of the relationship, assert their presence and challenge their opponents, whether or not the order is characterized by the active consent, passive resistance, militant organization or armed rebellion of the subordinated groups in society. These are the social forces that may reveal the contradictions in historical structures through their active and self-conscious forms of organization. If we consider the condition of hegemony, then, we are more likely to take seriously the role of oppositional social forces in challenging the boundaries of unequal social relations over time and in ways that do not always depend on cataclysmic events.

From a Gramscian perspective the concept of hegemony is meant to explain the more complex phenomena described by the 'consent given by the great masses of the population to the general direction imposed on social life by the dominant fundamental group' (Gramsci, 1971, p. 12). This is not the realist's version of hegemony as dominance. Rather a Gramscian view of hegemony rests upon the balance of consent and coercion that is achieved when even the subordinated groups in society support the order. If we consider the constant interplay between coercion and consent within the condition of hegemony we can evaluate the changing balance between them. As Augelli and Murphy (1993, p. 128) put it, 'these two forms of rule are mutually supportive and often combine in ambiguous ways'.

The strength of this definition rests on Gramsci's recognition of the agency of subordinated groups within a hegemonic structure. Here agency does not rest outside a structure but is an aspect of the social relations upon which structures are built. This may explain why the efforts, consciousness and self-organization of subordinated groups may at times stabilize a hegemonic structure. For example the strongest labour groups may support the order not because they are passive but because they perceive that their interests and the interests of their members will be furthered if they consent to the basic tenets of the order. This provides a partial explanation of why labour resistance movements can be defeated within their own organizations. Even when oppositional movements take power within a union, their contestation may abate when presented with an officially sanctioned model of labour relations. Hegemony depends on the ability of dominant groups to provide the intellectual and moral leadership required to produce widespread support for the order. This suggests something more complex than simple co-optation.

The concept of hegemony is relevant not only to national societies. Neo-Gramscians concerned with questions of world order have argued that a hegemonic world order was achieved after 1945 when the US made its particular interests appear to be in the general interest (for example Murphy, 1994). The convergence of ideas about economic development among the elites of the continent has been one of the most enduring characteristics of US hegemonic power (Cox, 1987).

Gramsci's concept of passive revolution offers insights into how, in the era of *Pax Americana*, such a convergence was reflected in peripheral societies such as Mexico.

Passive revolution and crisis in Mexico

Passive revolution

A hegemonic society can have an impact on other societies if the ideas and practices of the dominant class in the most powerful state are transmitted to less powerful states. According to Gramsci a passive revolution is present when:

> the impetus of progress is not tightly linked to a vast local development which is artificially limited and repressed, but is instead the reflection of international developments which transmit their ideological currents to the periphery – currents born on the basis of the productive development of the more advanced countries – then the group which is the bearer of the new ideas is not the economic group but the intellectual stratum, and the conception of the State advocated by them changes aspect; it is conceived of as something in itself, as a rational absolute. (Gramsci, 1971, pp. 116–17; see also Cox, 1993, p. 59)

For Gramsci, when elements of a new order are brought into a social formation from the outside, the emerging class may be unable to transform the old order fully. Although popular forces could not drive the transformation, neither would dominant forces emerge to lead society into the new moment. Rather the social order would appear more like an impasse (Gramsci, 1971, p. 54). Under conditions of passive revolution, the 'State which, even though it had limitations as a power "led" the group which should have been "leading" and was able to put at the latter's disposal an army and a politico-diplomatic strength' (ibid., p. 105).

Hegemony is not necessarily created under the leadership of the bourgeoisie during the emergence of the liberal state in peripheral countries (Cox, 1993). First of all, in the transition between the revolutionary direct frontal attack on the state and the struggle for hegemony in civil society, older social relations may be reconstituted and previous structures restored. It is possible that hegemony might be slow in coming or may not emerge at all. Again the concept of passive revolution is illuminating. Following a period of crisis and social upheaval, as Buci-Glucksmann (1980) argues, passive revolution may become the specific way in which the bourgeoisie continue to mount their struggle for a fully hegemonic capitalist society.

Although Gramsci was reflecting upon the particular historical experience of fascism in Italy in the 1930s, certain parallels were apparent in Mexico at the same time. Mexico was extraordinarily stable during the midtwentieth century but it was not hegemonic. Passive revolution emerged as an attempt to shape international dynamics to national priorities, first through the idealism of the Revolutionary Constitution and then under the direction of the Partido Revolucionario Institucional (PRI) in the 1930s. The ideological dimension of passive revolution reflected ideals constructed in combination with nationalist guarantees and internationalized production patterns that changed in relation to practices in the US. As late as the 1930s, however, Mexican structures of representation suggested that the active consent of the subordinated social groups had yet to be secured. Stability was achieved when the Mexican state presented itself in nationalist terms. By the middle of the twentieth century Mexican state leaders and the dominant class were able to argue that they had been successful in regulating the expansion of US influence in Mexican society and in the economy in particular. This idea, and the material conditions and institutions that went along with it, moved Mexico from a situation of open civil war (1910–17) to a period of stability that lasted from the 1930s to the late 1960s. This period can be characterized as one in which the passive revolution came to be temporarily institutionalized.

In Mexico passive revolution was not constructed entirely on the basis of capitalist class relations. Rather social relations other than class were central to stability in the middle part of the twentieth century. It was not just the state but also patriarchal historical structures, fashioned under colonialism and woven into capitalist society, that formed an important part of the passive revolution and stabilized Mexican society for much of the twentieth century. Moreover a particular form of hegemonic masculinity ensured that passive revolution was not blocked by patriarchal social forces, such as landowners or *caudillos*, as the latter were incorporated into the new social order in a manner that ruling groups found beneficial. When we look at the relative place of consent and coercion in historical structures to see whether or not they were hegemonic, we can look for their gendered counterparts in paternalism and authoritarianism.

Crisis

Along with hegemony and passive revolution there may also be a crisis of historical structures within the condition of hegemony. Such crises do not arise from the deterioration of material conditions only. They may also involve the discrediting of dominant ideas, as well as institutional impasses that combine to create a crisis of representation – that is, an irreconciled dissonance in the way that subjects identify themselves and their conditions, and the way in which these are represented in the paradigms of state and dominant civil societal institutions. In Mexico since 1968, the crisis has challenged the 'common sense' that informed the previous social compromise and intersubjective meanings corresponding to the passive revolution. The ascendance of neoliberalism has meant that the ideological basis of the old institutions has been called into question, while new forms of representation are either not yet accepted or have been rejected.

An extended crisis of representation is part of a deepening organic crisis. Such a crisis arises when:

> the ruling class has failed in some major political undertaking for which it has requested, or forcibly extracted, the consent of the broad masses (war, for example), or because huge masses (especially of peasants and petit-bourgeois intellectuals) have passed suddenly from a state of political passivity to a certain activity, and put forward demands which taken together, albeit not organically formulated, add up to a revolution. A 'crisis of authority' is spoken of: this is precisely the crisis of hegemony, or general crisis of the State. (Gramsci, 1971, p. 210)

As this quotation suggests, organic crises often emerge at moments when there are wider crises of world order. Thus given the simultaneous transformations that took place in *Pax Americana* and within Mexico, we need to explain Mexico's experience from the mid 1960s not only in national terms but also in terms of global processes.

By the end of the twentieth century the crisis in Mexico was of such proportions that Mexican society could be described as non-hegemonic at the time when NAFTA came into effect. By any measure, by the end of 1993 the set of institutions, social relations and ideas that once characterized the passive revolution had come apart, leaving Mexico in the throes of one of the most inconclusive moments of its history. This view of crisis emerges out of an analysis of historical structure and is located within the condition of hegemony.

The exhaustion of the passive revolution and its patriarchal construction of male workers as 'worker-fathers' became apparent in the late 1960s. Hegemonic masculinity, which had incorporated aspects of *caudillismo* into institutions of governance as well as ideological appeals to revolutionary nationalism, was called into question.[1] In part the crisis had structural and economic sources: the highly favoured masculine production pattern of state corporatism (discussed below) was contributing to the worsening economic conditions associated with the progressive stagnation of import-substitution industrialization. However the crisis also had politico-ideological sources, as indicated by the rise of subordinated groups and social movements that challenged the terms of the passive revolution and demanded autonomy and democracy. The massacre of unarmed students in Tlatelolco in 1968 is seen as a watershed, but the crisis of representation also extended deeply into parts of the labour movement. Movements calling for trade union independence challenged corporatism as well as the state's legitimacy as the guarantor of revolutionary ideals, and that demanded effective representation by union leaders.

The first attempt by state actors to respond to the crisis of *Desarrollo Estabilizador* (Stabilized Development) under the paternalistic terms of President Echeverría's social reforms failed to reconcile economic and legitimacy imperatives. On the one hand the cap on taxation – intended to encourage private investment – caused a shortage of credit to meet government expenditure so the government instead sought international credit and foreign investment. However because of profit repatriation this strategy increased the pressure on the current account (Sepúlveda and Chumacero, 1973; Aguilar García, 1984; Bennett and Sharpe, 1985; Álvarez Béjar, 1987) and caused – together with the external effects of 'Reaganomics' – the debt crisis in the 1980s. On the other hand the social reforms, subject to economic constraints, failed to integrate subordinate social forces. The reforms sought to rebuild the social compromise by expanding the internal market, redistributing income and extending public services and the social security system. However these initiatives depended on the gendered relations of the family and the social construction of the worker-father (Echeverría Álvarez, 1974). This construction increased the dependence of family members who were not considered to be workers, while exerting a disciplinary effect on those who were employed. In the wake of a stagnating economy, once a worker-father became unemployed his social benefits were lost, and since there was no unemployment insurance the loss of a job meant economic destitution for an entire family. Health care and housing rights were social rights based on the wage relationship.

Subordinated groups continued to mobilize as real incomes fell and unemployment rose to unprecedented heights in the 1970s. Labour groups organized legal and illegal strikes, and challenged the state corporatist leadership on local and regional levels. The wide variety of oppositional movements opened up divisions in the historical bloc that could not be reconciled by the PRI. However these mobilizations failed to forge a sufficiently strong counterhegemony. Their lasting significance lies in the shifting of the political terrain of conflict among social forces. In this sense militant labour movements were protagonists within the conditions of crisis. The severity of economic chaos and political turmoil indicated that the passive revolution would not be easily constituted, if at all. Indeed as the 1970s came to a close it seemed that authoritarianism rather than paternalism would be more able to resolve the immediate difficulties for the state (La Botz, 1988).

While subordinated groups continued to mobilize around the limits of the reform programme, the increasingly internationalized dominant groups came to resent the inflation and increased debt load. Consistent with Gramsci's concept of crisis of representation, the decomposition of historical blocs occasioned a recomposition of politics as established political parties became 'mummified and anachronistic' (Gramsci, 1971, p. 211). In the process ruling groups were freed from their attachment to the broader society and became not only unrepresentative but dominating and coercive as well. At the same time it would be a mistake to speak of this long crisis as if it were marked by excessive fragility on the part of state institutions. Many observers have noted the remarkable resilience of the governing PRI even after 1968 (Adler Hellman, 1983; Middlebrook, 1995).

Landowners and large agroindustrialists were disaffected by land reform (Adler Hellman, 1983), while industrialists began to convert their currency to dollars, fearing a devaluation of the peso (Alvarez, 1987). International capital exerted its dominance over the economy by forcing devaluation on 31 August 1976. A subsequent stabilization agreement with the IMF moved the economy further into the international sphere and state interventionist policies were abandoned in favour of a new phase of austerity. Where an expanding economy had once offered workers increased wages and state services, the López Portillo years saw the first moves towards trade liberalization, privatization and cuts to government spending, which started the trajectory that would continue in the 1980s and 1990s with structural adjustment programmes and culminate in the signing of NAFTA. With the outward turn, Mexican workers faced the disciplinary dynamics of the international market and these was increased repression of oppositional labour movements. Given the serious implications of unemployment, the costs of dissent were evident to any Mexican trade unionist engaged in an oppositional movement.

If there was one common understanding that emerged as a result of the failure of paternalism and the move towards authoritarianism, it was that reconstruction of the passive revolution was not in the offing. For the country's political elite the question was: upon what basis might a social compromise be reinvigorated? For the subordinated groups, the struggle for a form of social expression that could surmount and transform the crisis persisted.

Social relations of production in Mexico's passive revolution and crisis

One way of thinking about the crisis is to assess the condition of hegemony as it was manifested in production patterns. This requires an historical perspective. In the nineteenth century labour relations in Mexico were largely characterized by employers having direct power over workers in the form of the enterprise pattern. The 1917 constitution, which emerged out of the revolution, offered political actors an alternative in the form of the corporate pattern. This did not really become a stable institution in Mexico, but its powerful ideology was laid down in the constitution. Since the promise of paternalistic economic development under cooperative social relations was not realized in the period after the revolution, the social relations underpinning large-scale production came to be increasingly regulated by state corporatism. While labour organizations were accepted as legitimate entities under this state corporatism, they were not meant to mobilize workers in support of their collective interests and were subordinate to the national interest.

The legitimacy of the corporate pattern of social relations of production depended on both nationalism and paternalism, but it proved unstable and ephemeral. In the period immediately following the revolution, no coherent historical bloc was prepared to translate legitimate constitutional proclamations into a hegemonic order. It could be said, therefore, that a non-hegemonic situation existed. Social and military conflict persisted until the mid 1930s, when the developmental form of the state was consolidated. Despite persistent crises, however, some social practices remained deeply rooted in Mexican society. In other words, although many ideas lost their legitimacy during the non-hegemonic period, other gendered practices and shared meanings persisted many years after the onset of the prolonged crises. After the revolution, Mexican politics continued to be influenced by highly gendered social relations.

The transition from crisis to passive revolution depended on three dimensions of gender that developed in succession. These were (1) the paternalistic ideology incorporated into the constitution of 1917, in which the family, rather than the individual or class, was constructed as the basic unit of society; (2) institutionalized *caudillismo* as the hegemonic masculinity within the state and expressed through the power of the federal executive, the official union leadership and the universal father-worker; and (3) the masculinized character of the productive pattern favoured by the state and exemplified in the automotive industry (Healy, 1999).

With this pattern, while the idea of the workplace as a productive community gave way to more clearly defined social relations, the importance of the working-class family persisted. The revolutionary institutions of labour law organized a gendered terrain of labour struggle in which the gendered division of labour was strictly enforced. Women were excluded from the most favoured production pattern, under which the established male worker and the family wage were championed by the state.

Labour was now highly regulated by federal employment law, and official trade unions were more likely to present the demands of the state and capital to the workers than the other way round. At times, however, workers' militancy compelled the state to institutionalize some significant employment provisions for the worker-father in exchange for cooperation with the PRI. The state negotiated the terms of investment by both national and foreign capitalists and regulated labour through its ample legal framework. The benefits were not generalized. Given the highly skewed distribution of income and polarized class structure, indigenous peoples, peasants and women workers involved in other production patterns paid dearly for industrialization on these terms.

The masculinized and mestizo character of the automotive industry was apparent in its relation to other devalued productive patterns, such as the household and peasant agriculture. Even the Mexicanized car parts sector was subordinate to foreign assemblers. Technological innovations in the automotive industry set the pace for technological change elsewhere, as did patterns of work organization. The assemblers were concentrated in the industrial heartland of the country. To the extent that other production patterns were incorporated into the social formation, they supported the growing industrial base while their subordinate status was reinforced by regionalism. In addition patterns of class power, including the management structure and labour relations, depended on the paternalism and authoritarianism of *caudillismo* as the hegemonic masculinity. Feminized work and other devalued masculine productive patterns were constructed in opposition to this structure. Unequal gendered social relations were at the heart of a social order in which only a small and privileged sector of the population benefited from economic growth.

This social formation had a spatial dimension. In Mexico the consolidation of industrial production in the Valle de México accompanied the centralist patterns of corporatist development. A centrist ideology of participation became the national myth to which the state referred when defending the uneven outcomes of economic development. For example the national health care programme for workers in the private sector only applied to a minority of workers, most of whom were concentrated in the federal district. Moreover government leaders argued that the revolution was still in progress, that as descendants of the great heroes they were charged with the historic role of defending the revolution and over time, improving the situation for workers, peasants and employers, as set down in the constitution.

Working-class men in the Mexican automotive industry may have been considered to epitomize the relatively protected, well-paid worker with stable employment, but they continued to be subordinated, not only by their transnational employers but also by the state via the official labour movement. Hence we must not suppose that the 'Mexican miracle' was a golden age for workers. Car workers, together with textile workers, teachers, miners and railway workers, challenged the power of the official labour leaders and ushered in a period of national effervescence that began in the late 1950s and lasted until the organic crisis of the 1970s, as noted in the previous section.

In addition the passive revolution limited activities by social forces to those officially defined as legitimate collective identities. The popular discourse of the revolution persisted, but inclusion was limited to social forces within the official realm. Indigenous peoples were not present in corporatist structures, neither were women, the urban poor or workers in the informal economy. By the 1960s the degree of state violence to suppress popular demands had become incongruous with a stable society. With both the material and the ideological underpinnings of state corporatism weakened, the historical inequalities that existed between social forces in the Mexican political and economic structures could no longer be legitimated.

At present the productive pattern most favoured by capital and the state in Mexico is increasingly characterized by a combination of earlier material, institutional and ideological conditions and could be referred to as 'global corporatism'. In institutional terms the corporatist relationship between state institutions and officially sanctioned labour bodies continues to be used as a device for political domination in a non-hegemonic context to prevent democratic, independent and autonomous labour movements from emerging. The cooperative ideology of the corporate pattern and the family has re-emerged with the imposition of new forms of work organization and new representative structures within the workplace. The ideological commitment to cooperation is highly paternalistic, yet workers are subject to ruthless labour relations and gendered inequalities that structure an internationalized production system with dynamics arising outside the national context. The new pattern depends on authoritarianism by the state and employers as they deepen the integration of North America under NAFTA and other neoliberal trade and investment agreements. Through a brutal process, aspects of the enterprise pattern have also been reintroduced into the industrial heartland. The traditional labour rights once guaranteed to the worker-father no longer exist.

Global corporatism embodies the demand for flexibility, productivity and multitasking that global competitiveness demands of the working class. It rejects the legitimacy of both bipartite and tripartite production relations. Even solidarity is redefined under global corporatism as the responsibility of individual team members to one another and to the company. However, more than a decade after the imposition of NAFTA there are few signs that the crisis in Mexican production will be resolved by this new pattern. The next subsection will explore in further detail the current politics of production. It analyzes the gendered patterns of social relations of production, with special reference to the automotive industry.

Maquilization and labour militancy: the restructuring of gender and production patterns

In the 1980s the challenge to what remained of the state corporatist production pattern emerged from a double process aimed at restructuring the US and Mexican economies. Restructuring included the internationalization of production, the transformation of the state and the reorganization of work.

Austerity and restructuring came to dominate the setting of national priorities during the 1980s, not because of an inexorable process but because of the way in which dominant class priorities were reflected within and were reproduced by the state. In this period the coercive aspects of governing overcame any restrained appeal to paternalism. Radical social movements refused to accept a new social compromise under these conditions but there was no sign of a renewed passive revolution to overcome the political crisis. In fact the repression of oppositional movements increased as the state tried to force through the neoliberal agenda. Even though new social forces emerged among the urban poor and electoral contestation became a viable terrain of political struggle, the democratic trade union movements were consistently crushed.

The *Maquiladoras* originated in the mid 1960s, when the Mexican Border Industrialization Programme (BIP) replaced the 20-year-old Mexican Labour Programme, under which Mexican male farmworkers (*braceros*) had been encouraged to work in the US (Nash and Fernández-Kelly, 1983). When the agreement between the US and Mexico ended in 1964, 200,000 *braceros* were suddenly unemployed. Militancy by new peasant organizations and unemployment of up to 50 per cent in the border towns heightened the pressure on the state to respond to the worsening situation (Bustamante, 1983). The *Maquiladoras*, or 'in-bond plants', were developed according to a twinning arrangement with factories on the US side of the border. The Mexican government was keen to attract light assembly industries to the region, and therefore the laws restricting foreign ownership were lifted and domestic content levels were never imposed on these industries.

Labour relations in the *maquilas* resembled the enterprise pattern and were largely characterized by employers exerting power over workers. The BIP never resolved the problem of male unemployment in northern Mexico, since employers preferred female workers. Employment was unstable, and workers were subject to plant closures (Bustamante, 1983). Even so a shell of state corporatism was deployed to enforce the labour relations. Furthermore, as Fernández-Kelly (Nash and Fernández-Kelly, 1983) has shown, women's employment in the *maquila* industries did not change their subordinate position in Mexican society.

Most trade unions in the *maquilas* were oriented towards the objectives of the employer, rather than the workers' interests. Employers sought collective agreements with official unions so as to protect themselves against democratic labour movements. In turn these agreements offered the unions an important regional presence they otherwise would not have had (Carrillo and de la O, 1992).

There was another gendered dimension to this story. Although the *maquiladora* programme appeared to respond to issues that were specific to the northern border region, in fact it was closely related to problems in the industrial core in the centre of the country. In a spatial sense, as well as in terms of the dominant economic model, the *maquilas* were marginalized. Nonetheless the *maquiladoras*, a particular form of the enterprise pattern, offered a partial resolution to one of the central problems associated with import substitution under state corporatism; the automotive sector yielded a chronic balance of payments deficit (ibid., p. 6). By promoting the *maquiladora* programme the Mexican government expected to gain in terms of technology transfer, employment, foreign exchange and income generation in the border region (Bustamante, 1983). If the export-oriented *maquiladora* industries could replenish the national balance sheets with foreign exchange drained by the import-substituting industries they would serve an important function. This was far from a marginal initiative. The first *maquilas* were meant to complement state corporatism. In Mexico the verb *maquilar* means 'to assemble', while the verb *maquinar* means 'to machine'; the first is a highly feminized production operation while the second is highly masculinized. The similarity between the two verbs evokes the relationship the two forms of industrial production have had over time.

Whether or not the new export-processing zones would meet the government's economic objectives, the *maquilas* did respond to the crisis of legitimacy faced by dominant groups in Mexico. The new border industrialization programme showed them to be actively seeking out modern solutions to serious regional and national problems. The BIP met some of the ideological as well as material objectives of dominant groups as the limitations of import substitution became apparent. Not only did dominant groups argue in favour of a solution to the crisis that would not threaten their unequally high social standing, but also this strategy depended on the reproduction in the workplace of social practices that subordinated women workers to the demands of the 'common good'.

No longer restricted to the border areas, in the 1980s the *maquilas* began to lose their enclave status in the national economy, although this was not because they had provided backward and forward linkages or a solution to the country's employment problem, and certainly not because of the value they had added to the Mexican economy (Instituto Nacional de Estadística, Geografía e Informática, 1991). The physical relocation of the *maquilas* was not the most significant transformation, rather it was the ideological power of the transformation that we must acknowledge. The fact that the *maquilas* came to exist alongside old industries in the centre of the country bolstered the determination with which labour rights were dismantled in Mexico.

The *maquilas* represented a threat to established industrial male workers, who did not consider the opportunity for gendered solidarity when they witnessed economic restructuring with a feminized face in their workplace. The *maquilas* are critical to our analysis because theirs was the image in which labour relations were remade in Mexico. It was a gendered image and one that continues to divide workers both in Mexico and in North America in general.

In the car assembly plants in the centre of the country – a sector oriented towards production for the domestic market – the old plants were compelled to improve their productivity with a relatively minimal addition of new technologies (Arteaga *et al.*, 1989). The old plants did not disappear as a result of the transformations in the industry. Rather they too were reshaped. The assembly and parts industries became more and more like one another, and this was what some observers have come to call *maquilización* or 'maquilization' (Ramirez, 1988). The reclassification of jobs and skill, the intensification of work and the reduction of wages became the basis for international competitiveness (Arteaga *et al.*, 1989; Carillo, 1990). Together these factors were successful in bringing about higher productivity in the industry, but at a high cost to workers.

Struggles over maquilization in the Mexican automotive industry

This process was not left unchallenged by workers, who resisted restructuring as part of their contestation of the crisis of representation. This 'politics of production' can be analyzed in terms of Gramsci's three moments of relations of force. In the Mexican automotive industry these were elements of these three moments but they did not appear in neat stages from economic-corporate, to class solidarity, to political hegemony. Rather in real time and space the three stages were organically but unevenly linked, and they conditioned one another and had profound consequences for the strategies the social forces chose to pursue.

It was this unevenness that caused some of the most difficult challenges for social forces that had accepted the general framework of the previous compromise and their subordinate position within it. Their position in the newly emerging order was not yet determined and their ability to maintain a space for themselves during the crisis was partly conditioned by the extent to which the leadership of subordinated groups included, excluded or dominated their constituents in the previous order. For the subordinated groups the crisis became both a moment of opportunity and a necessity, during which time they had to organize to articulate their demands.

During such crises it is not always clear whether social movements will fight for the transformation of structures or for re-establishment of the old order. At the same time groups that were marginalized from the previous structures of representation may organize to subvert the internal hierarchies of their own organizations. This raises the possibility of social transformation, which for neo-Gramscians means the creation of a counterhegemony.

In Mexico, gender was a significant source of unequal power relations in these struggles. As the Volkswagen workers took up their struggle against neoliberalism, masculine authority was exerted through the office of the national presidency, which in turn faced unprecedented challenges to its position as the epitome of *caudillismo* during the 1990s. However the emblematic story of the Nissan workers' movement in the 1970s in Cuernavaca, Morelos, for example, shows that the ideology of trade union *caudillismo* could be reproduced in independent unions, despite the illegitimacy of the old trade union bureaucrats. Even though local community and regional labour leaders supported the workers in the plant, in the end this broadly based social unionism was defeated by a narrowly defined trade unionism that had become independent of the official labour organization, as well as reliant upon gendered practices relating to representation and closely associated with the modernization strategies of the employer and the state.

After 1968 the fact that masculinized workers' movements left the social relations of gender unproblematized meant that their efforts to contest the terms of crisis was seriously weakened. Gender was not made visible in contestations by oppositional social forces during this period of crisis, restructuring and globalization. By not politicizing the transformation of patterns of social relations of production in gendered terms, unions did not challenge the separate and unequal treatment of women workers, permitting the gendered division of labour in the household to justify the gendered division of labour in the paid labour force. The result was the failure, 'ethico-politically', to prevent the restructured production relations from pricing the worker-father out of the market in favour of the *maquila* girl. Hence neither the disintegration of the worker-father model, nor the feminization of manufacturing in general, were seen in relation to the way in which working-class men and women were divided by gender inequalities.

This process is illustrated most eloquently by the story of the Democratic Movement of Ford Workers as it confronted the deepening economic and political crisis in the 1980s. The movement grew increasingly conscious of the broad implications of its struggle and became a significant example of workers' efforts to contest the restructuring process at the level of class. However, here too the gendered character of the leading productive pattern conditioned the struggle, and rendered it much less effective as it faced the process of feminization or maquilization.

Labour conflict at Ford de México-Cuautitlán

The conflict at Ford-Cuautitlán centred on the character of working-class representation in state corporatism as this productive pattern, already in crisis, became more like the enterprise pattern. The state would no longer guarantee the minimal concessions through which the worker-father had been constructed. In this period the Confederación de Trabajadores de México (CTM) attempted to reassert its presence as a legitimate organization within the PRI, which was choosing new interlocutors in the realm of labour relations. Increasingly the CTM resorted to authoritarianism to hold on to its members, thus indicating that institutions of representation could no longer depend on their traditional bases.

For the most part the state supported the CTM against internal reform movements and heavily repressed oppositional labour and social movements. A significant reduction of wages and benefits was one of the consequences, although the expansion of management rights went beyond this. It was not just the lower wage bill, the possibility of relocation to northern greenfield sites or state support that benefited employers, but also the debilitation of labour representation meant that unions were unable to contest the reorganization of work. Employers prized the flexible nature of the new labour relations above all else. This social dimension is indispensable for understanding the reasons for the creation of new export-oriented plants in Mexico. It is also significant for understanding the demands that competition in the US market imposed on them (Arteaga *et al.*, 1989).

While in the earlier period the limits of passive revolution had enlivened oppositional movements within the unions, economic restructuring in the 1980s attacked acquired rights. The CTM leadership did not defend workers' rights, even though the *raison d'être* of the trade union was bound up with state corporatism. Instead the leadership presided over the dissolution of this masculine pattern and the incorporation of the feminized characteristics of the *maquila* pattern into the industrial centre. The movement of Ford workers, as it resisted the restructuring of production relations, was also a movement of resistance against the authoritarian *caudillismo* of the official trade union leadership. The Ford workers' movement was remarkable for its ability to analyze and organize on a number of levels over a relatively long period. The workers in this movement demonstrated a highly developed class consciousness in which they problematized questions of representation in relation to the need for a transformation of the form of the state. Their internationalism was in the service of this goal. Their direct challenge to the CTM was not an interunion dispute but a contestation of internationalized production relations within the terrain of the state itself. However the structures and transformation were not politicized in gendered terms.

The Ford Motor Company undertook to restructure its Mexican operations by first closing down two plants in the old industrial centre of the country. The Cuautitlán plant was spared, but the bulk of new investment went to an engine plant in Chihuahua and an assembly plant in Hermosillo (Arteaga, 1990). At the heart of Ford's restructuring process was the dismantling of the labour relations regime that had been constructed under state corporatism. This had implications for all three of Ford's Mexican assembly plants, as well as its parts suppliers and *maquilas*. Before the new northern plants were opened, Ford signed collective agreements with the National Union of Ford Workers, an affiliate of the CTM, and workers were organized into local unions at Ford-Cuautitlán in the central State of Mexico, Ford-Hermosillo in Sonora and Ford-Chihuahua in Chihuahua. Because of the collective agreements these factories were opened under conditions of maximum flexibility, including a steep reduction of the number of job classifications, for example to just one at the Hermosillo plant. By signing the collective agreements the National Union relinquished rights that had been acquired over years of struggle in the industrial centre of the country and undermined the strongest collective agreement in the automotive industry, that of the Cuautitlán plant in the State of Mexico. From the perspective of the Ford Motor Company, it was imperative that a new collective agreement be written for the Cuautitlán plant as well (ibid.).

Although the same union represented the workers in all three plants, they all had different contracts with different expiry dates. The fact that higher wages were paid to workers in the older plant in the state of Mexico was cause for discontent and mobilization in the newer northern operations. Wages at the Cuautitlán plant were 103.5 per cent higher than the average wage paid to workers at Ford-Chihuahua and 126.5 per cent higher than that paid to assembly workers at Ford-Hermosillo (ibid.). In part the strong collective agreement at Ford Cuautitlán reflected the age of the workers, who were well established and had built up years of seniority under the model of rights acquired by the worker-father. In Ford, as well as in other automotive companies, managers sought to enhance their control over the production process by changing the composition of the labour force in the plants (Carrillo, 1990).

The existence of the strong collective agreement at Ford-Cuautitlán was the central issue in a protracted conflict between management and the local union during the 1987 contract negotiations (Arteaga, 1990). In the summer of 1987 the federal government decreed emergency minimum wage increases for non-union workers and announced that increases in unionized workplaces would be negotiated between the employers and workers. With the National Union Executive pressing for an increase of 53 per cent, the Ford-Cuautitlán workers went on strike. The workers at Ford-Hermosillo and Ford-Chihuahua were granted the increase but went out on strike in solidarity with the Cuautitlán workers. As the strike moved into its second month the company announced it would close the Cuautitlán plant and terminate the contracts of all workers. Some argued that the conflict had been provoked by the National Union leadership and the company in order to create an impasse (ibid.). The secretary general of the National Executive Committee agreed to accept severances and the company dismissed the 3,200 workers (Talavera and Muñoz, 1993).

Less than three months later the company resumed operations in Cuautitlán and rehired 2,500 employees. By firing the workers and reopening the plant under a new collective agreement the management was able to change the character of the labour relations that had developed since 1964, when the plant was first opened. As a result the workers immediately went from holding the best contract with respect to employment rights in the country's automotive industry, to holding the worst (Arteaga, 1990). After the conflict at Ford Cuautitlán, skill levels and the number of job classifications were reduced (Carrillo, 1990), and seniority rights were replaced by management control over remuneration and job changes (Arteaga *et al.*, 1989). Moreover collective rewards were replaced by rewards for individual performance and productivity; negotiated productivity levels were replaced by management-dictated levels of productivity and efficiency; and management claimed the right to introduce productivity, quality and training programmes (Carrillo, 1990). Thus the collective agreement at Ford-Cuautitlán now conformed to the model of lean production that had been introduced in the north of Mexico.

When the workers returned to Ford they were told that a 'new Ford' now existed. Only uninjured workers were rehired. Conditions in the plant deteriorated in respect of workers' daily experience and high stress levels soon became evident. Ford was able to alter the working conditions in the plant by unilaterally asserting control over the production process, and as a result the stable labour relations that had existed under the old conditions disappeared. The company responded to dissent in two ways. First, the management introduced selective dismissals, and was able to do so easily since all workers were on temporary contracts. Second, the company instituted weekly quality-circle meetings in order to impress upon workers that it was in their self-interest to improve the plant's competitiveness. In effect the 'flattening' of labour relations devolved more responsibility to workers but reduced their control over the production process (Talavera and Muñoz, 1993).

Although Fidel Velázquez, president of the CTM, had appointed a new National Executive Committee for the National Union of Ford Workers, the resistance in the Cuautitlán plant was strong enough to ensure that the local union leadership was elected democratically after the plant reopened. This Local Executive Committee (LEC) mounted a campaign to challenge the unrepresentative character of the National Union. With the March 1989 contract negotiations approaching, the LEC convened a general assembly at which the workers elected representatives from each of the branches of the Cuautitlán plant. By forming a negotiating committee for the 1989 round of bargaining, the local leadership issued a direct challenge to the national leadership of the union as well as the company. Both Ford and the National Executive refused to recognize the negotiating committee, and the former argued that the committee should be formed by 'members of the union', which in contract language meant the National Executive Committee.[2] When this dispute was brought to the labour courts it was Ford's definition that was upheld (Arteaga, 1990).

The conflict between the local and national committees became irreconcilable as the local executive at Cuautitlán continued to demand democratic representation at the national level. On 17 June 1989 the local union held an assembly and declared its intention to campaign for the direct election of a new National Committee at the forthcoming congress of union delegates from the three Ford plants. A week later all the members of the LEC were fired from the plant (Abogado, 1992). The other workers responded by shutting down the plant.

Freed from the need to deal with the complaints from Cuautitlán, the union congress was held in July 1989 under the control of the national union and the CTM. In the lead-up to the congress the secretary-general of the National Union presented workers with an advance on their portion of the profit share, which in normal circumstances would have been allocated at the end of December. Although the advances had been distributed outside the legal provisions for the distribution of profits, the secretary-general's 'gift' ensured his continuation in his post and provided the company with a method of reducing dissent during a highly conflictual moment (Arteaga, 1990).

During the congress the delegates approved modifications to the statutes that governed the activities and role of the union. These had considerable implications for representation at the local level. One of the most significant changes was that to the definition of union member. To date union members had been defined as 'those workers who have offered their services to the Ford Motor Company in the automotive industry, in present installations or any that are established in the Mexican Republic in the future' (Article 51). In the July 1989 revision a sentence was added that blurred the definition. Along with *miembro* (member) the union added the category of *socio* (associate) to its constitution. Such associates could be either temporary or permanent. This formalized the union's acceptance of temporary workers and created a two-tiered structure of more and less entitled members of the union. By accepting the language of lean production the union also accepted the management's right to impose conditions that would foster insecurity among workers.

While most of the fired LEC members at Cuautitlán accepted their dismissal and took severance pay, some began a campaign to demand their reinstatement, believing that the problem required a political solution (Arteaga, 1990). By the end of 1989 there had been a series of unresolved conflicts in the Cuautitlán plant and labour relations were unstable. The conflict intensified when the company paid a very low profit share to the workers because tax had been deducted and the amount had been reduced to reflect the earlier payment. The infuriated workers initiated a wildcat strike and immediately elected a negotiating committee composed of 17 workers and five of the fired LEC members. The committee demanded an increased profit share and threatened to change labour centrals if the CTM did not take a harder line with the company (ibid.).

In response the company imposed a technical shutdown and closed the plant for longer than usual during the Christmas holidays. The conflict turned into a very violent confrontation. On 4 January the company circulated a letter in which it stated that 'outsiders had been attempting to destabilize production in the plant and distort information' (Talavera and Muñoz, 1993, pp. 51–3). The management members argued that they had nothing to do with the conflict and that it was an intra-union matter in which they would not involve themselves. Later the company was compelled to intervene since the workers refused to work until those who had been arrested were released. The latter were released and immediately took their demands to the Human Rights Commission in Mexico City (Arteaga, 1990).

On 8 January thugs were waiting when the workers arrived at the plant. They beat the workers with pistols, tubes and sticks, and then began shooting. One worker, Cleto Nigmo Urbina, was killed and ten others were wounded. Workers later reported that the armed band of thugs had entered the plant wearing company uniforms and badges that identified them as Ford workers. During the subsequent court cases, workers took some of the identification badges to court and showed that they lacked the federal registration number that appeared on all workers' badges. They argued that no one but the Ford Motor Company could have provided the thugs with the badges and uniforms (Talavera and Muñoz, 1993). Although the workers had captured three of the men involved in the assault, not one was brought to trial.

After the assault the company announced that work would be stopped until it could guarantee secure working conditions, whereupon workers occupied the factory. On 22 January more than 3,000 police were sent to remove them. After these events the Cuautitlán workers saw the negotiating committee (CN) as their only legitimate representative. Even though it existed outside the formal union structure, the CN was recognized in Mexico as the leadership of the Ford workers movement (Arteaga, 1990). In the US and Canada the CN became known as the leadership of the Ford Workers Democratic Movement (FWDM). The CN fought a long legal battle contesting the lack of representation within the union and the state. It fought for the reinstatement of fired workers, a political solution to the conflict and a new definition of solidarity within the context of North American integration. Their battle culminated in June 1991 in a referendum at the plant on union affiliation. A committee of independent observers, made up of trade unionists, lawyers and social activists from across Mexico and North America, argued that the ballot was not a secret one and declared the vote null and void.[3] But with the threat of mass dismissals and having once again lost the hearing into their appeal, the leaders of the democratic movement came to the end of their struggle. For Ford workers, economic restructuring meant the maquilization of the industrial heartland of Mexico.

Conclusion

Using the concept of 'condition of hegemony' we can conceptualize hegemony, passive revolution and crisis in such a way as to make apparent the continuities and disjunctures with previous orders. This permits a clearer view of the ongoing and less dramatic efforts of subordinated social forces to contest the processes that weaken or strengthen hegemony. These concepts are most helpful when applied to specific historical circumstances and the efforts of oppositional working-class movements to transform production patterns. They are usefully described in relation to the paternalistic and authoritarian dimensions of hegemonic masculinity experienced by working-class communities and movements in a period of globalization. To conceptualize these highly gendered historical structures aids our own understanding, but a gendered analysis could also aid the struggle by self-conscious, organized and solidaristic movements to transform the inequalities of power in an era of globalization.

In the case of Mexico, the reinvigorated discourse on family, loyalty and cooperation has not resolved the crisis of representation for the proponents of neoliberalism. Indeed the legitimacy of the state and the new hegemonic production pattern is reduced in the eyes of workers as labour opposition is repressed and democratic forms of representation are ignored and then closed off. What remains between the old revolutionary nationalist social compromise and the current crisis of representation is the highly gendered partnership between paternalism and authoritarianism, which limits the prospects of an effective counter hegemony.

Notes

1. *Caudillismo* can be equated with the more generally known term clientship. In Latin America clientship is associated with unequal relations between a patron and his subordinate. In more hierarchical societies, clientship depends on highly personal, cross-class alliances in which protection and access to resources are exchanged for loyalty and support. In Mexico a specific expression of clientship is found in the *caudillo*. *Caudillismo* has been a central characteristic of Mexican politics and explains how the apparently individualistic leadership by strong men is in fact a system of power that is tied to groups of other powerful men and regionally based structures of power (Eisenstadt and Lemarchand, 1981; Clapham, 1993). The concept of hegemonic masculinity comes from Connell (1987), who defines it as the dominant masculine ideal of a culture to which all femininities, as well as devalued masculinities, are subordinated. Connell suggests that hegemonic masculinity can be seen in relation to feminine forms such as 'emphasized femininity', in which compliance is highly valued. Other forms of femininity are hidden from view, while other masculinities are negated.

2. Confederación de Trabajadores de México, 'Estatutos, Sindicato Nacional de Trabajadores de Ford Motor Company', revised 1989. Article 18 states that the national executive of the union would be elected to six year terms. Article 19 states that the local executive would be elected to three year terms.

3. The observation committee was composed of national human rights activists, labour lawyers, union activists, UAW (United Auto Workers) and CAW (Canadian Auto Workers) members, among others. Interview by the author with the negotiating committee of the Movimiento Democrático de los Trabajadores de la Ford, Mexico, 12 May 1992; see also Talavera and Muñoz, 1993.

9
Globalizing Social Justice All the Way Down? Agents, Subjects, Objects and Phantoms in International Labour Politics

Dimitris Stevis and Terry Boswell

Introduction

The report of the seventeenth Congress of the International Confederation of Free Trade Unions (ICFTU) was entitled *Globalizing Social Justice* (ICFTU, 2000). What can the globalization of social justice mean from the point of view of any social entity, particularly a civil societal entity such as unions?

It seems to us that an analysis of social justice must address inequities both within the overall political economy – the external domain – and within the milieu or constituencies of a social actor – the internal domain. A socialist vision of the political economy leaves much to be desired if it is blind to 'lesser' inequities that are due to gender, colour or ethnicity. A liberal vision that is sensitive to these inequities but not those which are due to capitalism is even more unsatisfactory.

How does one go about deconstructing the social justice content of a social actor's preferences and practices? In recent decades there has been a move to cast societal politics ('civil society') as an ontologically separate sphere from which emanate the challenges to the democratic deficits of states and capitals. Such an approach obscures the variations among states, firms and societal entities and the significance of alliances that involve elements of all three. As various analysts have suggested, civil societal actors must be placed within the political economy, rendering apparent their position in and preferences about the social order (Harrod, 1972b; Sklair, 1997; Pasha and Blaney, 1998).

Unions are one of the most prominent categories of societal actor and have clearly influenced the political economy of the last century and a half in alliances or conflicts with states, capitals, churches and other societal forces. This chapter examines the attitudes of unions *vis-à-vis* 'unprotected workers', a key element of their internal domain, drawing upon the preferences and practices of global union federations from their inception to the present, although it should be noted that their views are a reflection of the debates within international union politics rather than concrete evidence of national union practices.

The chapter has both theoretical and empirical goals. Theoretically, the first section, situated in relation to the historical materialist analysis proposed by Cox (1987) and Harrod (1987), elaborates on the ways in which societal entities shape their internal domains, and offers a heuristic scheme that allows a more nuanced account of the complex and contradictory positions that social forces hold within a social order.

This scheme is then used in the second section to address our main empirical questions: how have global unions delineated their internal domains over the last 150 years, and do endogenous factors help explain their choices? While we recognize that exogenous factors have played a key role in shaping the practices and impacts of unions, we also argue that there is clear evidence of their own autonomous role in shaping their internal domains. The chapter closes with a short discussion of the possible reasons why global unions have become more inclusive, to the degree that they have done so.

Historical structuralism and hegemony from below

The historical structuralist (HS) emphasis on coexisting patterns of social relations of production forces us to disaggregate the category of worker, and to recognize the coexistence of various objective categories of worker well beyond those constituted within the dominant patterns. This disaggregation allows us to follow the formation of social alliances and of the cleavages that are often observed among workers, and to do so without rejecting the significance of class analysis or the dominant role of specific classes within historical formations (see also Chapters 3 and 4 of this volume).

Harrod and Cox's delineation of the 'unprotected worker' is more historical than it is formal, even though it does employ some formal criteria (Harrod, 1987; Cox, 1987; see also Chapter 2 of this volume). According to Harrod (1987, p. 38) the 'term *unprotected worker* is one of convenience and is intended to indicate the non established workers or least powerful of producers in the world labor force'. Most protected workers have historically been highly skilled and unionized while unprotected workers have historically been unskilled and non-unionized. However, one must not be too doctrinaire about the unionized/ skilled-non-unionized/unskilled delineation.

Highly skilled workers can be protected via provisions that do not involve unions – such as university tenure – as Cox and Harrod recognize. On the other hand very highly skilled workers, such as women in the garment industry, can be unprotected because their skills are not recognized as such. This is very much due to broader social norms that take these skills for granted (see Chapters 5 and 8 of this volume). Alternatively low-skill workers can be protected by unions, as is the case with caretakers. The point that we wish to make – and we think this is largely consistent with the historical spirit of Harrod and Cox – is that the patterns of social relations of production provide us with an approximation of the protected–unprotected continuum.

One of the key insights that the HS approach shares with other historical materialist and sociological analyses of social orders is that structurally subordinate social forces, such as skilled workers, can find their own *modus vivendi* with dominant forces at the expense of other fragments of the working class and the subaltern in general (Cox, 1987). While it may be convenient to talk about the result as consisting of dominant and subordinate forces, what actually occurs is a gradation of positions, depending on what the subordinate social forces want and can achieve and the price of hegemony that the dominant forces are willing or forced to pay. Such arrangements, however, require that forces further down in the social order become the managers of their own discontent, reinforcing the bargains that sustain hegemony by disciplining those beneath them (see Chapter 1 of this volume). This is what the term 'hegemony from below' refers to. In one sense this approach pays tribute to Foucault's (1980) view on the ubiquity of power relations. More profoundly, however, it recognizes the directionality of power that defines social orders but at the same time it does not absolve subordinate forces from the implications of their own choices.

How societal forces shape their internal domains

In line with the previous discussion, all social forces shape the political economy in terms of their visions and practices in what may be considered their external and internal domains. The internal–external distinction, however, is quite precarious, if analytically useful and historically valid, and something needs to be said about it before embarking on its use.

The key reason why the internal–external delineation is precarious is because internal politics is implicated in the constitution of the external domain while external politics is implicated in the constitution of the internal order. The internal and the external, in short, constitute a historical relationship. For instance it is not possible to talk about the internal politics of unions in the absence of the capitalist order that has produced unions and capital.

An additional reason why this delineation is precarious is because the internal–external boundary is the product of political struggles. What social forces identify as part of their milieu can be constructed in a variety of ways. From the very early years of the labour movement, for instance, unions disagreed among themselves as to who should be allowed to join. Without underestimating the formidable external obstacles that unions face – it is illegal, for example, to unionize various categories of public worker – there is plenty of evidence to demonstrate the role of unions in constructing their own milieu.

Finally, the external–internal distinction raises some significant problems of the kind that social scientists face routinely. When dealing with North–South issues, for instance, we often find ourselves supporting the legitimate demands of the South while at the same time recognizing that the advocates may be directly implicated in the production of social inequities. Similar dilemmas emerge within labour politics. How one can address the problems of internal politics without obscuring the significance of broader inequities is a considerable challenge, both politically and theoretically.

Societal forces shape their internal domain through inward and outward strategies. As noted above, unions have preferences about who they represent. The way in which unions define their constituencies to include some categories of people but not others has significant implications. This is not to say that anybody should join a union; rather it refers to whether unions exclude groups or categories of workers who, by some criteria, can be considered stakeholders.

Unions also constitute the political economy through their organization. At one level this refers to their representativeness and decision-making processes. At another level, societal politics in general and union politics in particular are intimately implicated in the production and reproduction of institutions we conventionally associate with other types of social entity. International union organizations, for example, are organized territorially, reproducing the geopolitical characteristics of the overall political economy.

It would be misleading, however, to limit ourselves to inward strategies. All societal actors also pursue outward strategies that, in addition to shaping the overall political economy, also shape their internal milieus.

The representatives of the middle classes did not demand voting rights just for themselves but for the whole social category they claimed to represent. The same applies to environmentalists, religious people, women and unions. Unions have called for a wide variety of rights and standards that cover whole categories of workers, and not only those organized. Voting rights, workplace standards, wage provisions and so on protect and empower workers at large.

In line with the above, it stands to reason that any discussion of hegemonic and counterhegemonic practices requires a more nuanced categorization of social actors, one that captures the gradation of power required to organize and legitimate a hegemonic order. Dichotomies such as 'capitalists' and 'workers' or 'North' and 'South' do provide us with the general picture, but cannot capture the important and contradictory dynamics played by the 'middle class' or the 'semiperiphery'. For this reason we employ an empirically more accurate heuristic distinction between agents, subjects, objects and phantoms.[1] The aim of this heuristic is not to be exclusive or exhaustive but to help map the complexities of power relations, whether in the overall political economy or within a societal entity's internal domain, as we do in this chapter. In the next few pages we shall outline how we derive our heuristic scheme and show, through examples, how it applies to labour politics.

Every preference, practice or institution delineates, explicitly or implicitly, which social entities or categories of people can have a voice, as well as what kinds of choice are considered legitimate and feasible.[2] The rules of voice cannot tell us who has power within a social order unless we also know what types of choice are feasible within its parameters. Similarly the rules of choice are an inadequate guideline if affected parties cannot participate in their elaboration and implementation. In general the issue is not whether procedure or substance is more important but how concatenations of procedural and substantive rules engender and regulate social relations.

We propose to examine voice and choice in simple terms. Accordingly we ask two closely related questions in each case: which stakeholders have a voice or choice (of any type); and, what kind of voice or choice do they have? The first question allows us to ascertain whether some stakeholders have no voice and whether some choices are illegitimate or unfeasible – in short these questions allow us to identify the boundaries between outsiders and insiders.[3] The second question allows us to examine the depth or strength of the voice or choice of the various insiders.

In the case of voice we utilize a simple continuum from silence to policy-making. At one extreme there are stakeholders who do not even have someone to advocate for them; at the other extreme are those who enjoy preponderant policy-making powers. A more democratic and just order would extend policy-making powers to all stakeholders. In the case of choice we employ a simple continuum from servitude to entitlements. At one extreme are stakeholders who cannot even use 'exchange', as would be the case with slaves; at the other are those whose entitlements do the talking. A more democratic and just order would extend entitlements equitably.

Who are the stakeholders? We do not know whether it is possible, or desirable, to provide an analytical answer to this question. We do think, however, that it is possible to provide criteria on the basis of which we can question why some entities are excluded. Clearly we cannot limit stakeholders to those who are louder or have revealed preferences. Even if we were not interested in equity and democracy, a thorough analysis demands that we identify all social entities and categories of people who are inescapably affected by a particular activity or policy, whether due to divisions of labour or power relations. There is certainly a point at which it will be difficult to say whether a particular entity is affected in any significant fashion. Inside that limit, however, we shall be well justified to interrogate exclusions. Such an approach suggests that the boundaries of a social formation are not always coincidental with those of a country and fit well with the more historical and sociological view of the state characteristic of historical structuralism (Cox, 1987).

How are stakeholders represented in the international political economy? The growth of global and regional institutions of governance, whose origins have been traced as far back as the mid-nineteenth century (Murphy, 1994), is one of the most important developments in the last twenty years. Yet no global institutions possess significant supranational capacities. Representation at that level is certainly important (O'Brien *et al.*, 2000), but in our view representation through state agencies and policies remains a central form of representation. Consistent with the historical materialist world view, states reflect social alliances and thus the power relations within them (Cox, 1987). As a result the role of state agencies varies according to the social alliances behind them. Where social welfare alliances are dominant, labour and social welfare ministries are more likely to play a central role (Rieger and Leibfried, 2003). Where liberal alliances are dominant, central banks or departments of the treasury are more likely to play such a role. When these alliances have imperial visions as well, military agencies are likely to have a central role. What this means is that particular societal forces with privileged access to these state agencies are more likely to shape foreign policy and influence international policy-making (for empirical evidence see Braithwaite and Drahos, 2000).

Thinking about stakeholders along these lines brings us up against the grand narrative of international politics. According to this narrative all states are functionally similar, and by virtue of having a formal voice in international fora all states have more voice than other types of entity. Starting from such a reification, mainstream analysts are then surprised to discover that non-state entities may be more powerful than some states, even though radicals have long pointed that out. What is more significant is that states are not functionally similar, state agencies do not have equal power over time, and so-called private entities routinely have access to and are shaped by their interactions with corresponding state agencies (Halliday, 1987). By focusing on who has an actual voice, rather than who is supposed to have one, we are forced to look for fragments of what seem to be cohesive categories and upon which hegemonic and counter hegemonic alliances are built.

Illustrations from union politics

It is on the basis of the above 'operationalization' that we categorize stakeholders as agents, subjects, objects and phantoms. Social entities are routinely some or all of these things, depending on the policy arena and issue. The distinguishing characteristic is that some are only phantoms most of the time while others have a great deal of agency. Agents in this spirit are stakeholders who have a strong voice and strong choice. In terms of the criteria just mentioned, they can play a policy-making role and the range of choices available empowers rather than constrains them. Some but not all states and state agencies are agents in world politics. To the degree that some private corporations are well situated in foreign policy-making or are the unique source of international rule-making, they are also agents in world politics (Braithwaite and Drahos, 2000).

Unions contribute to the creation of agents among workers through both inward and outward strategies. Internally they do so when they admit new categories of workers as equals in both membership and decision-making. The organizational changes within the ICFTU with respect to women workers are an example of this. Externally they can contribute to agency by advancing policies that empower workers as a whole, as is the case with workers' councils.

Subjects are entities who have, at a minimum, autonomous standing and some entitlements. While the range within which they can operate is largely shaped by agents, their rights are not discretionary, allowing them to defend and promote their interests as well as pursue agency. Corporate rights, canonical law and citizenship extend subjecthood to corporations, churches and individuals respectively. To the degree that these become international, they also make them subjects in international politics. Agents, of course, are also subjects.

Unions also create subjects through internal and external strategies. For much of the twentieth century industrial unions controlled national federations and shaped their priorities. The case of the Bolivian Confederation of Labour (COB) makes this very explicit. Because miners had the largest and most powerful union when the COB was created, they were guaranteed organizational and programmatic power in the confederation. Even after the miners had lost considerable ground compared with teachers and peasant workers the provision remained, causing serious frictions.

At its conception the American Federation of Labor (AFL) claimed to be inclusive of both black and white workers, but it soon abandoned this promise in order not to alienate all-white unions. As a solution it chartered all-black unions, who paid less in dues but also had less decision-making power and fewer rights.

Unions also enable unorganized and unprotected workers to gain subjecthood by their support of labour rights and standards that allow individual workers to organize or promote their rights through the legal system, and by the coverage of non-unionized workers via various arrangements, such as national pacts. They also do so when they commit themselves to listening to these categories of workers out of a commitment to their eventual organization and integration (ICFTU, 2000b) rather than paternalism.

Objects are entities that are regulated or protected through some clear legal or political commitments but have no standing of their own to defend or promote their interests. This does not mean that they do not engage in politics, but that someone else speaks on their behalf in the corridors of power. Children and nature fall into this category. Basically, then, objects are heteronomous and depend on the practices of agents and subjects.

Unions are also implicated in the creation of objects. One of the first union demands was the protection of children and women. For all of the nineteenth and much of the twentieth century their attitude towards women and children was paternalistic. In short the aim of their policy proposals was not a first step towards the complete integration of women but rather their protection, and in some cases their exclusion from certain professions.

Finally, phantoms are entities that are produced by the social processes at hand but have neither voice nor choice, and often no one to speak on their behalf. Women and slaves have been in this category for parts of history. In some cases they are regulated with an aim to contain or destroy them. In other cases they are invisible, as can be the case with temporary workers in academia or non-photogenic species.

Unions create phantoms, mostly through a combination of direct and indirect exclusion. Central to the creation of phantoms is the definition of certain practices as 'not work'. Household labour, for instance, has been considered as part of motherhood while some categories of migrant have been kept in permanent legal limbo. Historically the AFL has been rather punitive towards migrants, but its recent policy changes, as well as those of other national and international union organizations, illuminates how migrants can move towards subjecthood and agency within union politics.

A brief historical outline: towards less invisibility?

The world's major global federations represent most but not all of those who are organized. They probably also represent a large but smaller portion of people protected in some other fashion. For instance a substantial number of government employees cannot be unionized but do enjoy certain forms of protection. The overwhelming majority of the world's workers, however, are not unionized or protected. In short, unprotected work represents the great hinterland of union politics.

How to respond to unprotected and unorganized workers has been central to international union politics since its inception. Here we provide a preliminary outline of how global union organizations, primarily the ICFTU, have dealt with unprotected workers. Since these global organizations are confederal it is not appropriate to assume that their proposals will be adopted and implemented by the member unions. Rather we shall examine their views as part of the struggle for setting the agenda in global union politics.

It is not our goal to provide a comprehensive account of all relevant developments. Consequently we shall focus on major issues during each of six eras since the formation of the First International. These issues, some of which were more prominent in some periods than others, are organized in terms of the political geography of unions and their attitude towards natural characteristics such as gender, age, colour or ethnicity, and employment attributes such as sector or type of work. In line with the previous discussion, we aim to illuminate both their internal and their external strategies.

The First International: 1862–1876

The First International (FI) was largely European – the only exception being the US. In light of the fact that unionization was still in its infancy in Europe and the US, and even more so in other parts of the world, and the resources of the FI were quite limited, we can say that the FI was fairly inclusive in terms of countries where unions and related parties were emerging. While supportive of women's rights, the FI did not actively seek the participation of women workers (Freymond, 1962, vol 1). In fact there were serious disagreements over the rights and role of women (ibid.) The FI also placed child labour on its agenda. Its argument was that child labour should not be abolished but should be treated differently from adult labour. Accordingly children should be divided into three age groups – 9–12, 12–15 and 15–18 – with progressively more hours of work being allowed (ibid.) Its attitude towards emancipation was positive but not tested since it remained European, or made up of European migrants. It did not, however, limit itself to manual workers, even though that was one of the proposals. The FI was in favour of providing all migrant workers with equal rights but it was opposed to the importation of workers for strike-breaking. It must be noted, however, that the FI did not manage to attract the British Trades Union Congress (TUC), the largest union organization of the era. In fact the TUC did not agree with some of the most inclusive and radical proposals of the FI.

The period of the Second International: 1889 to World War I[4]

The nascent international union organizations and the Second International did make some small inroads beyond Europe, mostly industrializing countries with significant European populations, such as the US and Argentina. The international union movement, however, did not take up the plight of workers (mostly peasants) in the colonies. This was an issue that attracted a lot of discussion within the Second International. One view was largely supportive of colonial policies; a second view was critical but sought to work within them in order to mitigate their impact; a third view was opposed to colonialism and imperialism under all circumstances. Very few in the socialist and even fewer in the union movement, however, conceived of colonial peoples as possible partners in a global struggle for emancipation (for discussions see Braunthal, 1967; Kaarsholm, 1988; Tichelman, 1988).

With regard to employment attributes we can identify two tendencies. On the one hand, craft unions focused on skilled workers, on the other, emerging industry-wide unions also included less-skilled workers. On balance unions did manage to grow and include increasingly larger numbers and more categories of people. Yet they could not solve some important problems with unprotected work.

Neither the AFL nor the British committed themselves to extending membership rights to migrants. A review of the debates on international employment legislation during that era clearly underscores the centrality of migrant labour issues (US Department of Labor, 1920). It could not, of course, be otherwise given the enormity of migration.

It is worth noting that the international union movement was also blind to gender. This is particularly important given the role of women workers in the industrialization of a number of core countries and the prominent women's movements of the times. The limitations of international union politics in that regard was also underscored by its lack of policy on home work, much of which was undertaken by women (Milner, 1990) and which was on the agenda of advocacy organizations and the Socialist International (U.S. Department of Labor, 1920).

While the international union and socialist movements did advance proposals that would benefit all workers, such as workplace conditions and working time, this was a period in which industrial workers and work achieved hegemony in national and international union politics.

Another important characteristic of this period was the consolidation of the division of labour between parties and unions. Accordingly calls for social change were primarily the responsibility of socialist parties while unions focused on trade union issues. As unions, even in places such as Germany and Austria, gained weight in the social democratic countries, the overall politics of these parties also became more reformist.

The interwar period[5]

The International Federation of Trade Unions (IFTU) was formally reconstituted at the Amsterdam Congress of 1919, 'the first international trade union congress ever held' (Lorwin, 1929, p. 191). The IFTU came to include most of the largest European unions but could not achieve the inclusiveness of the years immediately preceding World War I. The AFL, which objected to the organizational and political priorities of the IFTU, decided not to join, taking along with it the Latin American unions – evidence of their relationship. Nor did the Russian unions join, while the Christian unions continued along their own independent trajectory.

The divisions within international union politics during this period were on the whole disastrous because of the rise of the right. There was, however, an expansion of the political geography of unionism. Because of its inability to make major inroads in Western Europe the communist international union organization sought, with some success, to expand into the rest of the world. In the case of Asia, it made significant inroads into the nascent union movement (Carr, 1964). Even though communist policies were often contradictory and sectarian, communist parties and unions were instrumental in initiating or supporting more socially inclusive unionization in parts of the South (for an overview see Carr, 1964; Simmons and Simmons, 1969). The IFTU eventually responded to the challenge. The first steps were taken in 1928 and were expanded during the 1930s (Schevenels, 1956; Saville, 1988; Van Goethem, 2000). In the end the IFTU was not particularly successful in the periphery, partly due to the quasi-imperial and sometimes racist attitudes of the British TUC.

All the major groups in international union politics advocated equal pay for equal work for women, but also maintained a paternalistic approach towards them (for the IFTU's agenda see Schevenels, 1956). During the interwar period the IFTU supported the Trade Union Women's Conferences but no woman reached a position of authority. Moreover many of the members of the IFTU did not organize women workers and often did not allow women workers into their ranks. Finally, the IFTU was well behind the communists in its response to black workers, as the case of South Africa shows (Simmons and Simmons, 1969). The high point during the interwar period was the admission of a black union from South Africa (whose representative, however, was not allowed to attend the TUC annual meeting so as not to offend white unions in South Africa) (ibid.).

As in the previous period, international unions continued to advance a number of policies that would affect all workers. During the very early years after World War I they adopted a rather broad agenda as socialist parties were in disarray. Increasingly, however, the IFTU returned to a more trade unionist agenda, consolidated by the leading role played by the British trade union movement.

The height of the Cold War: 1949 to the mid 1970s[6]

All the major federations sought to expand their constituencies to the South during this period. In Latin America the struggle was primarily between the AFL and an alliance of communists and nationalists. The former was also very much in support of decolonization and the creation of anticommunist unions in Africa, while the TUC was concerned about losing influence there. In the end all three international federations became very active in Latin America, in the World Federation of Trade Unions (WFTU) and the International Confederation of Free Trade Unions (ICFTU) in order to contain each other's influence and that of the Christian federation. The decision of the latter to move to the South was reflected in the allocation of its resources and in its organization. A valid argument can therefore be made that it was the only international union organization that saw the unions of the South as agents, or at least subjects, in international union politics (Pasture, 1999).

The membership of the ICFTU and the WFTU came to include unions from all continents, reflecting the changing world political economy.[7] The majority of members came from and authority remained in the hands of the unions from the core. The unions of the South did not become agents in the international union movement, and it can be said that they were not even viewed as subjects. An effort to give a voice to agricultural workers through their own International Trade Secretariat (ITS) was largely motivated by Cold War considerations in South East Asia. When that secretariat was absorbed by the main ITS dealing with agricultural workers it became apparent that it had been exaggerating the extent of its membership and activities.

The case of the International Solidarity Fund demonstrates the nature of North–South relations very clearly. The fund was set up in 1956 and reached its high point in 1961–63 (Wedin, 1974). Its purpose was to support union development in the South, and particularly in Africa. Central to any successes the fund may have had were the Scandinavian unions, particularly the Swedish unions. The AFL-CIO and the TUC lost interest rather quickly, preferring instead to pursue their own foreign policy programmes, as did many individual unions (Harrod, 1972a).

On balance, then, the early years after World War II were dominated by Cold War priorities. During the same period the dominance of industrial workers was further consolidated in the practices of national and international union organizations while their agendas became largely 'productionist'.

From détente to the end of the Cold War: the early 1970s to the early 1990s

The three global federations, as well as national federations and unions, continued to compete over the South, and increasingly over Eastern Europe. Because of its withdrawal from the ICFTU (1969–82), the AFL-CIO focused most of its resources on Latin America and Eastern Europe.

In the Americas it continued to support and train conservative trade unionists and oppose all others.

The most important development in the 1980s was the emergence of radical unions in the South. Right-wing dictatorships and apartheid resulted in the destruction of many existing unions, but they also engendered militant unions, as was the case in Brazil, South Africa and South Korea. These unions are now carrying their own weight in international and regional union politics, recasting the asymmetrical North–South relationship that characterized the twentieth century. It remains to be seen how broad and deep these rearrangements will become.

The temporary withdrawal of the AFL-CIO from the ICFTU allowed the latter to become a little less preoccupied with the Cold War and address some additional issues. A review of its reports reveals growing attention to a variety of social categories, particularly gender and young workers. Both of these remain priorities, indicating a broadening of the agenda and a move away from paternalism (ICFTU, 1988; Gumbrell-McCormick, 2000). The question of apartheid also appeared early in the 1970s but did not become a key issue until the 1980s. Towards the late 1980s issues related to rural employment and the informal sector were also placed on the agenda, albeit not with the force of the gender and apartheid questions.

A more important development in our view, and one with important implications for unprotected work, was the return of the ICFTU to the formulation of a comprehensive, if not always cohesive, view of the world political economy. During the 1970s and most of the 1980s this view was articulated with regard to multinational corporations. This dimension continued to be very important but it was increasingly complemented by the promotion of proposals to do with the overall world political economy, particularly in respect of the South (ICFTU, 1988; Gumbrell-McCormick, 2000). While not directly addressed to unprotected work, this agenda was more inclusive of non-unionized workers as it was predicated on measures that would affect society as a whole.

On balance, then, there was a broadening of the ICFTU's agenda during this period, although Cold War issues remained dominant. It is not clear, however, that there was much deepening of the agenda compared with that of more radical members of the organization or the early post World War I positions of the IFTU. Moreover the ICFTU paid little attention to unprotected workers, unlike the WCL after its move towards a more Christian socialist politics and greater attention to the South.

From the end of the Cold War to the present

The ICFTU and the associated Global Union Federations (GUFs) – as the International Trade Secretariats are now called – have now become the dominant global union organizations. A review of the ICFTU's public documents reveals a broadening of the agenda to include unprotected workers (through both inward and outward strategies) and a larger number of organized workers from the South. At the moment the majority of its members come from the South. Organizationally, however, the ICFTU/GUF network remains Northern, although the joining of important unions from the South, particularly from Brazil, South Africa and South Korea, are having an impact on the internal balance of the network. We must point out, however, that the majority of the members of Southern unions work in the industrial and service sectors, and on balance the ICFTU/GUF remains a network for workers in these sectors. Agricultural workers are severely underrepresented and 'under-advocated'. The same applies to household and home workers.

The ICFTU's efforts with regard to young workers and gender have been quite substantial (Gumbrell-McCormick, 2000; ICFTU, 2000a, 2000b). While it is possible to disagree about its methods and accomplishments, the truth of the matter is that the organization is at the forefront of international union politics in terms of gender. Not only has it strongly supported women, it has also introduced organizational changes to ensure representation by women on its executive board. Some of the GUFs also have an active gender policy (Reutter and Rütters, 2002).

The ICFTU has become an increasingly more vocal supporter of the rights of children, migrants, workers with disabilities, older workers and homosexual workers (ICFTU, 2000a, 2000b, 2004a–d), although not to the extent that it has done with women and young workers. Beyond these constituency strategies the ICFTU/GUF network has also sought to promote core employment rights that can benefit all workers and has sought to connect human rights with employment rights (ICFTU, 2000a).

More recently it has directly addressed the question of unprotected workers (ICFTU, 2001a, 2000b; Justice, 2002; interview with Dwight Justice of the ICFTU, July 2003). What emerges from the related debates is clear opposition to the use of the term 'informal sector', for two main reasons (see ICFTU, 2001a; Justice, 2002). First, it implies that there exists an informal sector that is similar to other sectors of the economy. Second, it obscures the fact that the employment denoted by the term is politically and legally unprotected.

In addition to addressing unprotected workers in its internal discussions, the ICFTU has played an important part in promoting the ILO's 'decent work' agenda. The membership and administration of the ICFTU and the GUFs does not reflect the changes that are evident in the case of gender and young workers, although some positive steps have been taken in that direction, particularly when unprotected work involves women (Gallin, 2002).

Beyond its constituency strategies the ICFTU has developed a broader agenda for rights that, if applied, would protect and empower individual workers regardless of whether or not they were union members. This agenda covers the prohibition of forced labour, the prevention of discrimination and the abolition of certain types of child labour (ICFTU, 2001b). Indeed, during the last decade or so the ICFTU's agenda has gone beyond economic issues to include democratization, human rights, health, education and other social rights (ICFTU, 2000a, 2000b, 2004a).

Findings and conclusions

We shall close by summarizing our findings and addressing some possible reasons why global union organizations have become more inclusive and why unions need to pay closer attention to unprotected workers.

As we have seen, the ICFTU has become more inclusive over the years and has sought to persuade the international union movement to adopt more inclusive constituency strategies. Both the ICFTU/GUF network and the world's unions as a whole remain most closely associated with the industrial and service sectors, which dominate the global political economy. Moreover even the more radical of the Southern union movements are primarily from these sectors. Thus the broadening that has taken place is more discursive than substantive, although it does reflect a strong commitment on the part of various members of the ICFTU/GUF network.

However, while the ICFTU and most of the GUFs have become more inclusive, this does not mean that they are advocating a social democratic turn to the world political economy – as some of the more radical members would like. On the other hand their agenda is broader than mere 'bread and butter' trade unionism. On balance the ICFTU is promoting an agenda of global social regulation that combines countervailing rights, such as democracy and unionization rights; protection from especially abusive employment practices and from abject poverty; and a continued tripartite dialogue at the national and global levels in order to create jobs, cushion the impact of transition and prevent crises. Importantly, the ICFTU's discursive goal is social development rather than simply growth or development.

What explains the inward and outward strategies outlined in the previous section? As noted earlier it is not our aim to offer detailed answers. Rather our major interest is whether endogenous factors have played a role. There is strong evidence to suggest that unions' move towards greater inclusiveness has been prompted by endogenous factors. For example no outside force made unions decide whether or not to represent crafts or industries or view the South as something to fight over rather than engage with. Similarly they have been free to choose whether to treat unprotected workers as phantoms or as potential agents within their own ranks and beyond.

It can be argued that the end of the Cold War and the relative decline of unionization – particularly in some countries at the core of the political economy – are the primary reasons why global union organizations are trying to shift the attention of their members to unprotected workers. Both these factors have clearly influenced global union organizations as well as national unions. However a number of developments preclude a direct connection. For example questions of gender were placed on the agenda before the end of the Cold War, and the rise of unionism in the semiperiphery resulted in a less paternalistic approach to Southern workers. Thus the inclusion of hitherto unprotected workers cannot only be a result of the end of the Cold War and the decline of unionization in the core. In addition there have always been forces within and in the interstices of global unions that have called for a broader delineation of the working class, although their efforts may have been facilitated by the end of the Cold War.

A second very important issue is the part played by global unions in mediating global hegemony. How has the end of the Cold War and the relative decline of their membership – and hence their prominence in mediating global hegemony – affected their move towards greater inclusiveness? Here global unions (and many national unions) are confronting a serious problem. On the one hand they are continuing to place a great deal of emphasis on influencing the work of global organizations, even though their actual capacity to do so has declined. Not only have some of the strongest supporters of the weak tripartism of the ILO lost ground in terms of influencing foreign policies, but also economic organizations are now more important in places where global unions have no representation. On the other hand global rule-making has become more consequential. Abandoning global policy-making is now less of an option than it was in the past.

How does the move to protect unprotected workers fit in with addressing this dilemma? Some view the broadening and deepening of the ranks as an attempt to recapture the glory days of tripartism (in comparison with the onslaught of hyperliberalism). For many, however, becoming more inclusive represents a step away from the 'march through the institutions' and towards more 'marches in the streets', and for a more critical approach to the institutions of global governance.

This brings us to the question of why unions ought to pay attention to unprotected workers – the vast hinterland of the working class. Because unions make choices and because their choices feed into the overall social order, there are good reasons why we should study the ways in which unions deal with unprotected work. One reason is that it is necessary to understand how the preferences and practices of unions affect the organization of power in the overall world political economy. Another is to sharpen our understanding of social democracy and justice.

While unions have lost ground in parts of the core, it is not possible to understand the organization of the global political economy without understanding how unions have been incorporated into the institutions of the core and the periphery. In some cases their incorporation has been narrow and particularistic; in others it has had broader social implications. In all cases the incorporation of unions has had a definite impact on the politics of work.

The incorporation of unions, of course, has not simply been a matter of the desire and capacity of unions. It has also been the product of the desire and capacity of other social forces. Some of these social forces have not limited themselves to the incorporation of unions but have also sought to incorporate additional categories of people. In some cases they have done so as part of a broad commitment to social equity similar to that of unions, as has been the case with social-democratic institutionalization. In other instances the aim has been to weaken or destroy the reach of unions or particular types of union or party. This was certainly the case in paternalistic corporatist countries, whether in Latin America or elsewhere. To put it differently, unions will be impervious to unprotected work at their own peril. There are good political reasons for broadening their constituencies, for example in order to grow or to prevent their opponents from outsmarting them (see Chapter 7 of this volume).

A second reason why it is important to study the ways in which unions deal with unprotected work has to do with social democracy.

Turning our analysis to unprotected workers, in the way that various analysts have done in the case of gender, age, ethnicity and other hitherto excluded social categories, forces us to rethink social democracy and social justice as it requires us to consider a wide range of stakeholders than those to which we are accustomed to researching.

Notes

1. The discussion in this section draws on Stevis (2002).
2. The discussion that follows draws on the debates on radical and social democracy (see for example Furniss and Mitchell, 1984; Esping-Andersen, 1990; Bachrach and Botwinick, 1992; Young, 2000; Boswell and Chase-Dunn, 2000).
3. It is worth noting here that some entities may choose to remain outsiders in order to avoid the constraints imposed by a policy. The emphasis is, therefore on those who are kept outside.
4. The key organizations were the Second Socialist International (1889–1914), the International Trade Secretariats (1889–) and the International Secretariat of National Trade Union Centres (1901–13), which became the International Federation of Trade Unions (1913 to World War I).
5. The key organizations were the International Federation of Trade Unions (1919–45), the 'Red International of Labour Unions' (1921–36), the Christian Confederation and the International Trade Secretariats.
6. The key organizations were the International Confederation of Free Trade Unions (1949 to the present), the World Federation of Trade Unions (1945 to the present), the International Federation of Christian Trade Unions (renamed the World Confederation of Labour in 1969) and the International Trade Secretariats.
7. The access of international union organizations to decolonized Africa was stymied during the 1960s by the formation of a state-sponsored African union confederation.

10
Power, Production and World Order Revisited: Some Preliminary Conclusions

Matt Davies and Magnus Ryner

The end of the Cold War fundamentally reshaped international studies. The *ceteris paribus* assumptions, which had made the interstate conflict dimension the privileged object of analysis and neorealism the dominant paradigm of the field, could no longer be plausibly maintained. The unequivocal victory of the US and the West in the Second Cold War, under the increasingly market oriented and neoliberal leadership of the Reagan administration, generated a fair degree of triumphalism and optimism in liberal academic circles. Expressed most strikingly by Francis Fukuyama's (1992) 'end of history' thesis, international politics was seen as increasingly devoid of conflict. In a world of 'complex interdependence' (Keohane and Nye, 1989), the realist games would be increasingly displaced by liberal games characterized by a rational, positive-sum politics of allocation, identity formation and cosmopolitan democracy.

Although this view of the world was articulated not long ago it already seems like an anachronistic echo of the past. Concrete events – such as the emblematic September 11, the subsequent 'war on terror' and the US-led invasion of Iraq – have clearly shattered this liberal idealist image. Of course it was argued strongly by many that this was indeed only an image – and not an accurate one at that. Realism, while embarrassed for not having predicted the end of the Cold War, never went away and it predicted a transition to a multipolar, or rather unimultipolar, world (Haass, 1999; Huntington, 1999). The 'end of history' thesis was also soon confronted with the competing 'clash of civilization' thesis.

It should be born in mind that by the 1980s, scholars drawing on historical materialism, critical theory, radical versions of constructivism and post-structuralism had begun to establish a niche for themselves in

223

the field of international studies. In different ways they expressed profound scepticism of the 'end of history' thesis and the 'spirit of the age' that it expressed. Whether taking the cue from Derrida's (1993) assertion of the perpetual ambivalence of social signifiers, Polanyi's (1957) concept of the 'double movement' or Marx's (1973) conception of capitalist dynamics as inherently contradictory and dialectical, they predicted that policies informed by the abstract-universal ideas of neoliberalism as rationalities of the narrow and special interests of the wealthy and powerful, when imposed on concrete social relations and practices, were bound to generate new sources of antagonism, conflict and change in the world order. At the same time, fully aware of the weaknesses of previous versions of historical materialism, which had been fiercely criticized at the theoretical level and discredited at the concrete level, this literature did not deterministically predict any particular content or direction of the double movement.

Whilst very much identifying with the latter intellectual tendencies, the present book has been written on the premise that not enough has been done in terms of advancing research on the 'double movement'. Related to this premise, it has been argued that it would be too costly for such research to ignore, as has hitherto been done, the potential contribution of Cox's and Harrod's concepts of 'patterns of social relations of production' and 'unprotected work' (see Cox, 1987; Harrod, 1987). The contributors to this book have made this case in different ways by highlighting the increased importance of poverty in world politics, and the ways in which the relationship between poverty and world politics is connected through unprotected work in the global political economy. In order to advance this research the chapters in this book – some of which are theoretical, explorative and wide ranging, and some more empirical, analyzing matters in particular contexts and locales – have engaged in an exercise of recovery and reconsideration of the 'power and production' approach to international studies (as formulated by Cox and Harrod) in order to rethink poverty as a social force and phenomenon of global politics. The contributors were asked to consider four broad questions when writing their chapters, questions that have continuing importance in the critique and development of this approach and of the field of international studies more generally:

- The ontological question of what international relations are and what place (unprotected) work has in international relations and the international political economy.
- The question of subject formation.

- The question of political mobilization and organization in social formation.
- The question of how the formation of subjects and modes of mobilization and organization contribute to the constitution of world politics.

In this final chapter the editors draw some conclusions from the findings of the contributors and propose an agenda for future research. Because the contributors have tended to arrive at different conclusions, the views in this chapter should not be taken as a synthesis of the findings of the contributors – their chapters speak for themselves – or as a summary of the 'state of the art' for this approach to the field. Rather it reflects the lessons learnt by the editors from the criticisms and observations offered by the contributors. Nevertheless, what is clear and consistent throughout this book is that the wilful neglect of work, of workers and of poor people by the field of international studies has greatly impoverished our understanding of global politics, both positively and normatively.

Unprotected work and the ontology of transnational relations

Gill (1993) raised the question of ontology for international studies in a now canonical essay. He set out to outline a new approach to the study of international relations not only in terms of respecifying the objects for analysis in the field, but also to critique the epistemological and methodological limitations of the predominant approaches. Bakker and Gill (2003) have returned to these questions, taking into consideration the contributions of feminist political economy and the topic of reproduction. We take it as a symptom of the continuing failure of the field of international studies to deal with such key questions that critical theorists such as Bakker and Gill have been obliged to return to the matter of the ontological status of international relations.

Approaching the field of international studies from the perspective of ontology presents certain problems. On the one hand, ontology as a philosophical concern – that is, as an investigation of the nature of being or existence – evidently lies beyond the overt concerns of the contributors to this volume. This is not to say that critical approaches to international studies cannot teach us important lessons about the nature of objects in the world, how they come to be and the relations or connections between them; on the contrary, these are the usual considerations of critical theory. What is more, international studies is always informed by implicit ontologies. However these ontologies are typically foundational assumptions that tend to remain unexamined.

On the other hand the term ontology is often used in a derivative sense as the set of things and relations that are matters of concern in a field, in the sense that there could be an ontology of international political economy (IPE), and this might be different from an ontology of the sociology of art. The danger with such an approach is that ontology could be reduced to empiricism or list-making, reifying the objects for investigation and closing the borders of the field to the concerns thus defined.

Here our approach to the question of ontology lies somewhere in between these two understandings. We shall deal with this question by asking what the power and production approach to international relations (IR) and IPE, as examined in this volume, can tell us about the things that make up the world we live in, the ways these things are connected to or implicated by one another, and the structure of the categories that IR and IPE use to analyze and understand reality.

In their original volumes, both Cox (1987) and Harrod (1987) indicate that production and power should be objects of analysis in IR and IPE. The chapters of this volume also understand production – mainly seen in the multiple social relations of production in a social formation and the patterns of power relations that are typical of these social relations of production – as objects for analysis. Thus Amoore argues in Chapter 1 that work and workers as global subjects must be core objects in our analyses. Similarly in Chapter 2 Harrod argues that work and production are the most important activities of humankind and that different patterns of power relations surround these activities, influencing the worldviews of people involved in the patterns.

However taking this approach demonstrates that power and production are not merely objects in the world. They are constitutive forces. As Niemann puts it in Chapter 6, we must understand production broadly, as society producing itself. The emphasis throughout this volume on the human activity of producing the world recalls Marx's emphasis on labour: 'Labour is the living, form giving fire; it is the transitoriness of things, their temporality, as their formation by living time' (Marx, 1973, p. 361). And because production is divided, fragmented and hierarchical, power constitutes the social relations in production.

Understanding reality as 'produced' allows us to address one of the most common criticisms of historical materialism as an approach to societies and international relations, namely that the approach reduces social relations to economic relations. Reductionism, or 'economism' as

Gramsci (1971) called it, rests on narrow conceptions of production, such as the notion that production is labour that adds value to commodities. Feminists have pointed out that this conception tends to exclude production in the household, which typically takes place outside market relations, even if it arguably adds value to the commodity of labour power. Davies (Chapter 4), for example, underscores Robert Cox's (1987, p. 50) description of the household as a 'producer of the last resort' in times of economic crisis when he explores the possible limits to shifting the burdens of reproduction onto the socially isolated household, and also when he examines the political and economic consequences of the migration of household labour to casual labour markets or enterprise labour markets.

Production in the narrow sense depends on a conception of the economy (and a practice of IPE) that takes the economy *a priori* as a separate and autonomous sphere of human activity that is governed by its own rules, which are generally conceived in terms of the market. The analytical shortcomings of such a conception have led Stevis and Boswell (Chapter 9) to insist on considering civil society actors within the political economy. In Chapter 3 Ryner makes a similar point against economism when he demonstrates that forms of consciousness cannot be derived mechanistically from relations of production because the so-called fundamental classes are fragmented: strictly economic explanations cannot account for the emergence of subjectivity, including class agency.

Thus production cannot be understood as belonging only to economic or market-oriented activities. Production is not only the production and reproduction of commodities such as labour power, for example, but also social relations must be produced and reproduced. Even space is produced: Niemann (Chapter 6), building on Henri Lefebvre's (1991a) spatial theories, analyzes how formally organized and informal migration have produced different spaces in Southern Africa. Thus production is not merely an object for IR and IPE; seen through the lenses of these fields, production is how objects and the relations between them come to be in the world. Production is an ontological category. Understanding objects as produced opens up the possibility of understanding them as dynamic, especially under the pressure of political struggles. Thus new configurations and new patterns can always be produced, as both Federici (Chapter 5) and Harrod (Chapter 2) remind us.

Consequently, as the contributions in this volume make clear, production implies both economic and political relations. Because production (in both the narrow and the broad sense) is fragmented and hierarchical, production necessarily implies power as an object for analysis. Indeed what Harrod (1987) calls a heuristic technique, we feel can be taken as an ontological statement: 'Even when [power] has not been ignored, the concentration has been on the question "who governs?" rather than on "what are the sources of power?", "how are they maintained?", and "what are its dynamics?", (ibid., p. 3).

When addressing such questions, Davies (Chapter 4) and Federici (Chapter 5) emphasize the part played by antagonism and struggle within and between the multiple social relations of production in explaining the political dynamics of social transformation; that is, how new patterns come to be. In his discussion of *habitus*, Ryner (Chapter 3) refers to the importance of antagonism and power when he argues that dispositions do not produce effects automatically; rather the socioeconomic context in which they are constructed 'offers an uneven terrain of potential articulations'. This can result in dissonance between the claims of hegemonic discourse and the everyday experiences of subordinates in the economic-corporate moment. In Chapter 9 Stevis and Boswell make a similar point when they argue that by 'focusing on who has an actual voice, rather than who is supposed to have one, we are forced to look for fragments of what seem to be cohesive categories and upon which hegemonic and counter hegemonic alliances are built'. This is precisely the analytical strategy pursued by Federici (Chapter 5), Niemann (Chapter 6), Clarke (Chapter 7) and Healy (Chapter 8).

These contributions empirically refocus the issue raised in the introduction to this volume: how can we conceptualize the role of the global poor in world politics? Mainstream analyses, it will be recalled, tend to assume that the global poor are a threat to world order, while the tendency in radical critiques is to assume that the poor will form a countermovement to challenge the neoliberal order. Given that production should be thought of as an ontological category – that is, that reality is produced – one of the tasks of this volume has been to revisit the patterns of production relations first elaborated by Harrod (1987) and Cox (1987) when they disaggregated the various blanket terms used in most analyses of social forces in global politics. Because production must not be thought of in narrowly economistic terms, the ontology proposed here must also account for the incidence of power in the production of the real. That is to say, just as production is not merely an object of analysis but also an ontological category, power is not merely an object: the real is produced under different and related patterns of power relations in production.

Unprotected work and subject formation

Analyses of and speculations about the role of the global poor in world politics posit the emergence of new social subjects, which also raises the issue of how to think about power. Are subordinates 'disciplined' by those who are dominant in these power relations or by their material conditions and the patterning of power itself? Drawing on the work of the Foucauldian theorist Nikolas Rose (1999), Amoore (Chapter 1) suggests that there is much to be said for such a contention. Instituted power relations in production contain 'technologies of the self' that help govern the way in which workers think about themselves. On the other hand, does the political fact of social struggle require us to reconsider power in terms that depart both from the traditional social scientific approaches that view power in terms of the capacity to oblige behaviours, and from critical theories, such as the materialist concept of structural power or the post-structuralist conception of disciplinary or biopower? Ryner (Chapter 3) suggests that these technologies of the self are not all pervasive, but instead stand in a relationship of tension and contradiction with the lived experience of the *habitus* (*pace* Bourdieu, 1977) of workers, which justifies Harrod's dialectical distinction between production rationalities and the 'basic consciousness' of unprotected workers as a dialectical source of sociopolitical dynamics. Be this as it may, whilst the contributors to this volume approach these questions differently, by foregrounding political antagonism, struggle and agency, the need for a sociologically thick account of power, as exercised and experienced in the social relations of production, is evident.

In Chapter 2 Harrod reflects critically on how political antagonism, struggle and agency have become topics of interest for IR and IPE. He points out that while these fields have recently taken up the idea that the global poor are either a threat to world order or a source of resistance, they still lack a theory of how and why this might be the case. To elaborate such a theory it is necessary to build upon the social ontology of power and production outlined in the previous section in order to establish how power relations in production shape the formation of subjects and societies.

Subjectivity and subject formation in the context of labour have been thorny issues for critical theory. Famously the members of the Frankfurt School, especially Habermas and Gorz, argued against viewing labour as determining the forms of subjectivity or the constitution of the social world, as do antihumanists in a structuralist idiom such as Althusser and a post-structuralist idiom such as Foucault. Implied in their criticisms is that reductionism reduces praxis to a technical matter (*techne*) and forgets the importance of the struggle for recognition. The question is, however, whether these theories have 'thrown the baby out with the bathwater' by negating, but not adequately transcending, the Hegelian–Marxist hermeneutics of the subject, based on what Harrod (1987) refers to as the limited two-class model of orthodox Marxism. It can be argued that the displacement of the industrial working class as the privileged subject in these accounts and the emphasis on new types of subjectivities are expressions of a particular configuration of patterns of power relations of production, whereby the welfare state and mass consumer society emerged against the backdrop of a social formation underpinned by tripartist and enterprise corporatist patterns. Whilst agreeing with the aforementioned critics of reductionism about the importance not to assume forms of subjectivity from economic positions, Federici's discussion in Chapter 5 of the deteriorating situation for prostitutes, who in the 1970s were seen as one of the new social movements celebrated by some authors, highlights the perennial contextual importance of social relations of production.

The contributors to this volume were not asked to consider the question of whether communication as a social logic is complementary to or subsumes the social forces expressed in production; however communication is at least an implicit concern when the questions of subjectivity and subject formation arise. Some of the findings in this volume point to a role by production (understood in a broad sense) in setting the context of subjectification. Despite the disagreement among some of the contributors about how best to specify and understand the patterns of social relations in production that shape the emergent subjectivities, there is broad agreement about the importance of social relations of production in accounting for both subject formation and social formation.

Thus we certainly accept the criticism that forms of subjectivity cannot be attributed mechanically to types of employment, and we agree with Harrod's cautioning that the 'emergence of a distinct consciousness from the social relations of production is a difficult process to chart' (Harrod, 1987, p. 33). The difficulties arise from a variety of factors. For example Harrod makes an analytical distinction between the material and psychological aspects of basic consciousness. With regard to the material aspect, 'each producer may be aware of his or her material interest within a certain form of social relations, that is, what actions will increase or decrease power and thereby affect return' (ibid., p. 33). However there is also a deeper consciousness that 'corresponds to a social character developed from adjustment to social relations or to the notion that the forms of social relations produce not only goods and services but also types of people' (ibid., p. 34). Consequently in adjusting to social relations, consciousness 'is affected by religion, culture, and traditions that are often residues of past, transformed social relations' (ibid., 1987, p. 33).

Thus forms of consciousness are subject to what Harrod calls rationalities, which disguise or mitigate hierarchical power. Moreover the insights into ontology of the power and production approach, as discussed above, lead us to underscore Harrod's notion that the patterns of social relations produce not only goods but also types of people. The complex array of patterns of power relations in a social formation and the migration of people between these patterns highlights the plurality of workers' experiences. As Niemann (Chapter 6) notes in his discussion of absolute space in Southern Africa, different patterns of social relations of production exist side by side and thus individuals can experience multiple contexts in their daily lives.

Amoore (Chapter 1) analyzes how flexibilization and the restructuring of work and of firms contribute to the differences among workers as subjects. She goes on to demonstrate how 'divisions at work are overlaid by other social divisions and inequalities so that, for example, some workers' experience of increased insecurity is ameliorated by financial security, and by inclusion in the defining of the terms of flexibility'. Other social divisions and inequalities, for example race and gender, are not ignored in a power and production approach. Niemann (Chapter 6) emphasizes how race has permeated the social relations of production in the mines in South Africa, and Healy (Chapter 8) emphasizes how gender permeates the social relations of production in Mexico. To stress the centrality of power in production relations is not, therefore, a reductionist approach to political analysis; rather it offers a means for understanding subjectivity in complex ways without resorting to pluralist notions of society that obscure the specific politico-economic conditions of societies.

Nevertheless not all of the contributors are satisfied with the specific rationalities or forms of consciousness and patterns of power relations that Harrod elaborated in his 1987 book. Clarke, for example, argues that COSATU has misunderstood the politics of casual workers. In Chapter 7 she focuses on the strategies of the union as an actor, rather than on the rationality of the workers, when criticizing the tendency to claim that casual workers, rather than the process of casualization, as are at the root of the problems caused by restructuring. However in her rejection of Harrod's claim that casual workers tend to embrace millenarianism or populism, she refers to some of the organizing efforts being made by this emergent section of the South African workforce. The importance of proximate political struggles is emphasized by Federici (Chapter 5). She commends Harrod's emphasis on the importance of power relations to the formation of consciousness, but points out that power relations can themselves be affected by political activity and social movements that redefine the main categories of social reproduction. The links between prostitutes' struggles, the feminist movement and women working in factories, offices and homes are exemplary in this regard, as are the difficulties presented by the decline of feminism and the weakening of workers' movements.

Thus when considering the production of political subjectivity – or in Stevis and Boswell's terminology (Chapter 9), the ways in which actors gain meaningful choice and effective voice if they shift their status from 'phantom' or 'object' to 'subject' or 'agent' – the migration of people between different forms of power relations is crucial. As Davies (Chapter 4) argues, the global poor can become formed as political subjects in public spheres, which must be conceptualized with regard both to the formation of the social context (what Negt and Kluge, 1993, call *Lebenszusammenhang*, or 'contexts of living') and to areas of social life that are excluded from the dominant conceptions of the public, namely work and family life. Such public spheres are formed by the migration of workers between different forms of production relations, and thereby circulating their struggles. We consider that this conception of the public sphere should be central to any theory of subject formation that is critical-materialist without being reductionist. To put it slightly differently, it should be central to a more refined understanding of the mechanisms by which subjects are formed beyond the Gramscian 'economic corporate moment' in order to become actors in the struggle over the ethico-political and hegemonic.

Subject formation and the organization and mobilization of unprotected workers

This brings us to the question of the importance of practices of social mobilization and social organization in civil society, or perhaps more to the point, the public sphere. It should be clear that this volume takes the view that the question of labour cannot be reduced to a matter of industrial relations and trade union politics. Such a view suffers from two major problems: it subscribes to an overly narrow conception of labour and work; and it conflates labourers and workers with a particular organizational representation of the interests of a particular category of workers. It should be added in this context that if trade unionists are, as C. Wright Mills (1948) once put it, 'managers of discontent' then a problematic politics of representation is attached to this relationship.

The concepts of labour and work obviously extend beyond these narrow confines – indeed we agree with Cox (1987) and Harrod (1987) that work is the key activity of humans – and cover a very diverse range of activities and relationships. The analytical approach to understanding labour in the global political economy suggested by Harrod is to disaggregate the global labour force, and the preferred method for doing this, as well as for analyzing the social formation, is to use the criteria of the power relations found in production. The analytical advantage of these criteria is that they do not elide different kinds of power relations in the way that the more common criteria of nationality, occupation, ethnicity or gender do. This gives the analysis a concrete basis for disaggregation and analysis. In Chapter 5 Federici provides an example of the importance of this when she highlights the complications with the notion of trafficking, which in some instances can be seen as entrapment, sexual slavery or debt bondage while in others it has more the appearance of a contract.

However disaggregation is merely an analytical tool, and we still need to understand how a social formation can bring together the different forms of power relations. Harrod (1987) argues that the social formation is constituted by the ensemble of patterns of power relations in production. Each pattern is itself organized by its internal power relations – that is, the power relations between the dominant and subordinate groups within the pattern – and by external power relations, namely 'the relationship between one form of social relations and the whole hierarchy of forms within any single social formation' (ibid., p. 31). Davies (Chapter 4) suggests that political transformations are more likely to result from political struggles that develop in the realm of external relations – that is, in the movement of people between proximate patterns of power relations – than from the political struggles that develop within any particular pattern. Nonetheless internal and external power relationships should be analyzed together. In Chapter 9 Stevis and Boswell argue that the 'key reason why the internal–external delineation is precarious is because internal politics is implicated in the constitution of the external domain while external politics is implicated in the constitution of the internal order'.

People migrate between proximate forms of social relations, and as they do so they may provoke changes in the consciousness and details of the power relations in the various patterns. This can work in both directions: people formerly employed in the enterprise pattern who are forced to migrate to a casual pattern may take the old forms of consciousness into the new pattern; or women who move between the household and the enterprise pattern may transform both patterns (see Chapters 4 and 8; this is also an important part of the argument in Chapter 7).

Thus the ensemble of patterns of power relations constitutes the social formation and these patterns have external relations with other patterns. The ensemble is structured hierarchically as dominant patterns extract from subordinate patterns. The ensemble of patterns is also linked by the movement of people between proximate patterns. This, however, raises the question of what constitutes proximity. Amoore (Chapter 1), Harrod (Chapter 2), Ryner (Chapter 3) and Davies (Chapter 4) all focus on the hierarchical ordering of the social relations of production, while Federici (Chapter 5) raises the issue of how proximate political struggles, such as for women's rights, civil rights or gay liberation, which are not necessarily definable in terms of production relations, may have important consequences for social and political mobilization. Clarke (Chapter 7) makes a similar observation regarding the different kinds of mobilization among casual labourers in South Africa.

The notion of proximity is also complicated because it is a spatial metaphor and, as Niemann's discussion of labour migration in Southern Africa (Chapter 6) reminds us, different social formations produce and depend on different kinds of space. In Chapter 3 Ryner's analysis of the interactions between changes in power relations in the core, semi-periphery and periphery also shows how proximate patterns are not necessarily spatially contiguous.

Of course these global relations must also be produced and reproduced. Thus Davies (Chapter 4), following Cox (1987) and Lefebvre (1976, 1991b), highlights the importance of the household in the production and reproduction of social relations; Federici (Chapter 5) analyzes how the labour of social reproduction is commodified; and Healy (Chapter 8) argues that passive revolution in Mexico depended not only on the state and concrete interclass relations but also on the patriarchal structures woven into Mexican society and social life.

One useful way in which to begin to think about the interactions between social formation and the organization and mobilization of unprotected workers is by considering the two dimensions of the concept of public sphere, as identified by Negt and Kluge (1993). In the previous section we covered one of these dimensions: the public sphere as a (produced) 'context of living' and 'horizon of experience'. However the public sphere also includes the instituted practices by which subjects orient themselves towards and articulate their demands and actions to political society, including state apparatuses and international organizations. In other words, it is through this dimension of the public sphere that subjects are politicized.

The contributors to this volume have intimated a number of ways in which unprotected workers are constituted as political subjects through organization and mobilization. Amoore (Chapter 1) points to the way in which transnational corporations condition these processes through the management of risk. Harrod and Ryner (Chapters 2 and 3) refer to the increased room for manoeuvre and populist and religiously inspired mobilization in the core as well as the periphery. Federici's contribution (Chapter 5) is well worth studying because of its engagement with the relationship between the conditions of the social relations of production, new social movements challenging *inter alia* conventional sexuality and Third World economic exploitation, and the international debates by feminist NGOs on how to address the question of prostitution. The chapter is also illustrative of an analysis becoming an active part of the politics of mobilization as it seeks to transcend the divided positions in international feminist mobilization and struggle.

The volume thus constitutes a critique of any conflation of the politics of work with trade unions. On the other hand it certainly does not suggest that trade unions are not important actors in the political economy of unprotected work. Ryner (Chapter 3) laments the decline of trade unions, which he interprets as part of the process of the 'ominous polarization of habitus' that he associates with populism. Three of the chapters analyze trade union politics in considerable detail. Far from seeing trade unions as passive victims of neoliberal globalization, Clarke and Healy (Chapters 7 and 8) suggest that corporatist practices and the failure to mobilize unprotected workers by means of more inclusive and gender-progressive strategies is part of the reason for trade union weakness. They do so, however (as trade union activists themselves), with full appreciation of the strategic dilemmas that South African and Mexican unions face within the confines of structural adjustment programmes and free trade agreements such as the North American Free Trade Agreement. Stevis and Boswell (Chapter 9), however, see some hope in the marginalization of trade unions from official political institutions. International trade unions are responding to the attendant crisis by becoming more attentive to the representation of unprotected workers.

Consistent with this theme, a number of the contributors consider the prospect of a 'social movement unionism', where by trade unions would respond to the decline of corporatism by broader membership mobilization. There are related questions about the prospect of trade unionism in the industrializing semiperiphery. These questions hinge in part on the degree of repression of trade unions involved in such endeavours, which is an example of how mobilization issues can spill over into formal politics. In any case, we would submit that the patterns of social relations of production approach contributes significantly to the question of the prospects of social movement trade unionism.

Implications for political society and transnational power politics

A general sentiment to which all the contributors to this volume seem to subscribe is exemplified by Harrod in Chapter 2: 'it might be considered strange [in discussions of international politics], if not eccentric, to start with an analysis of a small enterprise in an Indian industrial town or the pitch of a hawker in the Philippines'. However this is the case with an increasing number of studies that point to the importance the 'global poor' to global politics. In this volume Amoore's critical review of the IPE and globalization literature (Chapter 1), Harrod's and Ryner's critiques of 'work empty' discourses and orthodox Marxism (Chapters 2 and 3) and Davies's assertion that we should think more carefully about the subjects of resistance (Chapter 4), show that the conception of patterns of social relations of production and the attendant ideal types of unprotected work have a lot to offer to analyses of the global poor. In particular, by considering the global poor in this context we can understand how they are connected to global economic structures and the world order, and how they contribute to its reproduction and potentially to its transformation. The subsequent chapters demonstrate in more detail, and by means of more systematic empirical research, how these dynamics play themselves out in particular settings of the world order: Federici in relation to the sex trade and prostitution (Chapter 5), Niemann and Clarke in the case of postapartheid South Africa (Chapters 6 and 7), Healy in respect of the struggle over the 'condition of hegemony' in Mexico (Chapter 8) and Stevis and Boswell with regard to how international trade union organizations have responded to the phenomenon of unprotected workers (Chapter 9). Harrod's emphasis on power at the point of production suggests a conception of power that is the reverse of that in most approaches to international relations: power at its most basic is articulated in specific social relations in production, from which it accrues or flows to more general levels of social and political life, including international relations. Power at the global level flows from and depends on power at the local level.

What are the implications of this approach for the study of transnational political society and organization? Broadly speaking, on the basis of the approach one can argue that the study of transnational politics has a tendency to consider surface phenomena rather that the underlying social relations upon which the phenomena rest – what Marx called 'fetishism'. There is no doubt an affinity here with Enloe's (1996) feminist quest of rendering visible the hidden practices and actors upon which more formal power politics rests. Consider for example Harrod's observation in Chapter 2 that, at the immediate operational level, the war in Iraq is in large part being fought between people recruited from the American underclass and insurgents mobilized from the slums (for example the Mahdi Army). Beyond this, considering the old liberal functionalist concern with social integration, the approach has something to offer to a more in-depth analysis of the material sources of global conflict and disorder, as opposed to superficial rationalization of the causes as evil, fanaticism and so on.

From a critical theoretical point of view, if the objective is to understand how existing practices are constraining emancipatory potentials the focus should be on how power structures seek to mediate antagonisms and conflicts that arise from the power mobilization of unprotected work, with prevailing accumulation strategies. This attention to hegemonic accumulation strategies and concepts of social control has been the focus of critical IPE and IR up to this point, and it is here that it has made its most important contributions. Because this volume seeks to rebalance the critical research agenda it has not addressed these questions explicitly.

Nevertheless the volume points towards and begins to contribute to a synthesis. In its criticism of neoliberal transnational hegemony, critical IPE tends to highlight its limitation and the emergence of a Polanyian 'double movement'. But the nature of this double movement is not made concrete or specific. We contend that a systematic analysis of the configuration of transnational production patterns and attendant dispositions (Chapter 3), as well as the concrete configuration of public spheres (Chapter 4), provides the basis for such a synthesis and enables a more concrete and finely tuned understanding of the terms of counterhegemony. In different ways the more empirical chapters in this volume also contribute to such a synthesis.

This volume is not to be understood, then, as an analysis of local everyday life and the commonplace, rather than a top-down analysis. Indeed, because the conceptualization allows for the analysis of the connection of production patterns with the world order via social formations and public spheres, it integrally connects the local with the global.

Suggestions for future research

There should be no doubt that this volume constitutes a preliminary statement concerning the potential usefulness of the 'power and production' approach developed in 1987 by Cox and Harrod for the study of global politics in a new conjuncture. It is inevitable, then, that the volume is more interesting from the point of view of setting the agenda for future research than for the substantive conclusions it reaches. To return to the idea of the hermeneutic circle in Chapter 3, this is very much an exercise to obtain a well-considered initial understanding in preparation for obtaining a deeper understanding through systematic research.

The fact that there is still a need for systematic empirical research does not mean that the volume lacks careful empirical research. For example Federici (Chapter 5), Clarke (Chapter 7) and Healy (Chapter 8) summarize the conclusions of extensive studies and offer careful theoretical conceptualization and contextualization, using primary research material that is often exceedingly difficult to obtain. But these three case studies, while very important, cover just two countries and one sector. A more systematic analysis of unprotected work and world politics will require further analyses. A question that would need to be asked in this context is do we need exhaustive, representative or exemplary studies?

Producing an exhaustive collection of case studies would have obvious merits but would not always be realistic, given the scarcity of research resources. There is also the problem of trade-off between breadth and depth, which is classically encountered in comparative analysis (Ragin, 1987). Amassing quantitative analyses will be a desirable strategy and a legitimate part of a future research agenda. There are merits to attempting to determine the proportions and concentrations of different patterns of social relations of production, of which Ryner's study in this volume (Chapter 3) is a preliminary and impressionistic one. An important challenge here is to compile and organize census statistics. The ILO and UNDP statistics are far from satisfactory in this regard as they are not primarily concerned with multiple power relations in production.

Representative analysis is problematic as it is intimately associated with positivist and ahistorical assumptions, which are incommensurate with the historicism of the approach advocated here. 'Exemplary' studies, which on the basis of a contextually defined problematic can identify certain sectors, phenomena and countries that are particularly important from a general point of view, might constitute a more attractive approach. For example Harrod (Chapter 2), Ryner (Chapter 3) and Davies (Chapter 4) have pointed to the importance of millenarianism for unprotected work and the terms and sources of conflict in world politics. One could also consider analyzing the major international organizations, tracing the implications of their mode of governance for the social relations of unprotected work. The problem with such an approach is that critical researchers might be overly driven by their initial views of what should be considered important. Whatever approach is taken, future research has to consider case study selection with care, and the questions of representativeness and exemplarity are useful for orientating thought in this regard. It is certain that systematic analysis of counterpublic spheres, identified above as central to the problem, requires in-depth qualitative research, for which the question of case selection is unavoidable.

But avenues for future research are not only empirical. There are also important conceptual questions that cannot be resolved just by empirical analysis. There are many (implicit and explicit) conceptual debates in the pages of this book. Here we shall only focus on just one, namely that concerning patterns of social relations of production as ideal types.

Most of the contributors to this volume consider that the concept of patterns of social relations of production plays an indispensable part, and crucially enriches, the historical-structural analysis recommended in 1981 by Cox, who considered the interactive codetermination of material capabilities, ideas and institutions at the equally interactive levels of production, forms of state and world order. The contribution that is most faithful to Cox's original formulation is probably that by Ryner (Chapter 3), who also insists on situating the analysis of unprotected work in a Gramscian framework (more so than Harrod, who in Chapter 2 argues that the framework does not necessarily have to be associated with Gramsci, and also calls for a radically new materialism). Indeed much the first part of his chapter is devoted to defending such a procedure from semiotically based, post-structuralist theory. He then uses the Gramscian framework to reconstruct the 'economic corporate' moment of world order as one dimension of a Gramscian and Coxian 'relations of force'. He suggests that this gives us a critical politico-economic insight into what Huntington (1993) calls the 'clash of civilizations'. The other explicitly Coxian–Gramscian contribution is Healy's study of Mexico (Chapter 8). Healy demonstrates that any separation of production relations from other parts of the historical structure is always analytic, and if it is reified it can be distorting. Indeed she shows that gender relations are fundamentally constitutive of the terms of hegemonic struggle, and her chapter is an illustration of how feminist theory and Cox and Harrod's categories can mutually enrich one another.

The contributors who are more sceptical about a straightforward application of Cox and Harrod's categories of unprotected work include Federici (Chapter 5) and to a lesser extent Clarke (Chapter 7). Some of the issues and problems raised here are of an empirical nature and concern the applicability of the typology offered by Cox and Harrod. Federici's detailed analysis of prostitution questions the more sweeping accounts by Cox and Harrod, who tend to associate prostitution with the casual pattern of production. For Federici the sex industry is much more complex, both on the supply and on the demand side. One obvious response would be to categorize different prostitutes in terms of their location in different patterns (for example self-employment), which might help explain the divisions in prostitute's movements and feminist debates. However this would still leave the question of whether the recent trend in human trafficking is captured in the Cox and Harrod's categories. Is this form of indentured labour a new pattern, or a reemerging pattern that resembles slavery? Indeed is slavery re-emerging to such an extent in the new global political economy that it should be considered a new pattern? This question warrants further consideration and research from the point of view of the Cox–Harrod approach.

Clarke's research on South Africa raises similar questions. Whilst she agrees that Cox and Harrod's focus on disaggregation on the basis of power relations overcomes the limitations of the labour segmentation approach in terms of understanding the strategic terrain of workers' struggles, she is less certain about the direct applicability of their categories. She finds the distinction between protected and unprotected work (which admittedly is a distinction of convention) less than helpful and calls for greater differentiation of the wide variety of unprotected work. Things get even more problematic when one tries to categorize unionized black workers in South Africa in the final years of apartheid. For Clarke this is clearly not an instance of tripartism, given the degree and extent of the repression of trade unionists. Niemann (Chapter 6), whilst agreeing with Clarke on the matter of repression, still considers tripartism to be an apt term in connection with South Africa's 'racist Fordism', given that both the mining industry and the state recognized that they needed to find a *modus vivendi* with black trade unions. It should be also noted that problems can arise if analyses are based too closely on Cox and Harrod's framework. For example Ryner (Chapter 3) finds it hard to characterize the social relations of production for core workers in Europe as either corporate or tripartite. They still display tripartite traits, as centralized unions are involved both in social pacts to regulate wage increases and in concession bargaining over social benefits. However in the workplace benefits are increasingly individualized in a way that resembles the corporate pattern. Ryner calls this hybrid 'hollowed-out tripartism'. Similarly Healy (Chapter 8) argues that current patterns in the Mexican automotive industry are hybrids of the state-corporatist, enterprise and corporate patterns, where the former has the coercive power to restructure the patterns along the lines defined by the other two. What are we to make of all this?

In part the response has to be more careful research and possibly revision of the patterns identified by Cox and Harrod almost 20 years ago. Changes in what are, after all, ideal types are indeed implied in the dynamic and historicist nature of the approach. However the answer also lies in being clear about what it means methodologically to engage in heuristic and ideal-type reasoning.

Most of the confusion, we contend, could be redressed at this level, and here we can take a leaf from the founder of ideal-typical reasoning, Max Weber. As Harrod underlines in Chapter 2, the historical materialism advocated by him and Cox in 1987 implied a critique of the Marxian conception of an abstract capitalist mode of production as an achieved historical reality – a conception that became increasingly problematic in peripheral societies. This is something that Mao (1964) and Poulantzas (1973) recognized in different ways – the latter distinguishing between 'mode of production' and 'social formation' at different levels of abstraction – without taking the full consequences. Ryner puts it slightly differently in Chapter 3: the Marxian conception of capital as an emergent causal power and tendency can be accepted. However this tendency acts on countertendencies and historical legacies that make the social relations of the production of social formations much more complex than the Marxian two-class model and 'mode of production' imply. This is increasingly being recognized in Marxist research, and because of these complexities it is also being acknowledged that ideal types must be accepted as part of the toolkit for relating more abstract and concrete levels of analysis (see for example Albritton, 1986; Sayer, 1992). But what does it mean to use ideal types methodologically? Gerth and Wright Mills (1958, pp. 59–60) remind us that:

> The much-discussed 'ideal type', a key term in Weber's methodological discussion, refers to the construction of certain elements of reality into a logically precise conception … He felt that social scientists had the choice of using logically controlled and unambiguous conceptions, which are thus removed from historical reality, or of using less precise concepts, which are more closely geared to the empirical world … [C]omparison led him to consider extreme and 'pure cases'. These cases became 'crucial instances' and controlled the level of abstraction that he used in connection with any particular problem. The real meat of history would usually fall in between such extreme types; hence Weber would approximate the multiplicity of specific historical situations by bringing various type concepts to bear upon the specific case under his focus.

In other words the patterns of social relations of production are abstractions (though more concrete abstractions than the mode of production concept) – 'controlled and unambiguous conceptions' that are deployed heuristically in order to allow the analyst to assign some coherent analytical meaning to a complex reality. Moreover at this level comparative analysis – it is claimed – allows us to establish some relationship between similar power relations and rationalities and dispositions of consciousness. However as we move towards a more concrete and historical reality in our analysis there is less and less fit with the ideal type, be it in present-day Western Europe, Mexico, South Africa or the sex industry. This means that we should not try to fit this reality mechanically into the ideal typical categories. At the same time it does not mean that the ideal types – if they are any good – are irrelevant, because understanding is obtained by investigating how the concrete reality differs/varies from the ideal type. This is what it means to 'approximate' and 'bring to bear' the ideal types in concrete reasoning. It is in this context that Ryner's 'hollowed-out tripartism' (Chapter 3) and Healy's hybridic 'global corporatism' (Chapter 8) can be understood. It is also possible that this would resolve the disagreement between Niemann (Chapter 6) and Clarke (Chapter 7) over tripartism in South Africa.

At this stage it is appropriate to come full circle to the launching of the critical paradigm to which this book seeks to contribute, with a reminder of the way in which Cox, inspired by Gramsci (1971) and Braudel (1980), chose to define a 'historicist concept':

[The concepts are] constantly adjust[ed] to specific historical circumstances. The concepts cannot usefully be considered in abstraction from their applications, for when they are so abstracted different usages of the same concept appear to contain contradictions or ambiguities. A concept, in Gramsci's thought, is loose and elastic and attains precision only when brought into contact with a particular situation which it helps to explain – a contact which also develops the meaning of the concept. This is the strength of Gramsci's historicism and therein lies its explanatory power. (Cox, 1993, pp. 49–50)

References

Abogado, G. (1992) 'Movimiento Democrático de los Trabajadores de la Ford', interview by T. Healy, Mexico, DF, 12 May.

Adler Hellman, J. (1983) *Mexico in Crisis*, 2nd edn (New York: Holmes and Meier).

Agathangelou, A. M. (2004) *The Global Political Economy of Sex: Desire, Violence, And Insecurity in Mediterranean Nation States* (New York: Palgrave Macmillan).

Agnew, J. (1994) 'Timeless space and state-centrism: the geographical assumptions of International Relations theory', in S. Rosow, N. Inayatullah and M. Rupert (eds), *The Global Economy as Political Space* (Boulder, CO: Lynne Rienner).

Aguilar García, J. (1984) *La política sindical en México: industria del automóvil* (México, DF: Ediciones Era).

Ahmad, A. (1997) 'Postcolonial theory and the post-condition', in L. Panitch (ed.), *Ruthless Criticism of All That Exists, Social Register 1997* (London: Merlin), pp. 358–81.

Ahwireng-Obeng, F. and McGowan, P. (1998) 'Partner or hegemon? South Africa in Africa', *Journal of Contemporary African Studies*, vol. 16, pp. 5–37.

Albritton, R. (1986) *Towards a Japanese Reconstruction of Marxist Theory* (Basingstoke: Macmillan).

Alexander, P. (1998) 'Prostitution: still a difficult issue for feminists', in F. Delacoste and P. Alexander (eds), *Sex Work: Writings by Women in the Sex Industry*, 2nd edn (San Francisco, CA: Cleis Press), pp. 184–230.

Alvarez, E. (1979) 'Boerum Hill residents rally to rid local Church steps of prostitutes', *The (Brooklyn) Phoenix*, 23 August, p. 3.

Álvarez Béjar, A. (1987) *La Crisis Global del Capitalismo en México: 1968–1985* (México, DF: Ediciones Era).

Álvarez Béjar, A. (1993) 'Economic integration, social dislocation and political challenges in North America', paper presented at the 34th Annual Convention of the International Studies Association, Acapulco, Guerrero, México, 24–27 March.

Álvarez Béjar, A. and Borrego, J. (coords) (1990) *La inserción de México en la Cuenca del Pacífico, vol. II* (Mexico, DF: Facultad de Economía, Universidad Autónoma de México).

Amin, A. (1994) 'Post-Fordism: Models, Fantasies and Phantoms of Transition', in A. Amin (ed.), *Post Fordism: A Reader* (Oxford: Blackwell).

Amnesty International (2003) 'Intolerable killings: ten years of abductions and murders in Ciudad Juárez and Chihuahua' (www.amnestyusa.org/countries/mexico/document.do?id=3EC284DD25E3F2B080256D78005D4BB1).

Amoore, L. (2000) 'International Political Economy and the contested firm', *New Political Economy*, vol. 5, pp. 183–204.

Amoore, L. (2001) 'Work, production and social relations: repositioning the firm in the international political economy', in J. Harrod and R. O'Brien (eds), *Global Unions: Theory and Strategy of Organised Labour in the Global Political Economy* (London: Routledge).

References 245

Amoore, L. (2002) *Globalisation Contested: An International Political Economy of Work* (Manchester: Manchester University Press).

Amoore, L. (2004) 'Risk, reward and discipline at work', *Economy and Society,* vol. 33 (2), pp.174–96.

Amoore, L. (ed.) (2005) *Global Resistance Reader* (New York: Routledge).

Amoore, L. and Langley, P. (2000) 'Process, project and practice: the politics of globalisation', paper presented to 25th Annual Conference of the British International Studies Association, 18–20 December.

Amoore, L. and Langley, P. (2004) 'Ambiguities of global civil society', *Review of International Studies,* vol. 30 (1), pp. 89–110.

Anderson, B. (2000) *Doing the Dirty Work: The Global Politics of Domestic Labour* (London: Zed Books).

Anderson, G., Brosnan, P. and Walsh, P. (1994) 'Flexibility, casualisation and externalization in the New Zealand workforce', *The Journal of Industrial Relations,* vol. 36 (4), pp. 491–518.

Anderson, S. and Cavanagh, J. (2000) 'Bearing the burden: the impact of global financial crisis on workers and alternative agendas for the IMF and other institutions', *International Labor Rights Fund. Workers in a Global Economy* (www.ips-dc.org/reports/bearing.htm).

Archibugi, D., Held, D. and Köhler, M. (1998) *Re-imagining Political Community: Studies in Cosmopolitan Democracy* (Cambridge: Polity Press).

Arrighi, G. (1994) *The Long Twentieth Century* (London: Verso).

Arteaga, A. (1990) 'Nacido Ford, crecido flexible', *Trabajo,* vol. 2 (spring), pp. 66–7.

Arteaga, A., Jorge Carrillo V. and Jordy Micheli, T. (1989) 'Transformaciones tecnológicas y relaciones laborales en la industria automotriz', *Documentos de Trabajo,* vol. 19 (Mexico, DF: Fundación Friedrich Ebert).

Augelli, E. and Murphy, C. (1993) 'Gramsci and international relations: a general perspective and example from recent US policy toward the Third World', in S. Gill (ed.), *Gramsci, Historical Materialism, and International Relations* (Cambridge: Cambridge University Press), pp. 127–47.

Augustín, L. M. (2005) 'Cessons de parler de victimes, reconnaissons aux migrants leur capacité d'agir'. in C. Verschuur and F. Reysoo (eds), *Genre, Nouvelle Division Internationale du Travail et Migrations,* IUÈD-EFI, Cahiers: Genre et Développement, no 5 (Geneva: Editions L'Harmattan), pp. 109–18.

Bachrach, P. and Botwinick, A. (1992) *Power and Empowerment: A Radical Theory of Participatory Democracy* (Philadelphia: Temple University Press).

Bakker, I. (ed.) (1994) *The Strategic Silence* (London: Zed Books).

Bakker, I. (1998) *Unpaid Work and Macroeconomics: New Discussions, New Tools for Action* (Ottawa: Status of Women Canada).

Bakker, I. (2003) 'Neoliberal governance and the reprivatization of social reproduction: social provisioning and shifting gender orders', in I. Bakker and S. Gill (eds), *Power Production and Social Reproduction* (Basingstoke: Palgrave Macmillan), pp. 66–82.

Bakker, I. and Gill, S. (eds) (2003) *Power Production and Social Reproduction* (Basingstoke: Palgrave Macmillan).

Bales, K. (1999) *Disposable People: New Slavery in the Global Economy* (Berkeley, CA: University of California Press).

Balibar, E. (1993) 'Spinoza, the anti-Orwell: the fear of the masses', in E. Balibar (ed.), *Masses, Classes, Ideas: Studies on Politics and Philosophy Before and After Marx* (London: Routledge).

Barchiesi, F. (2005) *Class, Social Movements and the Transformation of the South African Left in the Crisis of 'National Liberation'*. Rcd 2004 http://www.red.m2014.net/article.php3?id_article=32 [cited August 17 2005].

Barkin, D. (1990) *Distorted Development: Mexico in the World Economy* (Boulder, CO: Westview Press).

Barrett, P. S. (2001) 'Labour policy, labour–business relations and the transition to democracy in Chile', *Journal of Latin American Studies*, vol. 33 (3), pp. 561–97.

Barry, K. (1981) *Female Sexual Slavery* (New York: Avon Books).

Barry, K. (1992) *The Coalition Against Trafficking in Women. History and Statement of Purpose 1991–1992* (Pennsylvania: CATW, State College).

Barry, K., Bunch, C. and Castley, S. (eds) (1984) *International Feminism: Networking Against Female Sexual Slavery* (New York: International Women Tribune Center).

Baskin, J. (1991) *Striking Back: A History of Cosatu* (London: Verso).

Basler, B. (1981) 'City prostitutes invade residential communities', *New York Times*, 15 August, p. 1.

Bassett, C. (2004) 'South Africa's trade unions and counter-hegemony: a great idea whose time came ... and passed', paper read at Canadian Political Science Association Annual Conference, June 2004, Winnipeg.

Bauman, Z. (1998) *Globalization: The Human Consequences* (Cambridge: Polity Press).

Beck, S. and Scherrer, C. (2003) 'The Red–Green attack on Modell Deutschland', paper presented at the Annual Meeting of the International Studies Association, Portland, Oregon, 26 February–1 March.

Beck, U. (2000a) *What is Globalization?* (Cambridge: Polity Press).

Beck, U. (2000b) *The Brave New World of Work* (Cambridge: Polity Press).

Belaala, S. (2004) 'Moroccco: slums breed jihad', *Le Monde Diplomatique* (English edition), November, pp. 4–5.

Bell, S. (1994) *Reading, Writing and Rewriting the Prostitute Body* (Bloomington, IA: Indiana University Press).

Bell, T. (2004) 'Women break new ground for farm workers', *Business Report*, 6 August, 2004 (www.busrep.co.za/index./php?fSectionld=559&Articleld=2177381).

Bennholdt-Thomsen, V., Faraclas, N. and von Werlhof, C. (eds) (2001) *There Is an Alternative: Subsistence and World Wide Resistance to Globalization* (London: Zed Books).

Bennett D. and Sharpe, K. (1985) *Transnational corporations versus the state: the political economy of the Mexican auto industry* (Princeton, NJ: Princeton University Press).

Bensusán, G. and León, S. (coords) (1990) *Negociación y Conflicto Laboral en México* (Mexico, DF: Friedrich Ebert Siftung).

Benzi, O. (2001) *Prostitute* (Milan: Mondadori).

Bernard, M. (2000) 'Post-Fordism and global restructuring', in R. Stubbs and G. R. D. Underhill (eds), *Political Economy and the Changing Global Order* (Don Mills, Ontario: Oxford University Press).

Bevir, M. (1999) 'Foucault, Power and Institutions', *Political Studies* vol. 47, pp. 345–59.

Bhorat, H. and Hinks, T. J. (2006) *Changing Patterns of Employment and Employer–Employee Relations in Post-Apartheid South Africa* (Cape Town: Development and Policy Research Unit (DPRU).

Bindman, J. and Doezema, J. (1997) *Redefining Prostitution as Sex Work on the International Agenda* (London: Anti-Slavery International).

Bittman, M., Matheson, G. and Meagher, G. (1999) 'The changing boundary between home and market: Australian trends in outsourcing domestic labour', *Work, Employment and Society*, vol. 13 (2), pp. 249–73.

Bohman, J. (1997) 'The public spheres of the world citizen', in J. Bohman and M. Lutz-Bachman (eds), *Perpetual Peace: Essays on Kant's Cosmopolitan Ideal* (Cambridge, Mass.: MIT Press).

Boswell, T. and Chase-Dunn, C. (2000) *The Spiral of Capitalism and Socialism: Toward Global Democracy* (Boulder, CO: Lynne Rienner).

Bourdieu, P. (1977) *Outline of a Theory of Practice* (Cambridge: Cambridge University Press).

Bowden, C. (1998) *Juárez: The Laboratory of Our Future* (New York: Aperture Foundation).

Boyer, R. (1997) 'Capital–labour relations in the OECD countries: from the Fordist Golden Age to contrasting national trajectories', in J. Schor and J. Il You (eds) *Capital, the State and Labour: A Global Perspective* (Aldershot: Edward Elgar).

Boyes-Watson, C. (2003) *Crime and Justice: A Casebook Approach* (Boston, Mass.: Allyn and Bacon).

Braithwaite, J. and Drahos, P. (2000) *Global Business Regulation* (Cambridge: Cambridge University Press).

Bramble T. and Barchiesi, F. (2003) *Rethinking the Labour Movement in the 'New South Africa'* (Burlington, Vt: Ashgate).

Braunthal, J. (1967) *History of the International. Volume 1: 1864–1914* (New York: Frederick A. Praeger).

Britto da Motta, A. (1999) 'Doing housework for pay: political struggles and the legal rights of domestic workers in Brazil', in M. Dalla Costa and G. F. Dalla Costa (eds), *Women, Development, and Labor of Reproduction* (Trenton, NJ: Africa World Press).

Britto da Motta, A., and Moreira de Carvalho, I. M. (1993) 'Pauperization and women's participation in social movements in Brazil', in M. Dalla Costa and G. F. Dalla Costa (eds), *Paying the Price: Women and the Politics of International Economic Strategy* (London: Zed Books), pp. 73–90.

Brodie, J. (1996) 'New State Forms, New Political Spaces', in R. Boyer and D. Drache (eds), *States Against Markets: The Limits of Globalization*, (London: Routledge).

Brown, B. (1977) 'Decriminalization of prostitution', *Boston Ledger*, 2 November.

Brown, D. E. (1991) *Human Universals* (New York: McGraw-Hill).

Buci-Glucksmann, C. (1980) *Gramsci and the State* (London: Lawrence and Wishart).

Burawoy, M. (1985) *The Politics of Production* (London: Verso).

Burnham, P. (1999) 'Historical materialism, getting it right: the politics of economic management in the 1990s', paper presented to the International Studies Association Convention, Washington DC, 16–20 February.

Bustamante, J. (1983) 'Maquilidoras: a new face of international capitalism on Mexico's northern frontier', in J. Nash and M. Patricia Fernandex-Kelly (eds), *Woman, Men and the International Division of Labour* (Albany, NY: State University of New York Press).

Butchtemann, C. F. and Quack, S. (1990) 'How precarious is "non-standard" employment? Evidence for West Germany', *Cambridge Journal of Economics*, vol. 14 (3), pp. 315–30.

CABIRIA (Community Health Project With Sex Workers) (2002) 'Stop the wave of repression and the municipal orders against prostitution', July (http://perso. wanadoo.fr/cabirialenglish/e_arrete01.html).

Caffentzis, G. (1993) 'The fundamental implications of the debt crisis for social reproduction in Africa', in M. Dalla Costa and G. F. Dalla Costa (eds), *Paying the Price: Women and the Politics of International Economic Strategy* (London: Zed Books), pp. 15–41.

Cafruny, A. (2003) 'Europe, America and the Neo-Liberal (dis)order: is there a coming crisis of the Euro?,' in A. Cafruny and M. Ryner (eds), *A Ruined Fortress? Neoliberal Hegemony and Transformation in Europe* (Lanham, MD: Rowman & Littlefield), pp. 285–305.

Cagatay, N. (1998) 'Gender and poverty', United Nations Development Programme, Social Development and Poverty Elimination Division Working Papers Series, no. 5 (www.undp.org/poverty/publications/wkpaper/wp5/wp5-nilufer.PDF).

Calhoun, C. (ed.) (1992) *Habermas and the Public Sphere* (Cambridge, Mass.: MIT Press).

Cameron, M. (1992) 'Micro and macro logics of political conflict: the informal sector and institutional change in Peru and Mexico', in A. Ritter, M. Eron and D. Pollock (eds), *Latin America to the year 2000: Reactivating Growth, Improving Equity, Sustaining Democracy* (New York: Praeger), pp. 215–19.

Campbell, D. (1996) 'Political prosaics, transversal politics, and the anarchical world', in M. J. Shapiro and H. R. Alker (eds), *Challenging Boundaries: Global Flows, Territorial Identities* (Minneapolis, MA: University of Minnesota Press), pp. 7–31.

Cant, M. and Brink, A. (1999) 'Black retailing in South Africa', *International Scope Review*, vol. 1 (2), pp. 1–15.

Carchedi, F. (ed.) (2004) *Prostituzione Migrante e Donne Trafficate: Il Caso delle Donne Albanesi, Moldave e Rumene* (Milan: Franco Angeli).

Carchedi, G. (1989) 'Classes and class analysis', in E. O. Wright (ed.), *The Debate on Classes* (London: Verso), pp. 105–25.

Carr, E. H. (1964) *Socialism in One Country, 1924–1926. A History of Soviet Russia*, vol. 3, part 2 (New York: Macmillan).

Carrillo, J. (coord.) (1990) *La Nueva Era de la Industria Automotriz en México: Cambio tecnológico, organizacional y en las estructuras de control* (Tijuana: El Colegio de la Frontera Norte).

Carrillo, J. and de la O, M. E. (1992) 'La reestructuración en la industria maquiladora', *El Cotidiano*, vol. 46 (Mar.–Apr.), pp. 54–9.

Carroll, J. (1976) 'Crackdown on S. F. prostitution', *San Francisco Chronicle*, 28 December.

Carroll, J. (1977) ' "Tough" cop to lead S. F. vice war', *San Francisco Chronicle*, 4 January.

Carroll, J. and Jarvis, B. (1977) 'Big police vice sweep of Union Square area', *San Francisco Chronicle*, 5 January.

Castiglioni, M. (ed.) (2001) *Percorsi di Donne Immigrate. Esperienze e Modellli di Intervento* (Milan: FrancoAngeli Editore).

Chamber of Mines (1994) *South African Mining Industry Statistical Tables* (Johannesburg: Chamber of Mines).

Chamber of Mines (1998) *South African Mining Industry Statistical Tables* (Johannesburg: Chamber of Mines).

Chamber of Mines (2001) *South African Mining Industry Statistical Tables* (Johannesburg: Chamber of Mines).

Chamber of Mines (2002) *South African Mining Industry Statistical Tables* (Johannesburg: Chamber of Mines).

Chamber of Mines (2004) *South African Mining Industry Statistical Tables* (Johannesburg: Chamber of Mines).

Chaney, E. M. and García Castro, M. (eds) (1989) *Muchachas No More: Household Workers in Latin America and the Caribbean, Women in the Political Economy* (Philadelphia, PA: Temple University Press).

Chang, G. (2000) *Disposable Domestics: Immigrant Women Workers in the Global Economy* (Cambridge, Mass.: South End Press).

Chang, K. A. and Ling, L. H. M. (2000) 'Globalization and its intimate Other: Filipina domestic workers in Hong Kong', in M. Marchand and A. S. Runyan (eds), *Gender and Global Restructuring: Sightings, Sites and Resistances* (London: Routledge), pp. 27–43.

Chapkis, W. (1997) *Live Sex Acts: Women Performing Erotic Labor* (New York: Routledge).

Cheadle, H. and Clarke, M. (2000) *Workers' Protection in South Africa: Country Study* (Cape Town: University of Cape Town).

Cheah, P. (1997) 'Posit(ion)ing Human Rights in the current global conjuncture', *Public Culture*, vol. 9 (2), pp. 233–66.

Cheru, F. (1989) *The Silent Revolution in Africa* (London: Zed Books).

Cheru, F. (1997) 'The silent revolution and the weapons of the weak: transformation and innovation from below', in S. Gill and J. Mittelman (eds), *Innovation and Transformation in International Studies* (Cambridge: Cambridge University Press), pp. 153–69.

Clapham, C. (1993) 'Patron-client politics', in J. Krieger (ed.), *Oxford Companion to Politics of the World* (New York: Oxford University Press), pp. 687–8.

Clarke, M. (2003) *Homeworking in the Clothing Industry, A Research Report on South Africa* (Cape Town: Labour and Enterprise Project).

Clarke, M. (2004) 'Challenging segmentation in South Africa's labour market: "regulated flexibility" or flexible regulation?', in L. Vosko and J. Stanford (eds), *Challenging the Market: The Struggle to Regulate Work and Income* (Montreal: McGill-Queen's University Press).

Clarke, M., Godfrey, S. and Theron, J. (2002) *Employment Standards in South Africa: A Country Study for the International Labour Organisation* (Cape Town: Labour and Enterprise Project Research Unit).

Clarke, M., Godfrey, S. and Theron, J. (2003) 'Globalisation, democratization and regulation of the South African labour market', unpublished research report for the UK research project *Globalisation, Production and Poverty: Macro, Meso and Micro Levels* (University of Cape Town).

Clarke, M. and Kenny, B. (2002) 'Falling out of the loop? Protection of casual and contract workers in the commercial, distributive sectoral determination', *Bargaining Indicators, Labour Research Service*, vol. 7, pp. 2–22.

Coalition Against Trafficking in Women (1993) *Coalition Report, Spring 1993* and *Summer 1993* (www.catwinternational.org/resources.php).

Coates, D. (1999) 'Labour power and international competitiveness: a critique of ruling orthodoxies', in L. Panitch (ed.), *Socialist Register 1999* (London: Merlin), pp. 108–41.

Cochran, M. (2002) 'A democratic critique of cosmopolitan democracy: pragmatism from the bottom-up', *European Journal of International Relations*, vol. 8 (4), pp. 517–48.

Cockburn, C. (1983) *Brothers: Male Dominance and Technological Change* (London: Pluto Press).

Cohen, S. (2003) 'Alienation and globalization in Morocco: addressing the social and political impact of market integration', *Comparative Studies in Society and History*, vol. 45 (1), pp. 168–89.

Colás, A. (2002) *International Civil Society* (London: Polity Press).

Colatrella, S. (2001) *Workers of the World. African and Asian Migrants in Italy in the 1990s* (Trenton, NJ: Africa World Press).

Connell, R. W. (1987) *Gender and Power: Society, the Person and Sexual Politics* (Stanford, CA: Stanford University Press).

Cooper, R. (2003) *The Breaking of Nations: Order and Chaos in the Twenty First Century* (London: Atlantic Books).

Corbin, A. (1990) *Women for Hire: Prostitution and Sexuality in France after 1850*, tr. A. Sheridan (Cambridge, Mass.: Harvard University Press).

Corporate Watch (2000) 'The Brave New World of work', vol. 9 (Summer).

Corso, C. and Trifiró, A. (2003) *Esiamo partite. Migrazione, tratta, e prositutzione straniera in Italia. Con un introduzione di Carla Corso e Ada Trifiró* (Milan: Astrea).

Corten, A. and Marshall-Fratani, R. (eds) (2001) *Between Babel and the Pentecost: Transnational Pentecostalism in Africa and Latin America* (Bloomington, IA: University of Indiana Press).

COSATU (1996) *Supplementary Secretariat Report on the Employment Standards Act Negotiations* (Johannesburg: COSATU).

Covarrubias A. (1992) *La Flexibilidad Laboral en Sonora* (Mexico, DF: El Colegio de Sonora y Fundación Friedrich Ebert).

Cox, R. W. (1971) 'Approaches to the futurology of Industrial Relations', *International Institute of Labour Studies Bulletin*, vol. 8, pp. 139–64.

Cox, R. W. (1981) 'Social forces, states and world order: beyond International Relations theory', in R. O. Keohane (ed.), *Neorealism and its Critics* (New York: Columbia University Press), pp. 204–54.

Cox, R. W. (1987) *Production, Power and World Order: Social Forces in the Making of History* (New York: Columbia University Press).

Cox, R. (1993) 'Gramsci, hegemony, and international relations: an essay in method', in S. Gill (ed.), *Gramsci, Historical Materialism, and International Relations* (Cambridge: Cambridge University Press), pp. 49–66.

Cox, R. W. (1995) 'Civilizations: encounters and transformation', in R. Cox and M. Schechter (eds), *The Political Economy of a Plural World* (London: Routledge), pp. 139–56.

Cox, R. W. (1996) *Approaches to World Order* (Cambridge: Cambridge University Press).

Cox, R. W. (ed.) (1997) *The New Realism* (London and Tokyo: Macmillan/UNU Press).

Cox, R. W. (1999) 'Civil society at the turn of the millennium: prospects for an alternative world order', *Review of International Studies*, vol. 25, pp. 3–28.

Coyle, D. (1997) *Weightless World* (Oxford: Capstone).

COYOTE (1977) 'Hookers' Rights Day', *Coyote Howls*, vol. 4 (1), p. 1.

Crouch, C. (1997) 'Skills-based full employment: the latest philosopher's stone', *British Journal of Industrial Relations*, vol. 35 (3), pp. 367–91.

Crouch, C and W. Streeck (eds) (1997) *Political Economy of Modern Capitalism* (London: Sage).

Crush, J., Ulicki, T., Tseana, T. and Van Vauren, E. J. (1999) *Undermining Labor: Migrancy and Sub-Contracting in the South African Gold Mining Industry* (Cape Town: IDASA).

Cully, M. (1999) *Britain at Work: As Depicted by 1998 Workplace Employee Relations Survey* (New York: Routledge).

Cutler, A. C. (2001) 'Critical reflections on the Westphalian assumption of international law and organization: a crisis of legitimacy', *Review of International Studies*, vol. 27, pp. 133–50.

Dalla Costa, M. and Dalla Costa, G. (1999) *Women, Development and the Labor of Reproduction: Struggles and Movements* (Trenton, NJ: Africa World Press).

Dalla Costa, M. and James, S. (1975) 'Women and the subversion of the community', in M. Dalla Costa and S. James (eds), *The Power of Women and the Subversion of the Community*, 3rd edn (Bristol: Falling Wall Press) pp. 21–56.

Danford, A. (1998) 'Work organisation inside Japanese firms in South Wales', in P. Thompson and C. Warhurst (eds), *Workplaces of the Future* (Basingstoke: Macmillan).

Danna, D. (2004a) 'Italy: the never-ending debate', in J. Outshoorn (ed.), *The Politics of Prostitution: Women's Movements, Democratic States and the Globalization of Sex Commerce* (Cambridge: Cambridge University Press), pp. 165–84.

Danna, D. (2004b) *Donne di Mondo. Commercio del Sesso e Controllo Statale* (Milan: Eleuthera).

D'Aquili, E. and Newberg, A. N. (1999) *The Mystical Mind: Probing the Biology of Religious Experience* (Minneapolis, MN: Fortress Press).

Davies, M. (2001) 'Problems in conceiving and realizing international public spheres', presented to the Hong Kong International Studies Conference, 27 July.

Davies, M. and Niemann, M. (2002) 'The everyday spaces of global politics: work, leisure and family', *New Political Science*, vol. 24 (4), pp. 557–77.

Davis, M. (2004) 'Planet of slums: urban involution and the informal proletariat', *New Left Review*, vol. 26, pp. 5–34.

Deakin, S. and Mückenberger, U. (1992) 'Deregulation and European labour markets', in A. Castro, P. Méhaut and J. Rubery (eds), *International Integration and Labour Market Organisation* (London: Academinc Press).

De Kiewiet, C. (1941) *A History of South Africa: Social and Economic* (New York: Oxford University Press).

Delacoste, F. and Alexander, P. (eds) (1998) *Sex Work: Writings by Women in the Sex Industry*, 2nd edn (San Francisco, CA: Cleis Press).

Denemark, R. A. and O'Brien, R. (1997) 'Contesting the canon: International Political Economy at UK and US universities', *Review of International Political Economy*, vol. 4 (1), pp. 214–38.

Deppe, F. (1998) 'Der Preis der neuen Sozialpartnerschaft, in R. Dreßler (ed.), *Jenseits Falsche Sachzwänge. Detlef Hensche zum 60* (Hamburg: Geburtstag), pp. 75–98.

Derrida, J. (1993) *Spectres of Marx* (London: Routledge).

Deyo, F. (ed.) (1987) *The Political Economy of New Asian Industrialism* (Ithaca, NY: Cornell University Press), pp. 182–202.

Diani, M. (2000) 'Simmel to Rokkan and beyond: elements for a network theory of (new) social movements', *European Journal of Social Theory*, vol. 3, pp. 387–406.

Dicken, P. (1998) *Global Shift: Transforming the World Economy* (London: Paul Chapman).

Dimendberg, E. (1997) 'Henri Lefebvre on abstract space', in A. Light and J. Smith (eds), *The Production of Public Space* (Lanham, MD: Rowman & Littlefield), pp. 17–47.

Doezema, J. (1998) 'Forced to choose: beyond the voluntary versus forced prostitution dichotomy', in K. Kempadoo and J. Doezema (eds), *Global Sex Workers, Rights, Resistance, and Redefinition* (London: Routledge), pp. 34–50.

Drainville, A. (2004) *Contesting Globalization: Space and Place in the World Economy* (London and New York: Routledge).

Dunaway, W. A. (2001) 'The double register of history: situating the forgotten woman and her household in capitalist commodity chains', *Journal of World-Systems Research*, vol. 2 (1), pp. 2–29.

Du Toit, A. and Alley, F. (2001) *The Externalization and Casualisation of Farm Labour in Western Cape Horticulture* (Cape Town: Centre for Rural Legal Studies).

Eagleton, T. (1991) *Ideology: An Introduction* (London: Verso).

Echeverría Álvarez, L. (1974) *Informes de Gobierno, 1971–1973* (Mexico, DF: Secretaría de la Presidencia).

Ehrenreich, B. (2003) 'Maid to order', in B. Ehrenreich and A. R. Hochschild (eds), *Global Woman: Nannies, Maids, and Sex Workers in the New Economy* (New York: Henry Holt), pp. 85–103.

Ehrenreich, B. and Hochschild, A. (eds) (2003) *Global Woman: Nannies, Maids, and Sex Workers in the New Economy* (New York: Henry Holt).

EIRO (1999) *Annual Review* (Luxembourg: EIRO).

EIRO (2000) *Outsourcing and Industrial Relations in Motor Manufacturing* (Luxembourg: EIRO).

Eisenstadt, S. N. and Lemarchand, R. (eds) (1981) *Political Clientelism Patronage and Development* (Beverly Hills, CA: and London: Sage Publications).

Elias, N. (1989) *The Germans* (New York: Columbia University Press).

Elmuti, D. and Kathwala Y. (2000) 'The effects of outsouricng strategies on participants' attitudes and organizational effectiveness', *International Journal of Manpower*, vol. 21 (1–2), pp. 112–28.

Elson, D. (1998) 'The economic, the political and the domestic: businesses, the state, and households in the organization of production', *New Political Economy*, vol. 3 (2), pp. 189–208.

Enloe, C. (1989) *Bananas, Beaches and Bases: Making Feminist Sense of International Politics* (Berkeley, CA: University of California Press).

Enloe, C. (1996) 'Margins, silences and bottom rungs: how to overcome the underestimation of power in the study of international relations', in S. Smith, K. Booth and M. Zalewski (eds), *International Theory: Positivism and Beyond* (Cambridge: Cambridge University Press), pp. 186–202.

Eschle, C. (2001) *Global Democracy, Social Movements, and Feminism* (Boulder, CO: Westview).

Esping-Andersen, G. (1990) *The Three Worlds of Capitalism* (Princeton, NJ: Princeton University Press).

Esping-Andersen, G. (1996) 'Welfare states without work: the impasse of labour shedding and familialism in continental European social policy,' in G. Esping-Andersen (ed.), *Welfare States in Transition: National Adaptations in Global Economies* (London: Sage/unrisd).

Euromonitor (2003) *Retail Trade International – South Africa Report* (www.euromonitor.com/report 2002).

European Commission (1997) 'Partnership for a new organisation of work', Green Paper, CEC (Brussels: European Commission).

Evans, P. (1987) 'Class, state and dependence in East Asia: lessons for Latin Americanists', in F. Deyo (ed.), *The Political Economy of the New Asian* (Ithaca, N.Y.: Cornell University Press), pp. 203–26.

Farnsworth, C. (1975) '200 prostitutes of Lyons in siege at Church', *New York Times*, 7 June, p. 2.

Farsakh, L. (2000) 'North African labour flows and the Euro-Med Partnership', *European Journal of Development Research*, vol. 12 (1), pp. 58–79.

Federici, S. (1975) 'Wages against housework' (Bristol: Falling Wall Press) repr. in E. Malos (ed), *The Politics of Housework* (London: Allison and Busby, 1980) and R. Baxandall and L. Gordon (eds), *Dear Sisters, Dispatches from the Women's Liberation Movement* (New York: Basic Books, 2000).

Federici, S. (1993) 'Economic crisis and demographic policy in Sub-Saharan Africa: the case of Nigeria', in M. Dalla Costa and G. F. Dalla Costa (eds), *Paying the Price: Women and the Politics of International Economic Strategy* (London: Zed Books), pp. 42–57.

Federici, S. (1999), 'Reproduction and feminist struggle in the new international division of labor', in M. Dalla Costa and G. Dalla Costa (eds), *Women, Development and the Labor of Reproduction: Struggles and Movements* (Trenton, NJ: Africa World Press).

Federici, S. (2001) 'War, globalization and reproduction', in V. Benhold-Thomsen, N. Faraclas and C. von Werlhof (eds), *There Is an Alternative: Subsistence and World Wide Resistance to Globalization* (London: Zed Books).

Federici, S. (2004) *Caliban and the Witch: Women, the Body and Primitive Accumulation* (New York: Autonomedia).

Federici, S. and Cox, N. (1975) 'Counter-planning from the kitchen' (Bristol: Falling Wall Press) repr. in E. Hoshino Altbach (ed.), *From Feminism to Liberation* (Cambridge, MA: Schenkman Publishing Company, 1980).

Fortunati, L. (1995) *The Arcane of Reproduction, Housework, Prostitution, Labor and Capital*, tr. H. Creek (New York: Autonomedia).

Foucault, M. (1976) 'Disciplinary power and subjection' in S. Lukes (ed.), *Power* (Oxford: Blackwell), pp. 229–42.

Foucault, M. (1980) *Power/Knowledge: Selected Interviews and Other Writings, 1972–1977* (New York: Pantheon Books).

Foucault, M. (2003) 'Governmentality', in P. Rabinow and N. Rose (eds), *The Essential Foucault* (New York: The New Press), pp. 229–45.

Fraser, N. (1992) 'Rethinking the public sphere: a contribution to the critique of actually existing democracy', in C. Calhoun (ed.), *Habermas and the Public Sphere* (Cambridge, MA: MIT Press), pp. 109–42.

Fraser, N. (1997) *Justice Interruptus: Critical Reflections on the 'Postsocialist' Condition* (New York: Routledge).

Freedman, M. (1976) *Labor Markets: Segments and Shelters* (London: Allanheld).

Freymond, J. (directeur) (1962), *La Première Internationale*, documents in 2 volumes (Geneva: Librairie E. Droz).

Friedman, S. (1987), *Building Tomorrow Today: African Workers in Trade Unions, 1970–1985*. (Johannesburg: Raven Press).

Fudge, J. (1997) *Precarious Work and Families* (Toronto: Centre for Research on Work and Society, York University).

Fudge, J. and Vosko, L. (2001) 'Gender, segmentation and the standard employment relationship in Canadian labour law and policy', *Economic* and *Industrial Democracy*, vol. 22, pp. 271-310.

Fukuyama, F. (1992) *The End of History and the Last Man* (Harmondsworth: Penguin).

Furniss, N. and Mitchell, N. (1984) 'Social welfare provisions in Western Europe: current status and future possibilities', in H. R. Rodgers Jr. (ed.), *Public Policy and Social Institutions* (Greenwich, CT: JAI Press), pp. 15–54.

GABRIELA (1997) *Globalization: Displacement, Commodification and Modern-day Slavery of Women*, Proceedings of the Workshop on Women and Globalization, 23 November 1996, Quezon City (Philippines) (Quezon: Final Proof Printing Inc.).

GABRIELA (2000) *KaWOMENAN*, Spring (www.gabnet.org/kawomenan.htm).

Gall, C. (2001) 'Poverty and a decade of Balkan conflicts feed a network of sex slavery', *Herald Tribune*, 31 July.

Gallin, D. (2001) 'Propositions on trade unions and informal employment in times of globalisation', *Antipode*, vol. 33 (3), pp. 531–49.

Gallin, D. (2002) 'Organizing in the informal economy', in *Unprotected Labour: What Role for Unions in the Informal Economy?* (Geneva: ILO), pp. 21–6.

Garrard-Burnett, V. (2004) 'The third Church in Latin America: religion and globalization in contemporary Latin America', *Latin American Research Review*, vol. 39, pp. 256–69.

Geldstein, R. N. (1997) 'Gender bias and family distress: the privatization experience in Argentina', *Journal of International Affairs*, vol. 50 (2), pp. 545–72.

Germain, R. D. (2000) 'Globalization in historical perspective', in R. D. Germain (ed.), *Globalization and its Critics: Perspectives from Political Economy* (Basingstoke: Macmillan), pp. 67–90.

Gerth, H. H. and Wright Mills, C. (1958) *From Max Weber* (Oxford: Oxford University Press).

Giddens, A. (1998) *The Third Way: The Renewal of Social Democracy* (Cambridge: Polity Press).

Gill, S. (1990) *American Hegemony and the Trilateral Commission* (Cambridge: Cambridge University Press).

Gill, S. (ed.) (1993) *Gramsci, Historical Materialism and International Relations* (Cambridge: Cambridge University Press).

Gill, S. (1995) 'Globalization, market civilization, and disciplinary neoliberalism', *Millennium: Journal of International Studies*, vol. 24 (3), pp. 399–423.

Gill, S. (1996) 'Globalization, democratization, and the politics of indifference', in J. Mittelman (ed.), *Globalization: Critical Reflections* (London: Lynne Rienner), pp. 205–28.

Gill, S. (1998) 'New constitutionalism, democratisation and Global Political Economy', *Pacifica Review*, vol. 10 (1), pp. 23–38.

Gill, S. (2002) *Power and Resistance in the New World Order* (Basingstoke: Palgrave Macmillan).

Gilpin, R. (1975) *US Power and the Multinational Corporation* (New York: Basic Books).

Godfrey, S. and Clarke, M. (2002) 'The basic conditions of employment act amendments: more questions than answers', *Law Democracy & Development*, vol. 6 (1), pp. 1–26.

González de la Rocha, M. (2000) 'Private adjustments: household responses to the erosion of work', in *SEPED Conference Paper Series no. 6* (available from: United Nations Development Program, www.undp.org/seped/publications/pvt_adjustments.pdf).

Government of Mexico (1992) *Nueva Ley Federal del Trabajo, Ley del Infonavit: Vista Panorámica y Leyes Complementarias*, 16th edn (Mexico, DF: Editorial Olguin).

Governmental of Mexico (1993) 'Exposición de motivos de la Ley del Seguro Social de 1973', *Diario Oficial de la Federación* (Mexico, DF: Editorial Alco) 12 March)

Government of South Africa (2001) *Labour Force Survey*, February (Pretoric: Government of South Africa).

Gramsci, A. (1971) 'Analysis of situations: the relations of force', in, Q. Hoare and G. Nowell Smith (eds), *Selections from the Prison Notebooks* (New York: International Publishers), pp. 175–85.

Gray, A. (2004) *Unsocial Europe: Social Protection or Flexploitation?* (London: Pluto Press).

Greenberg, S. (1987) *Legitimating the Illegitimate: State, Markets and Resistance in South Africa* (Berkeley, CA: University of California Press).

Greenfield, S. and Droogers, A. (eds) (2001) *Reinventing Religions: Syncretism and Transformation in Africa and the Americas* (Lanham, MD: Rowman & Littlefield).

Guha, R. and Spivak, G. (eds) (1988) *Selected Subaltern Studies* (New York: Oxford University Press).

Guillemaut, F. (2005) 'Lutte contre le traffic des femmes ou pour les droits de la personne, in C. Verschuur and F. Reysoo (eds) *Genre, Nouvelle Division Internationale du Travail et Migrations*, (Geneva: Editions L'Harmattan), pp. 325–38.

Gumbrell-McCormick, R. (2000) 'Facing new challenges: the International Confederation of Free Trade Unions (1972–1990s)', in M. van der Linden (ed.), *The International Confederation of Free Trade Unions* (Bern: Peter Lang), pp. 339–517.

Gutiérrez Garza, E. (coord.) (1989) *Reconversión Industrial y Lucha Sindical* (Mexico, DF: Fundación Friedrich Ebert).

Haas, F. (1977) 'The prostitution laws go on trial', *The Boston Phoenix*, 15 February, p.16.

Haass, R. (1999) 'What to Do with American Primacy', *Foreign Affairs*, September/October, pp. 37–49.

Habermas, J. (1975) *Legitimation Crisis* (Boston: Beacon Press).

Habermas, J. (1979) 'The public sphere', in A. Mattelart and S. Siegelabub (eds), *Communication and Class Struggle 1: Capitalism, Imperialism* (New York and Bagnolet, France: International General/IMMRC), pp. 198–201.

Habermas, J. (1989 [1962]) *The Structural Transformation of the Public Sphere* (Cambridge: Polity Press).

Habermas, J. (1991) *The Structural Transformation of the Public Sphere: An Inquiry into a Category of Bourgeois Society*, (Cambridge, Mass: MIT Press).

Habermas, J. (1992) 'Further reflections on the public sphere', in C. Calhoun (ed.), *Habermas and the Public Sphere* (Cambridge, MA: MIT Press), pp. 421–61.

Hall, S. (1988) 'The toad in the garden Thatcherism among the theorists', in C. Nelson and L Grossberg (eds), *Marxism and the Interpretation of Culture* (Urbana: University of Illinois Press), pp. 35–58.

Halliday, F. (1987) 'State and society in international relations: a second agenda', *Millennium: Journal of International Studies*, vol. 16 (2), pp. 215–29.

Handy, C. (1995) *The Future of Work* (London: Contemporary Papers).

Hanochi, S. (2002) 'Unprotected labour and trafficking capitalism', paper presented at the special workshop of the International Studies Association on The Political Economy of the Unprotected Worker in World Politics, ISA Annual Convention, New Orleans, 23 March.

Hardt, M. and Negri, A. (2000) *Empire*, (Cambridge, MA: Harvard University Press).

Harmes, A. (1998) 'Institutional investors and the reproduction of neoliberalism', *Review of International Political Economy*, vol. 5 (1), pp. 92–121.

Harries, P. (1994) *Work, Culture, and Identity: Migrant Laborers in Mozambique and South Africa, C.1860–1910* (Portsmouth, NH: Heinemann).

Harriss-White, B. and Gooptu, N. (2001) 'Mapping India's world of unorganized labour', in L. Panitch and C. Leys (eds), *Socialist Register 2001: Working Classes: Global Realities* (London: Merlin), pp. 89–118.

Harrod, J. (1972a) 'Ideology of international labour organisations towards developing countries', in *The Impact of International Organisations on Legal and Institutional Change in the Developing Countries* (New Haven, CT: International Legal Centre, Yale University Economic Growth Centre), pp. 184–210.

Harrod, J. (1972b) *Trade Union Foreign Policy: A Study of British and American Trade Union Activities in Jamaica* (Garden City, NY: Doubleday).

Harrod, J. (1987) *Power, Production and the Unprotected Worker* (New York: Columbia University Press).

Harrod, J. (1997) 'Social forces and IPE: joining the two IRs', in S. Gill and J. Mittelman (eds), *Innovation and Transformation in International Studies* (Cambridge: Cambridge University Press).

Harrod, J. (2000) 'The end of opposition?: market power as a rationality (or diverting the egalitarian neurological imperative?)', paper presented at the 41st annual convention of the International Studies Association, Los Angeles, 14–18 March (available from www.ciaonet.org/isa/har01).

Harrod, J. (2001a) 'Global realism: unmasking power in the international political economy', in R. Wyn-Jones (ed.), *Critical Theory in World Politics* (London: Lynne Rienner), pp. 111–25.

Harrod, J. (2001b) 'Power, production and the unprotected worker: rationalities, world views and global change', paper presented at the annual convention of the International Studies Association, Chicago, 20–4 February.

Harrod, J. (2003) 'The new politics of economic and social rights', in K. Arts and P. Mihyo (eds), *Responding to the Human Rights Deficit* (The Hague: Kluwer), pp. 61–71.

Harrod, J. (2004) 'Global unions: constraints in an age of the politics of the underclass', in B. Unfried and M. van der Linden (eds), *Labor and New Social Movements* (Vienna: ITH), pp. 91–102.

Harrod, J. (2005) 'The century of the corporation: dynamics and contradictions of the corporation in the 21st Century', in C. May (ed.), *Global Corporate Power: (Re)integrating companies into IPE* (London: Lynne Rienner).

Harrod, J. and O'Brien, R. (eds) (2002) *Global Unions? Theory and Strategy in the Global Economy* (London: Routledge).

Harvey, D. (1990) *The Condition of Postmodernity* (Oxford: Blackwell).

Hay, C. and Marsh, D. (1999) 'Introduction: Towards a New (International) Political Economy?', *New Political Economy*, vol. 4 (1), pp. 5–22.

Healy, T. (1999) 'Contesting Restructuring, Transforming Representation: Autoworkers and the Gendered Struggle for Counter-hegemony in Mexico', PhD dissertation, Carleton University, Ottawa.

Hegel, G. W. F. (1977) *Phenomenology of Spirit* (Oxford: Oxford University Press).

Held, D. (2003) *Cosmopolitanism: A Defence* (Cambridge: Polity Press).

Held, D., McGrew, A., Goldblatt, D. and Perraton, J. (eds) (1999) *Global Transformations: Politics, Economics and Culture* (Cambridge: Polity Press).

Herod, A. (2001) 'Labor internationalism and the contradictions of globalization: or, why the local is sometimes still important in a global economy', *Antipode*, vol. 33 (3), pp. 407–26.

Herrera Lima, F. (1992) 'Reestructuración de la industria automotriz en México y respuesta sindical', *El Cotidiano*, vol. 46 (Mar.–Apr.).

Higgins, W. (1985) 'Political unionism and the corporatism thesis', *Economic and Industrial Democracy*, vol. 6 (3), pp. 349–81.

Hoffman, J. (1979) 'The Times Square porno tour', *The Village Voice*, 17 September.

Hollis, M. and Smith, S. (1990) *Explaining and Understanding International Relations* (Oxford: Clarendon Press).

Holman, O. (2004) 'Asymmetrical regulation and multidimensional governance in the European Union', *Review of International Political Economy*, vol. 11 (4), pp. 714–35.

Hoogvelt, A. (1997) *Globalisation and the Postcolonial World: The New Political Economy of Development* (Basingstoke: Macmillan).

Hooper, C. (2000) 'Masculinities in transition: the case of globalization', in M. Marchand and A. S. Runyan (eds), *Gender and Global Restructuring: Sightings, Sites and Resistances* (London: Routledge), pp. 59–73.

Hopkins, D. N., Lorentzen, L., Mendieta, E. and Bastone, D. (eds) (2001) *Religions/Globalizations: Theories and Cases* (Durham, NC: Duke University Press).

Hsiung, P. C. (1996) *Living Rooms as Factories: Class, Gender, and the Satellite Factory System in Taiwan* (Philadelphia, PA: Temple University Press).

Humphries, J. (1977) 'Class struggle and the persistence of the working class', *Cambridge Journal of Economics*, vol. 1, pp. 241–58.

Huntington, S. (ed.) (1993) *The Clash of Civilizations? The Debate* (New York: Foreign Affairs).

Huntington, S. (1999) 'The Lonely Superpower', *Foreign Affairs*, Mar.–Apr., pp. 35–49.

Hyman, R. (1999a) 'Imagined solidarities: can trade unions resist globalization?', in P. L. M. Leisink (ed.), *Globalization and Labour Relations* (Cheltenham: Edward Elgar).

Hyman, R. (1999b) 'An Emerging Agenda for Trade Unions?', *Labour and Society Programme*, (Geneva: IILS).

Ibarra, M. D. L. (2000) 'Mexican immigrant women and the new domestic labour', *Human Organization*, vol. 59 (4), pp. 452–64.

ICG (2004) 'Iraq's transition: on a knife's edge', *ICG Middle East Report No 27*, 27 April (www.crisisgroup.org/home/index.cfm?id=2679&1=1).

IILS (1999) *Labour and Society Programme* (Geneva: International Institute for Labour Studies).

ILO (1972) *Employment, Incomes and Equality: a strategy for increasing productive employment in Kenya* (Geneva: ILO).

ILO (1990) *Yearbook of Labour Statistics: Retrospective Edition of Population Census 1946–1989* (Geneva: ILO).

ILO (1995) 'Deregulation, not a cure all', *World Employment Report* (Geneva: ILO).

ILO (1998a) *Statistics on Working Children and Hazardous Labour* (Geneva: International Labour Organization Bureau of Statistics).

ILO (1998b) *World Labour Report 1997–1998: Industrial Relations, Democracy and Social Stability* (Geneva: ILO).

ILO (2000a) *Labour Practices in the Footwear, Leather, Textiles and Clothing Industries* (Geneva: ILO).

ILO (2000b) *Yearbook of Labour Statistics* (Geneva: ILO).

ILO (2002) *ILO Compendium of Official Statistics on Employment in the Informal Sector*, STAT Working Paper 1 (Geneva: ILO).

Institut der Deutschen Wirtschaft (1999) *Trade Union Membership and Density in the 1990s* (Cologne: IDW).

Instituto Nacional de Estadística, Geografía e Informática (1991) 'Principales características de la industria maquiladora de exportación, por entidad federativa y municipio: 1979–1989, Cuadro No.1', *Estadística de la Industria Maquiladora de Exportación: 1979–1989* (Mexico, DF: INEGI).

International Confederation of Free Trade Unions (1988) *The Challenge of Change* (Brussels: ICFTU).

International Confederation of Free Trade Unions (2000) *Globalizing Social Justice: Trade Unionism in the Twenty-First Century* (Brussels: ICFTU).

International Confederation of Free Trade Unions (2001a) *Task Force on Informal or Unprotected Work: Background Document – May 2001* (Brussels: ICFTU).

International Confederation of Free Trade Unions (2001b) *A Trade Union Guide to Globalisation* (Brussels: ICFTU).

International Confederation of Free Trade Unions (2004a) *A Trade Union Guide to Globalization*, 2nd edn (Brussels: ICFTU).

International Confederation of Free Trade Unions (2004b) *Undocumented Migrants: Victims without a Voice* (Brussels: ICFTU).

International Confederation of Free Trade Unions (2004c) *Behind the Brand Names: Working Conditions and Labour Rights in Export Processing Zones* (Brussels: ICFTU).

International Confederation of Free Trade Unions (2004d) *India: economic boom masks widespread child labour* (Brussels: ICFTU).

International Labour Office, Bureau for Workers' Activities (ACTRAV) (2002) *Unprotected Labour: What Role for Unions in the Informal Economy?* (Geneva: ILO).

International Monetary Fund (2000) 'Pressing issues of globalization and poverty reduction are focus of 2000 IMF–World Bank Annual Meetings', *Finance and Development*, (Washington, DC: IMF).

Ismail, S. (2000) 'The Popular Dimensions of Contemporary Militant Islamism: Socio-Spatial Determinants in the Cairo Urban Setting', *Comparative Studies in Society and History*, vol. 42 (2), pp. 363–93.

Jaget, C. (ed.) (1980) *Prostitutes: Our Life* (Bristol: Falling Wall Press).

Jaggar, A. M. (1997) 'Contemporary Western feminist perspectives on prostitution', *Asian Journal of Women's Studies*, vol. 3 (2), pp. 8–29.

James, S. (1975) *Sex, Race and Class* (Bristol: Falling Wall Press).

James, W. G. (1992) *Our Precious Metal: African Labour in South Africa's Gold Industry, 1970–1990* (Bloomington, IA: Indiana University Press).

Jenness, V. (1993) *Making it Work: The Prostitutes' Rights Movement in Perspective* (New York: Walter de Gruyter).

Jessop, B. (1994) 'Post-fordism and the state', in A. Amin (ed.), *Post-Fordism: A Reader* (Cambridge, Mass : Blackwell), pp. 251–79.

Jessop, B. (1997) 'Changing forms and functions of the state in an era of globalization and regionalization', in R. Delorme and K. Dopfer (eds), *The Political Economy of Diversity* (Aldershot: Edward Elgar), pp. 102–25.

Jessop, B. and Sum, N.-L. (2006). 'Towards a cultural political economy: poststructuralism and the Italian School', in M. de Goede, *International Political Economy and Poststructural Politics* (Basingstoke: Palgrave Macmillan), pp. 157–76.

Johansson, I. and Liedman, S.-E. (1993) *Positivism and Marxism* (Gothenburg: Daidalos).

Jones, R. J. B. (1995) *Globalisation and Interdependence in the International Political Economy* (London: Pinter).

Justice, D. (2002) 'Work, law and the "Informality Concept" ', in International Labour Office, Bureau for Workers' Activities (ACTRAV), *Unprotected Labour: What Role for Unions in the Informal Economy?* (Geneva: ILO), pp. 1–5.

Kaarsholm, P. (1988) 'The South African War and the response of the International Socialist community to imperialism between 1896 and 1908', in F. van Holthoon and M. E. van der Linden (eds), *Internationalism in the Labour Movement (1830–1940)*, vol. 1 (Leiden: J. Brill), pp. 42–67.

Kempadoo, K. (1998) 'Introduction: globalizing sex workers' rights', in K. Kempadoo and J. Doezema (eds), *Global Sex Workers, Rights, Resistance, and Redefinition* (London: Routledge), pp. 1–28.

Kempadoo, K. (ed.) (1999) *Sun, Sex, and Gold. Tourism and Sex Work in the Caribbean* (Boulder, CO: Rowman & Littlefield).

Kempadoo, K. (2005) 'Globalizing sex workers' rights', in L. Amoore (ed.), *Global Resistance Reader* (London: Routledge), pp. 289–98.

Kempadoo, K. and Doezema, J. (eds) (1998) *Global Sex Workers, Rights, Resistance, and Redefinition* (London: Routledge).

Kennedy, I. and Nicotri, P. (1999) *Lucciole Nere: le prostitute nigeriane si raccontano* (Milan: Kaos Edizioni).

Kenny, B. (1998) 'The casualisation of the retail sector in South Africa, *Indicator South Africa*, vol. 15 (4), pp. 25–31.

Kenny, B. (2001) 'We are nursing these jobs: the impact of labour market flexibility on South African retail sector workers', in N. Newman, J. Pape and H. Janse, (eds), *Is There an Alternative? South African Workers Confronting Globalization* (Cape Town: ILRIG), pp. 90–197.

Kenny, B. (2003) 'Labour market flexibility in the retail sector: possibilities for resistance', in T. Bramble and F. Barchiesi (eds), *Rethinking the Labour Movements in the 'New South Africa'* (Burlington: Ashgate). pp. 168–83

Keohane, R. O. and Nye, J. (1989) *Power and Interdependence*, 2nd edn (Boston, Mass.: Little Brown).

Klein, N. (2000) *No Logo* (London: Flamingo).

Klerck, G. and Naidoo, L. (2003) 'In search of greener pastures: trade unionism in the agricultural sector', in T. Bramble and F. Barchiesi (eds), *Rethinking the Labour Movements in the 'New South Africa'* (Burlington: Ashgate), pp. 150–67.

Krieger, J. (ed.) (1993) *Oxford Companion to Politics of the World* (New York: Oxford University Press).

La Botz, D. (1988) *The Crisis of Mexican Labor* (New York: Praeger).

Laclau, E. and Mouffe, C. (1985) *Hegemony and Socialist Strategy* (London: Verso).

Lambert, R. (1999) 'International relations and industrial relations: exploring an interface', paper presented at the International Studies Association annual convention, Washington DC, 20 February.

Landes, J. B. (1998) 'The public and the private sphere: a feminist reconsideration', in J. Landes (ed.), *Feminism, the Public and the Private* (Oxford and New York: Oxford University Press), pp. 135–63.

Lash, S. and Urry, J. (1987) *The End of Organized Capitalism* (Madison, Wis.: University of Wisconsin Press).

Lefebvre, H. (1976) *The Survival of Capitalism: Reproduction of the Relations of Production* (London: Allison & Busby).

Lefebvre, H. (1984) *Everyday Life in the Modern World* (New Brunswick, NJ: Transaction Books).

Lefebvre, H. (1991a) *The Production of Space* (Oxford: Blackwell).

Lefebvre, H. (1991b) *Critique of Everyday Life*, vol. 1 (New York: Verso).

Light, J. (1999) 'Engendering change: the long, slow road to organizing women maquiladora workers' (www.corpwatch.org/issues/PID.jsp?articleid=691).

Linebaugh, P. (1992) *The London Hanged* (New York: Cambridge University Press).

Lipietz, A. (1985) *Mirages and Miracles* (London: Verso).

Lorwin, L. (1929) *Labor and Internationalism* (New York: Macmillan).

Lui, T. L. and Chiu, T. M. (1999) 'Global Restructuring and Non-Standard Work in Newly Industrialised Economies: the Organisation of Flexible Production in Hong Kong and Taiwan', in A. Felstead and N. Jewson (eds), *Global Trends in Flexible Labour* (Basingstoke: Macmillan), pp. 166–80.

Lynch, M. (2000) 'The dialogue of civilisations and international public spheres', *Millennium*, vol. 29 (2), pp. 307–30.

Maida, V. and Mazzonis, M. (2004) 'Il traffico di donne: il caso albanese', in F. Carchedi (ed.), *Prostituzione Migrante e Donne Trafficate: Il Caso delle Donne Albanesi, Moldave e Rumene* (Milan: Franco Angeli), pp. 53–76.

Malos, E. (1995) *The Politics of Housework* (Cheltanham: New Clarion Press).

Mansbridge, M. and Morris, A. (eds) (2001) *Oppositional Consciousness: The Subjective Roots of Social Protest* (Chicago, IL: Chicago University Press).

Mao Tse Tung (1964) 'Analysis of the classes in Chinese society' and 'Report on the investigation of the peasant movement in Hunan', in *Selected Works of Mao Tse Tung*, vol. 1 (Beijing: Peoples Publishing House), pp. 5–48.

Marchand, M. (1996) 'Reconceptualising gender and development in an era of globalisation', *Millennium: Journal of International Studies*, vol. 25 (3), pp. 577–604.

Marchand, M. and Runyan, A. S. (eds) (2000) *Gender and Global Restructuring: Sightings, Sites and Resistances* (London: Routledge).

Marcoux, A. (1997) *The feminization of poverty: facts, hypotheses and the art of advocacy* (Sustainable Development Department, Food and Agricultural Organization of the United Nations, www.fao.org/sd/WPdirect/WPan0015.htm).

Marginson, P. and Schulten, T. (1999) 'The "Europeanisation" of collective bargaining', *European Industrial Relations Observer*, vol. 4 (supplement), pp. 13–20.

Marsden, D. (1986) *The End of Economic Man* (Brighton: Harvester Wheatsheaf).

Marsden, D. (1992) 'Trade union action and labour market structure', in A. Castro, P. Mehaut and J. Rubery (eds), *International Integration and Labour Market Organisation* (London: Academic Press).

Martin, W. (1987) 'Incorporation of Southern Africa, 1870–1920', *Review*, vol. 10, pp. 849–900.

Marx, K. (1973) *Grundrisse* (New York: Vintage).

Matlosa, K. (1998) 'Basotho migrant miners in South Africa and Lesotho's future', in L. Sachikonye (ed.), *Labour and Migration in Southern Africa* (Harare: SAPES Trust), pp. 33–48.

Maurin, E. (2004) *Le Ghetto Francais* (Paris: Seuil).

McClintock, A. (1993) 'Sex workers and sex work: Introduction', *Social Text*, vol. 37 (Winter), pp. 1–10.

McDermott Hughes, D. (1999) 'Refugees and squatters: immigration and the politics of territory on the Zimbabwe–Mozambique border', *Journal of Southern African Studies*, vol. 25, pp. 533–52.

McDowell, L. (1991) 'Life without Father and Ford: the new gender order of post-fordism', *Transactions of the Institute of British Geographers, New Series*, vol. 16 (4), pp. 400–19.

McElroy, W. (2004) *Prostitutes, feminists, and economic associates* (www.zetetics. com/mac/vern/htm).

McGowan, P. and Harmer, F. (1979) 'Teaching international political economy: the role of values, history, and theory', *Teaching Political Science*, vol. 7, pp. 3–32.

McKeganey, N. and Barnard, M. (1996) *Sex Work on The Streets: Prostitutes and their Clients* (Buckingham: Open University Press).

McLaren, J. (1994) 'Book review of *Women For Hire: Prostitution and Sexuality in France after 1850*', *Canadian Journal of Women and the Law*, vol. 7, pp. 213–22.

Middlebrook, K. (1995) *The Paradox of Revolution: Labor, The State, and Authoritarianism in Mexico* (Baltimore: Johns Hopkins Universtiy Press).

Mies, M. (1998) *Patriarchy and Accumulation on a World Scale* (London: Zed Books).

Mies, M. and Benholdt-Thomsen, V. (1999) *The Subsistence Perspective: Beyond the Globalised Economy* (London: Zed Books).

Milkman, R. (1998) 'The new American workplace: high road or low road?', in P. Thompson and C. Warhurst (eds), *Workplaces of the Future* (Basingstoke: Macmillan), pp. 25–39.

Mills, C. (1948) *The New Men of Power: America's Labor Leaders* (New York: Harcourt, Brace).

Milner, S. (1990) *The Dilemmas of Internationalism: French Syndicalism and the International Labour Movement 1900–1914* (New York: Berg).

Mittelman, J. (2000) *The Globalization Syndrome: Transformation and Resistance* (Princeton, NJ: Princeton University Press).

Mlambo, K. (1998) 'Capital flows, savings and investment in SADC', in C. Chipeta (ed.), *Trade and Investment in Southern Africa: Towards Regional Cooperation and Integration* (Harare: SAPES Books), pp. 95–105.

Moghadam, V. M. (2000) 'Transnational feminist networks: collective action in an era of globalization', *International Sociology*, vol. 15 (1), pp. 57–85.

Montali, L. (2000) 'Família e trabalho na reestruturação produtiva: ausência de políticas de emprego e deterioração da condições de vida' [Family and work in the restructuring of production: the absence of employment policies and the deterioration of living conditions], *Revista Brasileira de Ciências Sociais*, vol. 15 (42), pp. 55–71.

Moody, K. (1997) *Workers in a Lean World* (London: Verso).

Moody, K. (1998) 'American labor: a movement again?', in E. M. Wood, P. Meiksins and M. Yates (eds), *Rising from the Ashes? Labor in the Age of 'Global Capitalism'*, (New York: Monthly Review Press), pp. 57–72.

Moroli, E. and Sibona, R. (1999) *Schiave D' Occidente: Sulle Rotte dei Mercanti di Donne* (Milano: Mursia).

Munck, R. and Waterman, P. (eds) (1999) *Labour Worldwide in the Era of Globalization: Alternatives for Trade Unions in the New World Order* (London: Macmillan).

Murphy, C. (1994) *International Organization and Industrial Change: Global Governance Since 1850* (Cambridge: Polity Press).

Murphy, C. (1996) 'Seeing women, recognising gender, recasting international relations', *International Organization*, vol. 50 (3), pp. 513–38.

Murray, A. (1998) 'Debt-bondage and trafficking: don't believe the hype', in K. Kempadoo and J. Doezema (eds), *Global Sex Workers, Rights, Resistance, and Redefinition* (London: Routledge).

Murray, C. (1999) *The Underclass Revisited*, Amercan Enterprise Institute: Papers and Studies (www.aei.org/publications/pubID.14891, filter.all/pub_detail.asp).

Mwangi wa Githinji and Cullenberg, S. (2003) 'Deconstructing the peasantry: class and development in rural Kenya', *Critical Sociology*, vol. 29 (1), pp. 73–86.

Naidoo, R. (2003) *The Union Movement and South Africa's Transition, 1994–2003* (Johannesburg: National Labour and Economic Development Institute).

Nash, J. and Fernández-Kelly, M. P. (eds) (1983) *Women, Men and the International Division of Labor* (Albany, NY: State University of New York Press).

Nasr, V. (2000) 'International politics, domestic imperatives, and identity mobilization: sectarianism in Pakistan, 1979–1988', *Comparative Politics*, vol. 32 (2), pp. 171–90.

Nathan, D. (1997) 'Death comes to the maquilas: a border story', *The Nation*, 13–20 January, pp. 18–22.

Negt, O. and Kluge, A. (1993) *Public Sphere and Experience: Towards an Analysis of the Bourgeois and Proletarian Public Sphere* (Minneapolis, MA: University of Minnesota Press).

Newitt, M. (1995) *A History of Mozambique* (Bloomington: Indiana University Press).

Nichiporuk, B. (2000) *The Security Dynamics of Demographic Factors* (Santa Monica, CA: Rand).

Niemann, M. (2003) 'Migration and the lived spaces of Southern Africa', *Alternatives*, vol. 28, pp. 115–40.

Nitzan, J. and Bichler, S. (2000) 'Capital accumulation: breaking the dualism of "economics" and "politics"', in R. Palan (ed.), *Global Political Economy: Contemporary Theories* (London: Routledge), pp. 67–88.

O'Brien, R. (2000) 'Workers and world order: the tentative transformation of the international union movement', *Review of International Studies*, vol. 26 (4), pp. 533–56.

O'Brien, R. (2001) 'A proposal for evaluating the emergence of a global labour movement', paper presented at ISA annual convention, Chicago, 22 February.

O'Brien, R., Goetz, A. M., Scholte, J. A. and Williams, M. (2000) *Contesting Global Governance: Multilateral Economic Institutions and Global Social Movements* (Cambridge: Cambridge University Press).

OECD (1996) *The OECD Jobs Strategy: Pushing Ahead with the Strategy* (Paris: OECD).

OECD (1997) *Implementing the OECD Jobs Strategy: Lessons from Member Countries, Experience* (Paris: OECD).

Office of the US Assistant Secretary of Defense (1998) *Executive Summary: Population Representation in the Military Services: Fiscal Year 1997* (Washington, DC: GPO).

Omer-Cooper, J. D. (1994) *History of Southern Africa* (Portsmouth: Heinemann).

Oppermann, M. (ed.) (1998) *Sex Tourism and Prostitution: Aspects of Leisure, Recreation, and Work* (New York: Cognizant Communication).

Outshoorn, J. (ed.) (2004) *The Politics of Prostitution. Women's Movements, Democratic States and the Globalization of Sex Commerce* (Cambridge: Cambridge University Press).

Outsourcing Institute (2000) *Outsourcing Index 2000: Strategic Insights into US Outsourcing* (New York: Outsourcing Institute and Dun and Bradstreet).

Panitch, L. (1985) *Working Class Politics in Crisis* (London: Verso).

Panitch, L. (2001) 'Reflections on strategy for labour', in C. Leys and L. Panitch (eds), *Working Classes, Global Realities: Socialist Register* (London: Merlin Press).

Parenti, C. (1999) *Lockdown America: Police and Prisoners in the Age of Crisis* (London: Verso).

Pasha, M. K. and Blaney, D. L. (1998) 'Elusive paradise: the promise and peril of global civil society', *Alternatives*, vol. 23 (3), pp. 417–50.

Pasture, P. (1999) *Histoire du Syndicalisme Chrétien International: La Difficile Recherche d'une Troisième Voie* (Paris: Èditions L'Harmattan).

Pedrero Nieto, M. and Saavedra, N. (1987) *La Industria Maquiladora en México*, Working Paper no. 49 (Geneva: ILO).

Peterson, A., Vasquez, M. and Williams, P. (eds) (2001) *Christianity, Social Change and Globalization in the Americas* (New Brunswick: Rutgers University Press).

Petrakos, G. Maier, G. and Gorzelak, G. (eds) (2000) *Integration and Transition in Europe: The Economic Geography of Interaction* (London: Routledge).

Petras, J. and Wongchaisuwan, T. (1993) 'Thailand: free markets, Aids, and child prostitution, *Z Magazine*, September, pp. 35–8.

Pheterson, G. (ed.) (1989) *A Vindication of the Rights of Whores* (Seattle, Wash.: Seal Press).

Phoenix, J. (1999) *Making Sense of Prostitution* (New York: Palgrave).

Piore, M. (1980) 'The technological foundations of dualism and discontinuity', in S. Berger and M. piore (eds), *Dualism and Discontinuity in Industrial Societies* (Cambridge: Cambridge University Press), pp. 55–81.

Plantet, J. (2003) 'Prostitution: le choix de rèprimer plutôt que de rèinsèrer', *Lien Social*, no. 668 (5 June), pp. 4–5.

Platt, L. (2001) 'Regulating the global brothel', *The American Prospect*, vol. 12 (12) (www.prospect.org/print/V12/12/platt-l.html).

Polanyi, K. (1957) *The Great Transformation* (Boston, MA: Beacon Press).

Pollert, A. (1999) *Transformation at Work: The New Market Economies of Central Eastern Europe* (London: Sage).

Portes, A., Castells, M. and Benton, L. (1989) *The Informal Economy: Studies in Advanced and Less Developed Countries* (Baltimore, MD: Johns Hopkins University Press).

Poulantzas, N. (1973) *Political Power and Social Classes* (London: Sheed and Ward).

Prandy, K. (2002) 'Ideal types, stereotypes and classes', *British Journal of Sociology*, vol. 53 (4), pp. 583–602.

Punto Crítico (1980) *Problemas y Perspectivas del Movimiento Obrero: 1970–1980* (Mexico, DF: Punto Crítico).

Radice, H. (2000) 'Responses to globalisation: a critique of progressive nationalism', *New Political Economy*, vol. 5, pp. 5–19.

Ramírez, J. C. (coord.) (1988) *La Nueva Industrialización en Sonora: El Caso de los Sectores de Alta Tecnología* (Hermosillo: El Colegio de Sonora).

Raymond, J. (1989) 'At issue: the international traffic in women; women used in systems of surrogacy and reproduction', *Reproductive and Genetic Engineering*, vol. 2 (1), pp. 51–7.

Raymond, J. (1998) 'Prostitution against women: NGO stonewalling in Beijing and elsewhere', *Women's Studies International Forum*, vol. 21 (1), pp. 1–9.

Reich, R. (1991) *The Work of Nations: Preparing Ourselves for Twentieth Century Capitalism* (New York: Simon and Schuster).

Reutter, W. and Rütters, P. (2002) 'International trade union organizations and women's policy', *Economic and Industrial Democracy*, vol. 23, pp. 35–58.

Rey, P. -P. (1976) *Les Alliances de Classes* (Paris: Maspero).

Reysoo, F. (2005) 'Féminization de la migration', in C. Verschuur and F. Reysoo (eds), *Genre, Nouvelle Division Internationale du Travail et Migrations* (Geneva: Editions l.'Harmattan).

Reysoo, F. (ed.) (2002) *Economie Mondialisée et Identités de Genre* (Geneva: Institut Universitaire d' Études du Développement).

Rieger, E. and Leibfried, S. (2003) *Limits to Globalization: Welfare States and the World Economy* (Cambridge: Polity Press).

Robinson, V. (2004) 'Breaking the unions' backs', *Mail and Guardian*, 5 March.

Rogers, G. (1989) 'Precarious work in Western Europe', in G. Rodgers and J. Rodgers (eds), *Precarious Jobs in Labour Market Regulation: the Growth of Atypical Employment in Western Europe* (Geneva, Switzerland: ILO Publications), pp. 1–16.

Rose, N. (1999) *Governing the Soul: The Shaping of the Private Self* (London: Free Association Books).

Ross, A. (2001) 'No-collar labour in America's "new economy" ', in C. Leys and L. Panitch (eds), *Working Classes, Global Realities: Socialist Register* (London: Merlin), pp. 77–88.

Rubery, J. (1978) 'Structured labour markets, worker organisation and low pay', *Cambridge Journal of Economics*, vol. 2 (1), pp. 17–37.

Rubery, J. and Wilkinson, F. (1981) 'Outwork and segmented labour markets', in F. Wilkinson (ed.), *The Dynamics of Labour Market Segmentation* (London: Academic Press).

Ruggie, J. G. (1998) *Constructing the World Polity* (London: Routledge).

Ruggiero, V. (2000) *Crime and Markets: Essays in Anti-Criminology* (Oxford: Oxford University Press).

Rupert, M. (1995) *Producing Hegemony: The Politics of Mass Production and American Global Power* (Cambridge: Cambridge University Press).

Rupert, M. (2000) *Ideologies of Globalization* (London: Routledge).

Ryner, M. (2002) *Capitalist Restructuring, Globalisation and the Third Way* (London: Routledge).

Sabel, C. (1982) *Work and Politics* (Cambridge: Cambridge University Press).

Said, E. (1993) *Culture and Imperialism* (New York: Vintage).

Sally, R. (1994) 'Multinational enterprises, political economy and institutional theory: domestic embeddedness in the context of internationalisation', *Review of International Political Economy*, vol. 1 (1), pp. 163–92.

Salzinger, L. (2001) 'Making fantasies real: producing women and men on the maquila shop floor', *NACLA: Report on the Americas*, vol. 34 (5), pp. 13–19.

Sandoval Godoy, S. (1990a) 'Conflictos laborales y relaciones capital-trabajo en la planta Ford de Hermosillo, 1986–1989', *Estudios Sociales*, vol. 1 (1), pp. 117–40.

Sandoval Godoy, S. (1990b) *Equipos de trabajo: la experiencia de Ford Motor Company en Hermosillo Sonora* (Hermosillo, Sonora: Centro de Investigación en Alimentación y Desarrollo), pp. 1–40.

Sandoval Godoy, S. (1990c) 'Los equipos de trabajo en la planta Ford', *Revista de El Colegio de Sonora*, vol. 2 (Dec.), pp. 106–25.

Sassen, S. (1994) *Cities in a World Economy* (Thousand Oaks, CA: Pine Forge Press).

Saul, J. and Leys, C. (1999) 'Sub-Saharan Africa in global capitalism', *Monthly Review*, vol. 51 (3), pp. 13–30.

Saville, J. (1988) 'Britain: internationalism and the labour movement between the wars', in F. van Holthoon and M. van der Linden (eds), *Internationalism in the Labour Movement (1830–1940)*, vol. 2 (Leiden: E. J. Brill), pp. 565–82.

Sayer, A. (1992) *Methods in Social Science: A Realist Approach*, 2nd edn (London: Routledge).

Schevenels, W. (1956) *Forty-Five Years: International Federation of Trade Unions* (Brussels: IFTU Board of Trustees).

Scholte, J.-A. (2000) *Globalization: A Critical Introduction* (Basingstoke: Macmillan).

Schulten, T. and Stueckler, A. (2000) 'Wage policy and EMU', *European Industrial Relations Observer*, vol. 4, pp. i–viii.

Scott, J. (1990) *Domination and the Arts of Resistance: Hidden Transcripts* (New Haven, CT: Yale University Press).

Seabrooke, L. (2001) *US Power in International Finance: The Victory of Dividends* (Basingstoke: Palgrave Macmillan).

Selznick, P. (1969) *Law, Society and Industrial Relations* (London: Russell Sage Foundation).

Sepúlveda B. and Chumacero, A. (1973) *La inversión extranjera en México* (México: Fondo Cultura Económico).

Sheppard, N. Jr (1976) 'More teen-aged girls are turning to prostitution, youth agencies say', *New York Times*, 5 April, p. 41.

Sheppard, N. Jr (1978a) 'Minneapolis steps up fight on prostitution', *New York Times*, 7 February, p. 6.

Sheppard, N. Jr (1978b) 'Private morals of public aides set off debate', *New York Times*, 9 November, p. 28.

Silver, B. J. and Arrighi, G. (2001) 'Workers North and South', in C. Leys and L. Panitch (eds), *Working Classes, Global Realities: Socialist Register 2001* (London: Merlin), pp. 53–76.

Simmons, H. J. and Simmons, R. E. (1969) *Class and Colour In South Africa 1850–1950* (Harmondsworth: Penguin).

Simon, R. (1982) *Gramsci's Political Thought* (London: Lawrence and Wishart).

Sinclair, T. J. (1999) 'Synchronic global governance and the international political economy of the commonplace', in M. Hewson and T. J. Sinclair (eds), *Approaches to Global Governance Theory* (New York: State University of New York Press), pp. 157–71.

Sindicato Nacional de Trabajadores de Ford Motor Company (1989) *Estatutos* (México, DF: Sindicato Nacional de Trabadajores de Ford Motor Company).

Sklair, L. (1991) *Sociology of the Global System* (London: Harvester Wheatsheaf).

Sklair, L. (1997) 'Social movements for global capitalism: the transnational capitalist class in action', *Review of International Political Economy*, vol. 4 (3), pp. 514–38.

Sklair, L. (2001) *The Transnational Capitalist Class* (Oxford: Blackwell).

Skrobanek, S., Boonpakdi, N. and Janthakeero, C. (1997) *The Traffic in Women: Human Realities of the International Sex Trade* (London: Zed Books).

Smith, S. (1996) 'Positivism and beyond', in S. Smith, K. Booth, and M. Zalewski (eds), *International Theory: Positivism and Beyond* (Cambridge: Cambridge University Press), pp. 11–46.

Smothers, R. (1976) 'Prostitution loitering bill passes Albany legislature', *New York Times*, 11 June, p. B4.

Soja, E. W. (1996) *Thirdspace: Journeys to Los Angeles and Other Real-and-Imagined Places* (Cambridge, Mass.: Blackwell).

Soldatenko, M. A. (1999) 'Made in the USA: Latinas/os, garment work and ethnic conflict in Los Angeles sweat shops', *Cultural Studies*, vol. 13 (2), pp. 319–34.

Somavia, J. (1999) 'Trade unions in the 21st Century', Keynote Speech, ILO, Geneva (www.ilo.org/public/english/bureau/dgo/speeches/somaria/1999/network.htm).

Southall, R. (1999) *South Africa in Africa: Foreign Policy Making During the Apartheid Era* (Johannesburg: Institute for Global Dialogue).

Statistics South Africa (2000) *October Household Survey, 1999* (Pretoria: Statistics South Africa).

Statistics South Africa (2002) *Labour Force Survey: September 2001* (Pretoria: Statistics South Africa).

Staudt, K. (1998) *Free Trade: Informal Economies at the U.S–Mexican Border* (Philadelphia, PA: Temple University Press).

Stevis, D. (1998) 'International labour organizations, 1864–1997: the weight of history and the challenges of the present', *Journal of World-Systems Research*, vol. 4 (1), pp. 52–75.

Stevis, D. (2002) 'Agents, subjects, objects, or phantoms? Labor, the environment and liberal institutionalization', *The Annals of the American Academy of Political and Social Science*, vol. 581 (May), pp. 91–105.

Stokes, H. S. (1979) ' "Sex package tours" are protested in Japan', *New York Times*, 8 May.

Stopford, J. M. and Strange, S. (1991) *Rival States Rival Firms: Competition for World Market Shares* (New York: Cambridge University Press).

Talavera, F. and Muñoz, F. (1993) 'Testimonios de Ford: el movimiento democrático de los trabajadores de la Ford, 1987–1991', *Síntesis de Coyuntura 8*, pp. 1–100.

Taylor, M. (2004) 'Labor reform and the contradictions of "growth with equity" in postdictatorship Chile', *Latin American Perspectives*, vol. 31 (4), pp. 76–93.

Taylor, P. (1994a) 'On the nation-state, the global and social science', *Environment and Planning A*, vol. 28, pp. 1917–28.

Taylor, P. (1994b) 'The state as container: territoriality in the modern world-system', *Progress in Human Geography*, vol. 18, pp. 51–62.

Tello, C. (1990) *La Política Económica en México 1970–1976*, 10th edn (Mexico, DF: Siglo Veintiuno Editores).

Theron, J. and Godfrey, S. (2000) *Protecting Workers on the Periphery* (Cape Town: Institute of Development and Labour Law).

Thompson, E. P. (1963) *The Making of the English Working Class* (Harmondsworth: Penguin).

Thompson, E. P. (1993) 'The Patricians and the Plebs', in *Customs in Common* (New York: The New Press), pp. 16–96.

Thompson, L. (1995) *A History of South Africa* (New Haven and London: Yale University Press).

Tichelman, F. (1988) 'Socialist internationalism and the colonial world', in F. van Holthoon and M. van der Linden (eds), *Internationalism in the Labour Movement (1830–1940)*, vol. 1 (Leiden: E. J. Brill), pp. 87–108.

Tola, V. (2004) 'Postfazione', in F. Carchedi (ed.), *Prostituzione Migrante e Donne Trafficate: Il Caso delle Donne Albanesi, Moldave e Rumene* (Milan: Franco Angeli), pp. 208–16.

Tooze, R. and Murphy, C. (1996) 'Poverty of epistemology in IPE: mystery, blindness, and invisibility', *Millennium: Journal of International Studies*, vol. 25 (3), pp. 681–707.

Torres L., Drury, D., Eldring, L., Lewis, P. and Vass, J. (2001) *The Mesebetsi Labour Force Survey: Top Line Report* (Oslo: Fafo Institute for Applied Social Science).

Towers, B. (1997) *The Representation Gap: Change and Reform in the British and American Workplace* (Oxford: Oxford University Press).

Traverso, C. (1998) 'Genova: convegno sulla prostituzione, cinquantamila sulla strada della schiavitú' (Genoa. Conference on Prostitution. Fifty Thousand on the Road of Slavery), *Manifesto*, p. 18.

Truong, T.-D. (1990) *Sex and Morality. Prostitution and Tourism in South-East Asia* (London: Zed Books).

UNDP (1995) *Human Development Report* (New York: Oxford University Press).

UNDP (1996) *World Development Report* (Oxford: Oxford University Press).

UNDP (1999) *Human Development Report* (New York: Oxford University Press).

UNDP (2002a) *Human Development Report* (Oxford: Oxford University Press).

UNDP (2002b) 'A Future for All', in *Arab Human Development Report* (Oxford: Oxford University Press).

United Kingdom HMSO (2000) *Eliminating World Poverty: Making Globalisation Work for the Poor*, white paper on International Development (London: HMSO).

United Nations (1995) *Beijing Declaration and Platform for Action Adopted by the Fourth World Conference on Women: Action for Equality, Development and Peace* (Beijing: United Nations).

US Department of Labor, Bureau of Labor Statistics (1920) *Historical Survey of International Action Affecting Labor* (Washington, DC: GPO).

Van der Anker, C. (ed.) (2004) *The Political Economy of New Slavery* (Basingstoke: Palgrave Macmillan).

Van der Pijl, K. (1998) *Transnational Classes and International Relations* (London: Routledge).

Van Goethem, G. (2000) 'Conflicting interests: the international federation of trade unions, 1919–1945', in M. van der Linden (ed.), *The International Confederation of Free Trade Unions* (Bern: Peter Lang), pp. 73–163.

Verschuur, C. and Reysoo, F. (eds) (2005) *Genre, Nouvelle Division Internationale du Travail et Migrations* (Geneva: Editions L'Harmattan).

Vilrokx, J. (1999) 'Towards the denaturing of class relations? The political economy of the firm in global capitalism', in P. Leisink (ed.), *Globalization and Labour Relations* (Cheltenham: Elgar), pp. 57–77.

Volpi, F. (2003) *Islam and Democracy: The Failure of Dialogue in Algeria* (Ann Arbour, Mich.: University of Michigan Press).

Vosko, L. (2000) *Temporary Work: The Gendered Rise of a Precarious Employment Relationship* (Toronto: University of Toronto Press).

W&R SETA (2001) *Wholesale and Retail Trade Sector Skills Plan* (Johannesburg: Wholesale and Retail Sector, SETA).

Waltz, K. (1979) *Theory of International Politics* (Reading, MA: Addison-Wesley).

Watanabe, S. B. (2000) *Women's Struggle and Female Migration Into Japan in the 1980s and 1990s.*(Ann Arbor, Mich.: Bell & Howell).

Waterman, P. and Wills, J. (2001) 'Introduction: space, place and the new labour internationalisms: beyond the fragments', *Antipode*, vol. 33 (3), pp. 305–11.

Wedin, Å. (1974) *International Trade Union Solidarity: ICFTU 1957–1965* (Stockholm: Prisma).

Wilkinson, F. (1988) 'Deregulation, Structured labour markets and unemployment, in P. J. Pedersen and R. Lund (eds), *Unemployment: Theory, Policy, Structure* (Berlin: Walter de Gruyter).

Williams, S. (1997) 'The nature of some recent trade union modernization policies in the UK', *British Journal of Industrial Relations*, vol. 35 (4), pp. 495–514.

Williams, G., Vernon, R., Corbridge, S. and Srivastava, M. (2003) 'Participation and power: poor peoples' engagement with India's Employment Assurance Scheme', *Development and Change*, vol. 34 (1), pp. 163–92.

World Bank (1995) *Workers in an Integrating World: World Development Report* (New York: Oxford University Press).

World Bank (2001) *Attacking Poverty, World Development Report* (New York: Oxford University Press).

Wright, E. O. (ed.) (1989) *The Debate on Classes* (London: Verso).

Wynter, S. (1998) 'WHISPER: Women Hurt in Systems of Prostitution Engaged in Revolt', in F. Delacoste and P. Alexander (eds), *Sex Work: Writings by Women in the Sex Industry*, 2nd edn (San Francisco, CA: Cleis Press), pp. 266–270.

Young, B. (2001) 'The "mistress" and the "maid" in the globalized economy', in L. Panitch and C. Leys (eds), *Working Classes, Global Realities: Socialist Register 2001* (London: Merlin), pp. 315–28.

Young, I. M. (2000) *Inclusion and Democracy* (New York: Oxford University Press).

Index

Notes: n = note; **bold** = extended discussion or heading emphasized in main text.

Printed in the United States
101145LV00001B/59/A

9 781403 996978